"Now it came about in the four hundred and eightieth year after the sons of Israel came out of the land of Egypt, in the fourth year of Solomon's reign over Israel, in the month of Ziv which is the second month, that he began to build the house of the LORD" (1 Kings 6:1).
• Solomon became king in 970 BC and began building the temple in 966 BC.
• The year of the exodus = 1446 BC (966 + 480)

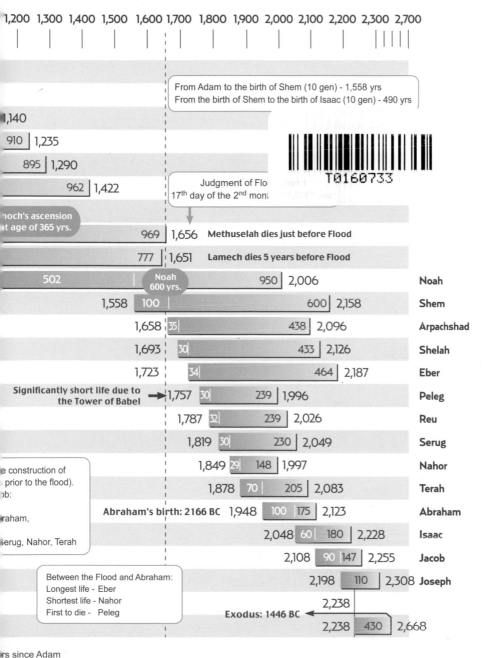

| 1,200 | 1,300 | 1,400 | 1,500 | 1,600 | 1,700 | 1,800 | 1,900 | 2,000 | 2,100 | 2,200 | 2,300 | 2,700 |

From Adam to the birth of Shem (10 gen) - 1,558 yrs
From the birth of Shem to the birth of Isaac (10 gen) - 490 yrs

1,140

910 | 1,235

895 | 1,290

962 | 1,422

Judgment of Flo...
17th day of the 2nd mon...

T0160733

Enoch's ascension at age of 365 yrs.

969 | 1,656 **Methuselah dies just before Flood**

777 | 1,651 **Lamech dies 5 years before Flood**

502   Noah 600 yrs.   950 | 2,006   **Noah**

1,558 | 100 | 600 | 2,158   **Shem**

1,658 | 35| 438 | 2,096   **Arpachshad**

1,693 | 30| 433 | 2,126   **Shelah**

1,723 | 34| 464 | 2,187   **Eber**

Significantly short life due to the Tower of Babel → 1,757 | 30| 239 | 1,996   **Peleg**

1,787 | 32| 239 | 2,026   **Reu**

1,819 | 30| 230 | 2,049   **Serug**

1,849 | 29| 148 | 1,997   **Nahor**

...e construction of ...prior to the flood). ...ob:

1,878 | 70 | 205 | 2,083   **Terah**

...raham,

Abraham's birth: 2166 BC 1,948 | 100 | 175 | 2,123   **Abraham**

...erug, Nahor, Terah

2,048 | 60 | 180 | 2,228   **Isaac**

2,108 | 90 |147 | 2,255   **Jacob**

Between the Flood and Abraham:
Longest life - Eber
Shortest life - Nahor
First to die - Peleg

2,198 | 110 | 2,308 **Joseph**

2,238

Exodus: 1446 BC ←
2,238 | 430 | 2,668

...rs since Adam

...t death   * The years are based only on biblical accounts and estimations may vary slightly.

THE GENESIS GENEALOGIES

THE GENESIS GENEALOGIES

God's Administration in the History of Redemption

NEW REVISED EDITION

Rev. Abraham Park, D. Min., D. D.

PERIPLUS EDITIONS
Singapore • Indonesia

Unless otherwise indicated, scriptural verses quoted in this book are taken from the *New American Standard Bible*, © The Lockman Foundation 1960, 1962, 1963, 1968, 1971, 1972, 1973, 1975, 1977 and 1995.

Published by Periplus Editions (HK) Ltd.

www.periplus.com

English Translation Copyright © 2009, 2018 Periplus Editions (HK) Ltd.
First Korean edition published by Huisun in 2007. www.pyungkang.com

Library of Congress Control Number: 2009926227

ISBN 978-0-7946-0816-3 (hc)
ISBN 978-0-7946-0815-6 (pb)

Distributed by:

North America, Latin America & Europe
Tuttle Publishing
364 Innovation Drive
North Clarendon, VT 05759-9436 U.S.A.
Tel: 1 (802) 773-8930
Fax: 1 (802) 773-6993
info@tuttlepublishing.com
www.tuttlepublishing.com

Japan
Tuttle Publishing
Yaekari Building, 3rd Floor
5-4-12 Osaki, Shinagawa-ku
Tokyo 141-0032
Tel: (81) 3 5437 0171
Fax: (81) 3 5437 0755
sales@tuttle.co.jp
www.tuttle.co.jp

Asia Pacific
Berkeley Books Pte. Ltd.
3 Kallang Sector #04-01
Singapore 349278
Tel: (65) 6741-2178
Fax: (65) 6741-2179
inquiries@periplus.com.sg
www.tuttlepublishing.com

Indonesia
PT Java Books Indonesia
Jl. Rawa Gelam IV No. 9
Kawasan Industri Pulogadung
Jakarta 13930
Tel: (62) 21 4682-1088
Fax: (62) 21 461-0206
crm@periplus.co.id
www.periplus.co.id

Printed in Malaysia
26 25 24 23 22   10 9 8 7 6 5 4 3 2   2205VP

Contents

Foreword

All too often genealogies are viewed as uninteresting or, even worse, boring. However, Dr. Abraham Park's new book, *The Genesis Genealogies: God's Administration in the History of Redemption*, demonstrates the great value and even excitement of an in-depth study of biblical genealogies. A strong foundation is necessary for any enduring structure. And so it is also true that the book of Genesis is a firm foundation for our biblical faith. Genesis is not only the groundwork for understanding our beginnings, but also the basis for understanding ourselves as well as our relationship with God and one another. One simply cannot overstate the importance of Genesis as the foundational paradigm for all Christian thinking. Dr. Abraham Park is to be congratulated for his important and worthy contribution to our understanding of this foundational book.

Dr. Park displays a remarkable facility with the Hebrew language. Time and again, his linguistic skills are on display. This indicates not only the seriousness of his research, but also his love for the book of Genesis. He has rightly understood that one cannot fully grasp God's work of salvation unless one digs deeply into the book of beginnings. The old adage that one cannot understand the future without first understanding the past holds true in biblical studies. Dr. Park takes this adage to heart in this remarkable book.

The biblical point of departure for Dr. Park is Deuteronomy 32:7, where the Song of Moses declares, "Remember the days of old, consider the years of all generations . . . ." He carefully considers the ten genealogies of Genesis (of heaven and earth, of Adam, of Noah, of Noah's sons, of Shem, of Terah and Abraham, of Ishmael, of Isaac, of Esau, and of Jacob), and through each of these, the history of redemption is clearly expounded. Dr. Park employs these genealogies, which find their ultimate expression in the work of Jesus Christ, to reveal the core of God's work of redemption in history.

There are several distinguishing features of Dr. Park's important book. First, it is a book suffused with Scripture. It is absolutely clear that Dr. Park loves the Bible, and it is obvious that he drinks deeply from the fountain of biblical study. Second, it has a clear evangelistic thrust. At many points the clear implication of his exposition is a warm invitation to embrace Jesus as Lord and Savior. Dr. Park, it would seem, has never lost sight of the Great Commission in Matthew 28:19–20.

> Go therefore and make disciples of all the nations, baptizing them in the name of the Father and the Son and the Holy Spirit, [20]teaching them to observe all that I commanded you; and lo, I am with you always, even to the end of the age.

Third, I was delighted to see that he takes the historicity of the Genesis account seriously. In a day when many modern theologians cast doubt on the historicity of Adam, for example, it is refreshing to see a firm affirmation of historicity. Finally, the text is clear and well written. The average reader will not get lost in technical jargon, but will indeed see the teaching of Scripture with ease.

This book is a sweeping vista of God's plan of redemption from Genesis down through the ages to its final expression in the person and work of Jesus Christ. Dr. Park's book is a journey worth taking. I heartily recommend this insightful work for seminaries and colleges. I can assure readers that this book will not disappoint. Read it, study it, pray over it, and then put its wisdom to work in your life and ministry.

Dr. Frank A. James III, Ph.D., D.Phil.
President and Professor of Historical Theology,
Biblical Theological Seminary, Orlando

Preface

In the beginning God created the heavens and the earth.

—Genesis 1:1

The book of Genesis is called the book of the beginning because it is a record of the origin of the universe, the creation of man, the origin of the fall, and the commencement of God's work of salvation. At the same time, Genesis is an introduction to the entire Bible and the blueprint of the history of redemption (Isa 46:10; 48:3).

The study of genealogies תּוֹלְדוֹת (*toledoth*), which are the core of Genesis, has profound soteriological (salvational) value. The genealogies in Genesis are not merely enumerations of the life and death of generations. They contain God's amazing plan for salvation which suffuses the entire Bible. In-depth study and research into the lives and ideologies of the patriarchs, as well as accounts of significant events, will greatly help us understand God's administration in the history of redemption which permeates through the Bible.

As I read the Bible, I took special interest in the years of generations recorded in the Genesis genealogies. I focused on the Scripture verses, "Remember the days of old, consider the years of all generations" (Deut 32:7) and "Stand by the ways and see and ask for the ancient paths, where the good way is, and walk in it" (Jer 6:16). In order to understand the true meaning of the genealogies, I researched for a long period of time, carefully read through the Bible, and referenced various books and resources.

I studied the years of the generations that are recorded in the genealogies in the book of Genesis and was able to view the history of redemption in a three-dimensional form according to their years. Immediately, time and space that were once trapped in the rigid structure of the genealogies began to come alive, releasing an infinite measure of

God's providence that had been hidden in it. I was able to discover the living and active faith of the patriarchs in the Genesis genealogies. Each and every step they took in faith left a clear imprint. They lived in eager anticipation of the woman's seed (Gen 3:15) and the stirring sound of their beating hearts still reverberates today. Tears overwhelmed me and sleep escaped me as I was moved by the grace that led me to understand the hidden meaning of the years of generations.

Grace abounded in great measures as I shared my newfound understanding with the beloved members of Pyungkang Cheil Church during weekly services and special gatherings. I testified of the grace I received from my studies for the first time in 1968 and then in 1983 during six months of expository Bible studies at the Wonji-Dong Retreat Center. Since then, I have modified the studies and shared them on different occasions both in the country and abroad throughout the year 2005. Both the congregation and I were blessed by these studies through the overflowing inspiration of the Holy Spirit.

Despite the long years of my ministry, I delayed publishing this book because I did not feel that it was necessary for a person like me to publish a book. However, in response to the strong urgings from my fellow ministers and beloved congregation, I organized some of my studies into an expository format and published it in the year 2007, the golden jubilee anniversary (50 years) of this servant's ministry. Although this book may be inadequate as fruit presented before God, I took the courage to share it with the world because of the abounding grace that the congregation and I had received. I earnestly hope that God's grace may allow this book to cause even larger waves of blessings to sweep across the churches throughout the world.

This book is certainly not a theological or scholarly treatise. I merely organized what I had preached by the grace that I had received through the enlightenment of the Holy Spirit after repeatedly kneeling in prayer and reading the Bible through and through. I was greatly blessed by the writings of the forerunners of faith as I referred to them in my research for this book. I borrow the words of the author of Ecclesiastes and confess, "That which has been is that which will be, and that which has been done is that which will be done. So there is nothing new under the sun" (Eccl 1:9).

The content of this book can hardly be considered complete in explaining the infinite Word of God, which is a mystery that cannot be understood entirely even through a lifetime of research and study. I ask you to read this book with a Christlike heart of understanding. Please forgive any awkward sentences and generously tolerate any unintended mistakes.

When Peter asked, "Lord, how often shall my brother sin against me and I forgive him?" Jesus answered, "I do not say to you, up to seven times, but up to seventy times seven" (Matt 18:22). I ask you to overlook my shortcomings with the love and mercy of Christ. If anything has been accomplished through this inadequate servant, I confess that it was not the work of this eighty-year-old sinner, but completely the work of the Lord.

Just as King David confessed, "My times are in Your hand" (Ps 31:15), the life I have lived and the history of the Pyungkang Cheil Church are wholly in God's sovereign hand of grace. Truly, the mighty strength of God and the power of the Holy Spirit have been present. As I advance beyond the fiftieth year of my ministry made possible only by the grace of God, I feel immensely grateful for the opportunity to leave behind a trace of this insignificant life in the form of this meaningful book.

Finally, I take this opportunity to express my gratitude to my fellow ministers, elders, leaders, and the congregation of Pyungkang Cheil Church, as well as my wife and children, for all of their prayers and support for this inadequate servant. In addition, I would like to thank every helping hand that has made the publication of this book possible.

I pray that Jesus Christ, the only Savior who died on the cross for all of our sins and rose again on the third day, will always be with His churches around the world. Furthermore, I yearn for the day when the sinful land and all of its people are filled with the knowledge of the Lord as the waters cover the sea (Matt 28:20; Isa 11:9; Hab 2:14). I lift up all the glory to our only living God. Hallelujah!

October 27, 2007
From the prayer room at the Pyungkang Cheil Retreat Center
Servant of Jesus Christ,

朴潤植

Abraham Park

Abraham Park

PART ONE

Consider the Years of All Generations

"Remember the days of old,

Consider the years of all generations.

Ask your father, and he will inform you,

Your elders, and they will tell you."

—Deuteronomy 32:7

The book of Deuteronomy is comprised of three farewell sermons that Moses preached after the completion of the forty-year wilderness journey before his impending death. At the end of his remarkable 120-year life, Moses proclaimed these final words and exhortations to the Israelites with resolute determination. His first sermon was "The Recollection of God's Past Work of Salvation" (Deut 1:1–4:43); his second sermon, "The Reiteration of the Law" (Deut 4:44–26:19); and his third sermon, "The Future Foretold" (Deut 27–30). The book concludes with Moses' death and the commissioning of Joshua as Israel's new leader (Deut 31–34).

Moses delivered his sermons near the end of the long wilderness journey, on the first day of the eleventh month in the fortieth year of the exodus. Hence, it was two months and ten days before the emotional entry into Canaan (Deut 1:3–5). The main audience was the second generation of the exodus since all the soldiers of the first generation had died before crossing the brook Zered (Deut 2:13–15). Moses preached with the earnest hope that this second generation would become a generation of faith that would continue to obey the Word of God even after they enter Canaan.

Moses' song in Deuteronomy 32 addressed the somber subject of Israel's betrayal, fall, and God's subsequent judgment. The sincere message of this song, however, is God's boundless love and His merciful promise to His chosen people. Calling the Israelites by the affectionate name, "Jeshurun"[1] (Deut 32:15), Moses desired to ingrain in their hearts the truth about God who had chosen them from before the beginning of time. God is sovereign over all history. He is the source of all their blessings, and He governs their future.

In Deuteronomy 32:7, Moses expressed great concern for the dismal events that might unfold after the Israelites enter and settle in the land of Canaan. He gave them three specific commands that could help them avoid and overcome such events: "Remember the days of old," "Consider the years of all generations," and "Ask your father and elders." This was surely a demonstration of God's fervent love for His chosen people. In drawing their attention to the walk of faith during the "days of old" and the "years of all generations," Moses hoped that the Israelites, who would soon possess the land of Canaan, would carry on this walk of faith.

Moses declared that God had chosen the Israelites as His heirs even before creation (Deut 32:8–9; Eph 1:4–5) and prepared the land of Canaan as an inheritance for His people (Deut 32:49). Thus, they were to adhere strictly to the three commands in order to completely inherit this land. Today, these three commands are the basic code of conduct for Christians who are journeying toward the kingdom of heaven, the spiritual Canaan.

CHAPTER 1

The First Command:
Remember the Days of Old

> [זְכֹר יְמוֹת עוֹלָם]
> **Do not forget the many days that have passed in history.**

1. The "Days of Old" in Light of God's History of Salvation

The Hebrew term for the *days of old* is יְמוֹת עוֹלָם (*yemoth olam*). It does not simply refer to history, but rather to a history marked by the fulfillment of God's good Word and His promise to save mankind (Deut 4:32; Isa 46:9; Ps 77:5–6, 11–12; 78:1–8; 143:5). In the original language, the term "days of old" encompasses a comprehensive period of time and includes the entire time in which God's work of salvation has been in progress. The expression "days of old" is composed of two Hebrew words: יְמוֹת (*yemoth*), the plural form of יוֹם (*yom*) meaning "day," and עוֹלָם (*olam*), meaning "long duration," "antiquity," "eternity," or "everlasting." This shows that its scope traces back to ancient history.

For Moses, the "days of old" encompass the following events:

1. The fall of Adam and Eve in the garden of Eden
2. Cain's gruesome murder and the faithless deeds of his descendants
3. The overflowing sin and wickedness of Noah's time
4. The hubris of those who built the tower of Babel
5. The covenant of the torch made with Abraham in Genesis 15
6. Israel's 430 years of slavery in Egypt
7. The glorious exodus from Egypt
8. The forty years of trial in the wilderness

God's commitment to the work of salvation was steadfast despite man's increasing sins since the fall and expulsion from the garden of Eden until today. Thus, the "days of old" are the days and years of God's work marked by His fervent love and tears. The prophet Jeremiah referred to these days as the "ancient paths" and the "good way" (Jer 6:16).

This was the path of faith that believes in and fulfills the messianic promise. It was a path of suffering that required people of faith to engage in ongoing battles against evil and overcome any affliction that came along the way in order to preserve the good (Heb 11:36). Gratefully, this path promised the blessing of peace in the end (Jer 6:16). This entire path is compressed into the genealogies in the book of Genesis. In other words, the traces of the events of old, the good way, God's fervent love, and His tears and zeal, which we need to remember, are melded into the genealogies.

2. Remember

In Hebrew, the term *to remember* is זָכַר (*zakhar*). This word means (1) "to recall a memory" (Exod 13:3), (2) "to consider" (Job 7:7), (3) "to recollect" (Ps 63:6), (4) "to think in light of the future" (Isa 47:7), and (5) "to remind." In the original Hebrew text, this word *zakhar* appears fifteen times in the book of Deuteronomy (Deut 5:15; 7:18 [two times]; 8:2, 18; 9:7, 27; 15:15; 16:3, 12; 24:9, 18, 22; 25:17; 32:7). Human beings have a tendency to forget critical events after a long period of time or as generations pass. The chief cupbearer whose dream Joseph interpreted is an excellent example of a person who forgot an important event (Gen 40:23).

The history of the Israelites is, undeniably, full of events that are too shameful to recall. They spent 430 years as slaves in a foreign country (Exod 12:40–41) and wandered in the wilderness for forty years with no land to call their own. God sent Moses and other prophets throughout the ages to urge the Israelites to remember their detestable years of slavery in Egypt (Exod 13:3, 14; 20:2; Deut 5:6, 15; 6:12; 7:8; 8:14; 13:5, 10; 15:15; 16:12; 24:18, 22; Josh 24:17; Judg 6:8; Jer 34:13; Mic 6:4). The 430 years in Egypt were so bitter that the Bible often likens Egypt to an iron furnace (Deut 4:20; 1 Kgs 8:51; Jer 11:4). Moreover, God commanded them to remember how He had made them walk the path of suffering in the wilderness (Deut 8:2; 9:7). Nations that easily forget their times of suffering are doomed to experience greater suffering in the future.

God did not just instruct the Israelites to "remember." He also designated various objects as memorials to help the chosen people remember. The noun form of the verb *to remember* (*zakhar*) is זִכָּרוֹן (*zikkaron*), meaning "memorial" or "reminder." God gave the Israelites various memorial days and objects so that the "days of old" would be embedded in their memories.

First, God instituted memorial days to commemorate great historical events. He instituted the Feast of Passover and commanded His people to "celebrate it as a permanent ordinance" (Exod 12:14, 17, 24). Accordingly, the Israelites observed Passover by eating unleavened bread and bitter herbs to commemorate God's saving work before the exodus when the angel of death passed over their homes and spared their lives (Exod 12:8; Num 9:11).

> **Exodus 13:16** So it shall serve as a sign on your hand and as phylacteries on your forehead, for with a powerful hand the LORD brought us out of Egypt.

The Israelites were to observe three great feasts, the Feast of Passover, the Feast of Weeks, and the Feast of Booths (Exod 34:22–23; Deut 16:16). They were reminders of the enormous and wondrous grace of salvation that He had poured upon them throughout their history. Furthermore, God commanded them to keep His Sabbaths holy: "You shall surely observe My sabbaths; for this is a sign between Me and you throughout your generations" (Exod 31:13). He also said, "Also I gave them My sabbaths to be a sign between Me and them" (Ezek 20:12, 20).

Second, after God began to intercede in human history, He urged the people to preserve certain objects as memorials. He did this so that they would remember His grace that He poured upon them in times of distress and give thanks to Him.

The following are some examples of memorials that appear in the Bible. When 250 leaders of the congregation, along with Korah and his companions, assembled together against Moses and Aaron (Num 16:1–3), the earth opened its mouth and swallowed them up with their households and all the men who belonged to Korah (Num 16:31–35). Then, God instructed Moses to tell Eleazar, "The censers of these men who have sinned at the cost of their lives, let them be made into hammered sheets for a plating of the altar . . . and they shall be for a sign to the sons of Israel" (Num 16:36–40).

When the Israelites challenged Moses and Aaron's authority, God caused Aaron's rod to bud in order to stop their murmurings. He instructed Moses to place this rod in the ark of the covenant to be kept as a sign against the rebels (Num 17:10). God also commanded them to preserve manna, the food with which God had sustained the Israelites in the wilderness, in a jar to be kept in the ark of the covenant for their descendants (Exod 16:32–34). Finally, He commanded that the two tablets of the covenant be kept in the ark of the covenant (Deut 10:2, 5). Consequently, Aaron's budded rod, the jar of manna, and the two tablets of the covenant were preserved in the ark of the covenant as memorials to remind the people of God's grace throughout the generations (Heb 9:4).

The bronze serpent that Moses made and erected on a pole during the wanderings in the wilderness was also preserved as a memorial (Num 21:4–9; 2 Kgs 18:4). When the Israelites grumbled against God, they were bitten by fiery serpents and were about to die. Then, God commanded them to make a serpent of bronze and look at it so that they might be healed and live. This bronze serpent foreshadowed Jesus Christ who would be lifted on the cross for all eyes to behold (John 3:14–15). It was a perpetual reminder that God is merciful even in wrath.

Also, when God allowed Joshua to lead the people across the Jordan River after Moses' death, He commanded them to set up a memorial to commemorate the miracle of the parting of the waters and the drying of the land (Josh 3). God commanded them to set up twelve stones in two different places as a perpetual sign of the crossing of the Jordan River (Josh 4:6). One set of twelve stones was to be taken from the middle of the Jordan to be set up in Gilgal (Josh 4:8, 20). The second set was to be placed in the middle of the Jordan at the site where the priests had stood with the ark of the covenant (Josh 4:9). In Joshua 4:7, God said, "So these stones shall become a memorial to the sons of Israel forever." The command to "remember the days of old" is a call to discover God's fervent love, grace, and guidance throughout times of suffering, affliction, and trials so that we may come to truly fathom His amazing administration of redemption.

CHAPTER 2

The Second Command: Consider the Years of All Generations

[בִּינוּ שְׁנוֹת דּוֹר־וָדוֹר]

Take interest in the years of the passing generations.

Moses' second command was to "consider the years of all generations." This command may appear similar to the first command, "remember the days of old," but there is a distinct difference.

1. Years of All Generations

The "years of all generations" and the "days of old" are similar in that both refer to the past, but the expression "years of all generations" refers to a more defined and specific point in history than the expression "days of old." In Hebrew, the term *years* is שְׁנוֹת (*shenoth*), the plural form of שָׁנָה (*shanah*). The term "days of old" refers to a general time in the past, whereas the term "years" refers to a significant and meaningful point in time within the "days of old." The word "generations" is composed of two consecutive occurrences of the Hebrew word דּוֹר (*dor*), which means "time period" or "generation," and thus refers to each of the generations that appears within the history of salvation.

Therefore, if the "days of old" refer to God's entire history of salvation, then the "years of all generations" refer to God's specific administration of redemption in each generation within the history of salvation.

The genealogy is the most condensed record of the core of God's administration of redemption in each generation. Thus, if we study God's work of redemption revealed in the genealogies through the help of the Holy Spirit, then God's amazing providence of salvation concealed within each generation can be clearly understood.

2. Consider

The word *consider* in the phrase "consider the years of all generations" is בִּין (*bin*) in Hebrew and means "to discern" or "to have insight." It refers to the act of closely observing or studying the principle of a matter or event in order to gain thorough understanding and insight. Thus, the command to "consider the years of all generations" does not simply mean to reminisce about the past. It is an exhortation to gain understanding through careful research and study. Prophet Isaiah also repeatedly urged the Israelites to "consider" in the following passage:

> **Isaiah 51:1–2** Listen to me, you who pursue saving justice, you who seek Yahweh. Consider the rock from which you were hewn, the quarry from which you were dug. ²Consider Abraham your father and Sarah who gave you birth. When I called him he was the only one but I blessed him and made him numerous. (New Jerusalem Bible)

This passage is a call to consider the events and experiences of different persons in the years of all generations. Isaiah urged the people to consider the faith of their ancestors, Abraham and Sarah, as well as the history of Israel. He encouraged them not to lose hope even though their return from captivity in Babylon seemed impossible at the time. He also beseeched them to reflect upon God's covenant with Abraham and to think about all of His great works during the years of slavery in Egypt.

CHAPTER 3

The Third Command: Ask Your Father, and He Will Inform You, Your Elders, and They Will Tell You

> [שְׁאַל אָבִיךָ וְיַגֵּדְךָ זְקֵנֶיךָ וְיֹאמְרוּ לָךְ]
> **Entreat your father, he will explain to you, and your elders will tell you.**

Moses' third command was "Ask your father, and he will inform you, your elders, and they will tell you."

1. Your Father and Elders

The Israelites were to ask their fathers and elders. The Hebrew word for *father* is אָב (*av*) and generally refers to the male parent, but it also means "forefather." In the context of this verse, *father* refers to the patriarchs of faith from all the previous generations. The Hebrew word for *elder* is זָקֵן (*zaqen*) and means "elder," "aged," "senior," or "old man." Elders were leaders of the people, not just aged men. God commanded Moses to call the elders of Israel together and consult with them about the plans for the exodus (Exod 3:16, 18).

Thus, the father and the elders in this verse are the patriarchs of faith, such as Abraham and the leaders of the people. They kept God's commands and never strayed outside the boundaries of God's Word and His law. They were profoundly experienced and well-trained in God's work through oral narratives passed down by their ancestors.

It is crucial to note that most patriarchs enjoyed astonishing longevity. While there are certain things in life that can be learned relatively quickly, other things can only be learned through experience over an extended period of time. Imagine the extent of spiritual truths the godly patriarchs must have come to understand during their long lives. For them, the Word of God was not just knowledge; it was living wisdom deeply rooted in their lives. Job 12:12 states, "Wisdom is with aged men, with long life is understanding." Leviticus 19:32 states, "You shall rise up before the grayheaded and honor the aged, and you shall revere your God; I am the LORD." Proverbs 16:31 also states, "A gray head is a crown of glory; it is found in the way of righteousness."

God granted spiritual leadership to the patriarchs, who lived godly lives throughout their long years, and charged the people to go to them and ask. Just as a nation turns to the seniors of society in times of crisis, God commanded His people to seek the advice of their fathers and elders without hesitation if their faith ever wavered as they acclimated themselves to a new society and culture in Canaan.

2. Ask

The word *ask* is שָׁאַל (*shaal*) in Hebrew and means "to inquire," "to make a request," or "to beg" and connotes a desperate plea. This phrase strongly urges the Israelites to proactively seek after their ancestors, ask questions, and plead for answers just as a starving beggar cries out for food. God commanded the sons of Israel to take special interest and be diligent in learning about all the great works that He had accomplished for them.

In the past, the Israelites and their kings either went directly to God or to His prophets when they faced difficult problems that they could not solve (1 Kgs 22:7; 2 Kgs 3:11; 22:13; 2 Chr 18:6). In 1 Kings 22:7, King Jehoshaphat cried out in the midst of battle, "Is there not yet a prophet of the LORD here that we may inquire of him?" King David also looked to God countless times and in every moment of his life (1 Sam 23:2; 30:8; 2 Sam 5:19, 23; 1 Chr 14:10). God answered each time David sincerely inquired of Him. As a result, David experienced the glory of victory in all his battles. On the contrary, because Joshua did not seek God's counsel, he made the grave mistake of agreeing to a peace covenant with the inhabitants of Gibeon who had come to him in disguise (Josh 9:14–15).

3. He Will Inform You and They Will Tell You

God assured the Israelites that they would certainly receive an answer when they inquire of their fathers and elders. He confirmed this in Deuteronomy 32:7: "Ask your father, and he will inform you, your elders, and they will tell you." The fathers will diligently answer those who inquire of them, and the elders will explain in elaborate detail. The Hebrew verb for *inform* is נָגַד (*nagad*) and is derived from the word that means "to place an object on a high place for all to see." The word *nagad* is used when God reveals His will to His people. This word is also used when God reveals His will in a dream (Gen 41:25) and when the prophets proclaim the Word of God (Deut 4:13).

The Hebrew word for *tell* is אָמַר (*amar*), meaning "to speak," "to prove," or "to answer." This means that the leaders will not only tell, but will also explain the matter clearly when the people inquire. The people were to go to the fathers of faith, like Abraham, for issues concerning faith. For issues concerning their communal or social lives, they were to go to their leaders responsible for administrative duties.

With the passage of time, these "fathers and elders" have faded into history. Nevertheless, they live on today providing answers for their inquiring descendants. We must learn about the divine administration of redemption that is concealed within their generations by inquiring of the numerous patriarchs of faith. Armed with insight, we must go on to live our lives fulfilling God's will in our generation.

4. The Unchanging Word of God

Everything in this world changes constantly, making it meaningless to distinguish between what is old and what is new. The Word of the living God, however, is eternally unchanging; it is the same yesterday, today, and forever (Heb 1:12; 13:8). It does not corrupt or rust away. The Word is alive today and is being witnessed to us as a sharp two-edged sword (Heb 4:12; 1 Pet 1:23). Thus, if we obey Moses' command in Deuteronomy 32:7 to remember the days of old and to consider the years of all the generations, we will be able to realize the true meaning of learning from the past to build the new. God's Word itself is a new work. However, when we forget the Word or when it is taken away, corruption, defects, and perversity will emerge (Deut 32:5).

As believers looking forward to the spiritual Canaan, our land of the eternal sabbath (kingdom of God, heaven), we must open our ears to Moses' earnest cry to the Israelites before their entry into Canaan and embrace it as a message for us today. When we continue to study and delve into the genealogies and contemplate the "days of old" and the "years of all generations," we will discover the great treasures hidden in God's redemptive administration through the help of the Holy Spirit.

However, this finding must not be kept just for ourselves. We must teach it and pass it on to the godly descendants who will remain on this earth until the day of the Lord's return. This is God's purpose for us on this earth. It is His redemptive providence to preserve the covenantal offspring until the end of the world (Gen 45:7). I am sure that those who understand God's will and follow in the footsteps of the godly forefathers mentioned in the days of old and the years of all generations will enter into the sabbath rest that remains for His people (Heb 4:1–11).

PART TWO

God's Administration of Redemption and the Genesis Genealogies

The Bible is not only a historical account of the Israelites. It is a magnificent record that contains the grand theme of God's work of redemption. It begins with the historical account of creation (Gen 1–2) and concludes with the completion of the new heaven and the new earth (Rev 21–22).

Similar to the meaning of the word *liberation*, the word *redemption* in the phrase *history of redemption* refers to salvation, which is freedom from the bondage of sin obtained through a ransom payment. Redemption requires a ransom payment for our sins because the wages of sin is death (Rom 6:23). Jesus is the only One in heaven and on earth who has given up His own life as a ransom to redeem us from death (Matt 20:28). First Timothy 2:6 testifies of Jesus as One "who gave Himself as a ransom for all." Matthew 20:28 states that Jesus came "to give His life a ransom for many" and Ephesians 1:7 states, "In Him we have redemption through His blood, the forgiveness of our trespasses." First Peter 1:18–19 further explains, "knowing that you were not redeemed with perishable things like silver or gold from your futile way of life inherited from your forefathers, but with precious blood, as of a lamb unblemished and spotless, the blood of Christ."

God transferred all the sins of mankind onto Jesus, who was without sin (Heb 4:14–15), and imparted His righteousness as a gift to those who believe in Jesus (Rom 8:3–4; 4:25; 2 Cor 5:21; Eph 2:8; Col 1:20–22; 1 Pet 3:18). God paid the ransom for our lives by sending His Son in the likeness of sinful flesh, so that His Son may give up His life in fulfillment of the "requirement of the Law" (Rom 8:3–4). Colossians 1:21–22 states, "And although you were formerly alienated and hostile in mind, engaged in evil deeds, yet He has now reconciled you in His fleshly body through death [v. 20: the blood of His cross], in order to present you before Him holy and blameless and beyond reproach."

Thus, the history of redemption refers to the entire course of history in which God saves sinners through the death and resurrection of Jesus Christ. A broader definition of the history of redemption is God's administration to renew mankind and all creation in order to recover the paradise that was lost through the fall of Adam and Eve (Rev 21:5).

Therefore, the history of redemption lies at the heart of world history, and Jesus stands at the center of the history of redemption. Jesus Christ, as the dividing point between BC and AD, is the Lord of the new epoch; He is the consummation of the Old Testament and the basis of the New. He is the focus in both the Old and New Testaments. All history that unfolds in this world is centered on Jesus Christ, fulfilled through Him, and will be completed at His return.

Colossians 2:2 confirms that Jesus Christ is "God's mystery." Colossians 1:26-27 states, "that is, the mystery which has been hidden from the past ages and generations, but has now been manifested to His saints, to whom God willed to make known what is the riches of the glory of this mystery among the Gentiles, which is Christ in you, the hope of glory."

The history of this world is founded upon the history of God's work of salvation because God is the origin of all history and sovereign over its development and changes (1 Chr 29:11–12; Job 12:23; Ps 103:19; Dan 4:25; Eph 1:11). The history of God's redemptive work is not separate from the history of this world; God works with, through, and upon the foundations of secular history. Therefore, careful study of the Bible provides us with deeper insight into the truth regarding the past, the present, and the future of this world.

Although we believe in God and have become His children, we fail to fathom the greatness of God who is sovereign over the history of this immense world. We do not understand the enormity of His heart or the intricacy of His plan. It is my prayer that after studying God's administration of salvation in detail from its beginning, we will discover His greatness and praise His works. Moreover, I pray that each one of us may come to realize our respective duties and calling, and understand where we stand in the progression of God's redemptive history.

CHAPTER 4

God's Administration
of Redemption

1. The History of Redemption as a Part of God's Administration

The history of mankind is the history of redemption, which unfolds according to God's administration. It is the history that God the Father devised after the fall, which Jesus the Son fulfilled, and the Holy Spirit completed.

(1) What is God's administration?

The word *administration* is οἰκονομία (*oikonomia*) in Greek and is used three times in the letter to the Ephesians (Eph 1:9; 3:2, 9). It can be translated as "manager" (Luke 16:2–4; Gal 4:2), "stewardship" (1 Cor 9:17), "divine administration" (Col 1:25), or "the mystery of His will" (Eph 1:9). A steward manages and administers a house. Likewise, the Lord of the universe governs the heavens and the earth for the purpose of saving His chosen people according to His divine administration through Jesus Christ and His church. God's administration includes the entire process of managing, allocating, arranging, planning, governing, and ministering the order, movement, and time of all things in the universe (Col 1:25). Its sole focus is in achieving complete salvation for mankind, and the accomplishment of this administration is entirely dependent on Christ and His Church (Eph 1:20–23).

Let us now briefly sum up the relationship between administration and the history of redemption. God's administration entails all the work of governing and managing which He performs within the history of this world and the universe to achieve His decree which was planned before the ages. The core of the history of redemption is the messianic prophecies and their fulfillment.

(2) God's administration is only fulfilled according to His decrees and predestined will.

Divine decree refers to God's eternal plan or purpose which He established before eternity and creation (Eph 1:4–5; 3:11). Our salvation has been predestined from before creation (Titus 1:2; 2 Tim 1:9). In Matthew 25:34, the King says to those on His right, "Inherit the kingdom prepared for you from the foundation of the world." God planned and prepared for the salvation of His people through Jesus Christ before the creation of this world (John 1:1–4, 18; 17:5, 24; Prov 8:22–23). For this reason, Ephesians 1:9–10 describes Jesus' coming as the "administration suitable to the fullness of the times," signifying that God's plan for salvation was finally fulfilled through Jesus Christ, the Word incarnate. Just as Apostle Paul emphasized, God's administration is realized only in Christ (Eph 1:3, 4, 7, 9, 10, 12, 15, 20).

However, Apostle Paul was astounded to realize that the notion of the Israelites as the sole "elect people" had crumbled after Jesus' coming; God's plan to save the Gentiles had been actualized. He described this as the "administration of the mystery" (Eph 3:9), because it had been kept hidden until then.

Even now, God continues to intercede in the history of mankind and brings to fruition His will according to the blueprint of the "administration suitable to the fullness of the times" and the "administration of the mystery." God's work of redemption will proceed without ceasing until His predestined will and plan are completely fulfilled at the second coming of Jesus Christ.

2. The Focus and Scope of Redemptive History

(1) The focus of redemptive history is the salvation of fallen mankind.
God's grace springs forth from the center of His redemptive work. Redemptive history is not characterized by fearful judgment and wrath, but by the patience, grace, and mercy of God, whose desire is to bring more people to salvation (1 Thess 5:9; 1 Tim 2:4; 2 Pet 3:9). There was not a single moment when God relinquished His will to save mankind. He granted unexpected grace every time mankind was on the brink of destruction resulting from their overflowing sin and wickedness. He desired to preserve the "godly seed" (2 Pet 2:5) and to save the holy tree "stump" for the end (Isa 6:13). In times of total despair, He infused life

with soaring vitality. The greater the sins of mankind, the brighter His grace and mercy shined (Rom 5:20).

(2) The scope of redemption encompasses the redemption of the whole man and the recovery of the entire universe.

The sin of one man, Adam, caused God's wrath and curse to fall upon all mankind and all creation (Rom 5:12, 15, 17, 20). Thus, God's redemption pertains to the holistic man, the spirit, the soul, and the body (Rom 8:19–23), as well as the entire universe.

In Romans 8, Apostle Paul spoke of three types of universal groaning that resulted from the fall. The first is the groaning of all creation (Rom 8:22). Because the curse had fallen upon all creation (Gen 3:17–19), all creation eagerly waits for the glorious day when the sons of God will be restored from the fall (Rom 8:19). This will be the day when the curse upon creation will be lifted to finally redeem it to its original state.

The second is the groaning of the saints (Rom 8:23). Although they have already become God's children through faith in Jesus Christ, they are still in an imperfect state bound by the sickness and death of the body. Thus, they eagerly long for the redemption of the body at the second coming of the Lord (1 Cor 15:50–58).

The third is the groaning of the Holy Spirit (Rom 8:26). The Holy Spirit intercedes in prayer for all saints with "groanings too deep for words" in hope that they may soon be redeemed. Upon the completion of God's redemptive work, all groanings will cease, and the glorious restoration of the entire universe will come to pass.

(3) The method of redemption is the atoning work of Jesus Christ.

The history of redemption began with the promise of the "woman's seed" made after the fall of Adam and Eve (Gen 3:15). After making this promise, God Himself made garments of skin and covered Adam and his wife (Gen 3:21). The garments were made of animal skin, indicating that a blameless animal was sacrificed in order to cover mankind that had sinned. This was a foreshadowing of how Jesus, who was without sin, would come as the sacrificial lamb and shed His blood on the cross to redeem and save mankind (John 1:29; 1 Cor 5:7; Rev 5:6). Only Jesus' atoning work on the cross has the power to resolve the issue of sin and pain. Sinners must receive Jesus Christ's righteousness through the precious blood of the cross; then the shame of their sins will be completely covered (Rom 3:25; 13:14; Gal 3:27; Eph 4:24; Col 3:10).

God Himself made the garments and clothed them (Gen 3:21), demonstrating that sinful mankind is entirely incapable of saving themselves (Rom 3:10). It establishes that salvation is possible only through God's sovereign grace.

While the first proclamation of the gospel was made in Genesis 3:15, the first proclamation of atonement was made in Genesis 3:21. Here, through the account of Adam and Eve, God foretold of His sovereign plan to redeem mankind through the sacrifice of Jesus Christ and the shedding of His precious blood. From this perspective, Genesis 3 contains the origin of the fall, the origin of the gospel that would open up the path to life for mankind, and the origin of the gospel of atonement.

3. Christ, the Apex of Redemptive History

The incarnate Jesus Christ stands at the apex of redemptive history because God's administration for redemption is fully revealed and fulfilled through His crucifixion.

(1) The Bible progressively introduces the Messiah.

The Old and New Testaments progressively introduce the Messiah in relation to all the events and the tide of each era (John 5:39, 45–47; Heb 1:1–2). As we read the Bible, we must focus solely on the Messiah and the redemptive history fulfilled by Him—how God saved mankind through Christ and how He will complete the work of salvation.

The messianic promise was first made in Genesis 3:15, which revealed that He would come as the woman's seed. The method by which this promise would be fulfilled was progressively revealed through Isaiah's prophesy: "A virgin will be with child and bear a son" (Isa 7:14). It was finally fulfilled through the conception of Jesus Christ by the Holy Spirit and His virgin birth (Matt 1:18–25).

(2) Jesus Christ's death on the cross was predestined as part of God's administration of redemption.

Jesus' crucifixion was not a coincidental or sudden event. When the time to bear the cross was imminent, Jesus said, "For indeed, the Son of Man is going as it has been determined" (Luke 22:22) and "For this purpose I came to this hour" (John 12:27). In His prayer at the garden of Gethsemane, Jesus sought to do the Father's will and not His own (Matt 26:38–42; Luke 22:42; Heb 5:7). Apostle Paul added that Christ died for our sins "according to the Scriptures" (1 Cor 15:3). Thus, our Savior Jesus Christ came to this earth, lived on the earth, and died on the cross according to the Scriptures. Furthermore, He rose again on the third day after destroying the power of death in accordance with the Scriptures. He remained on earth for forty days after His resurrection and ascended into heaven in accordance with the Scriptures. His second coming will also be fulfilled in accordance with the Scriptural prophecies. All these events were predestined as part of God's administration of redemption.

(3) Jesus Christ accomplished redemption once and for all through the cross, and its efficacy is everlasting.

Concerning Jesus Christ's redemptive work, the author of Hebrews states, "But through His own blood, He entered the holy place once for all, having obtained eternal redemption" (Heb 9:12).

The crucifixion of Jesus Christ was not a single independent event that occurred two thousand years ago. Its power continues to save today, and its efficacy is everlasting. The Old Testament priests were replaced continuously as each priest died. Sacrifices of atonement had to be prepared again and again, and the blood of the sacrifice had to be offered repeatedly (Heb 7:20–28). In contrast, Jesus Christ is the everlasting priest (Heb 7:21–24) and the perpetual sacrifice offered once for all (Heb 7:26–28; 9:26, 28; 10:10; Rom 6:10). The Greek word for *once* is ἐφάπαξ (*ephapax*) and means "once for eternity." Thus, Jesus' atoning sacrifice on the cross did not achieve temporal salvation; it is the accomplishment of eternal salvation.

(4) The work of redemption will be completed through the second coming.

The Old Testament testified of Jesus Christ numerous times and in various ways (Heb 1:1). Jesus Christ is the Word who came in the flesh according to the prophecies of the Old Testament. He came at the fullness of time and proclaimed the Word without rest while He was on the earth until His death on the cross (Gal 4:4; John 5:17). This was God's zeal to save sinners who were predestined for salvation from the beginning of time (Isa 9:7; 2 Cor 11:2; Isa 62:1). He demonstrated His boundless love for mankind by shedding His blood on the cross (Rom 5:8; 1 John 4:10), thereby completing the work of redemption. Subsequently, the Holy Spirit bestows the virtues of Jesus Christ's work upon all who are called in order to guide them onto the path of salvation. Now, God, who fulfilled the work of redemption through the first coming, will perfect it through the second coming.

When the Lord returns, those who died in Christ will be resurrected to a transformed body, and those who are alive will be transfigured to the completion of God's saving work (1 Cor 15:51–54; 1 Thess 4:16–17). After the thousand-year reign, the devil, who had caused the fall of this world, will be thrown into the lake of fire and brimstone. Then, the first heaven and the first earth will pass away, and the new heaven and the new earth will at last be established (Rev 20:1–10; 21:1).

The history of God's work of redemption, which has tirelessly run its course since the fall of Adam, will arrive at its glorious completion through the second coming of Christ. It is our calling to become God's precious vessels until His work of redemption is complete.

CHAPTER 5

God's History of Redemption and the Genealogies

1. The Redemptive-Historical Significance of the Genealogies

Man was created in God's likeness, but sinned and fell to the path of death. The history of redemption is the entire history of the salvation of mankind and the restoration of all creation. Thus, the major themes of redemptive history are creation, fall, and restoration. All attention is focused on who the Messiah is and how God's people would be saved through Him. These major themes are clearly depicted through each person that appears in the genealogies. The history of redemption is concisely compressed into the names and ages of the persons recorded in the genealogies.

The Bible addresses the broad themes of redemptive history through various sets of genealogies. For example, Genesis 5 records Adam's genealogy—ten generations from Adam to Noah. Genesis 11 records Shem's genealogy—ten generations from Shem to Abraham. Together, these genealogies clearly reveal that the Messiah would ultimately come as a descendant of Abraham. The genealogies in Genesis 5 and Genesis 11 are unique in that they include a complete record of each person's birth, age at procreation, and life span even though they lived 4,000–6,000 years ago. The completeness of the genealogies affirms that God's redemptive work did not cease in any generation, but continued throughout history.

The genealogy in Ruth (Ruth 4:18–22), which comes after the Genesis genealogies, is brief. Yet, it compresses the history of all the people who lived from the birth of Judah's son Perez to the birth of King David (approximately 840 years) into just ten names. This genealogy confirms that the Messiah will come through the line of Judah, the fourth among Jacob's twelve sons. The book of Chronicles, the last book of the Hebrew Bible, contains genealogies from chapters 1–9. It records numerous people who lived from Adam until before the Dark Age (over 3,600 years) from a redemptive-historical perspective. Furthermore, the genealogy in Matthew 1 summarizes the complete flow of the redemptive history of the Old Testament. The book opens with the verse, "The record of the genealogy of Jesus the Messiah, the son of David, the son of Abraham" (Matt 1:1). It introduces Jesus as the Messiah who came through the path revealed in the genealogies in Genesis 5 and 11, the genealogy in Ruth, and the genealogy in the book of Chronicles (1 Chr 1–9).

Careful study of the Genesis genealogies will lead us to a clearer understanding of God's administration of redemption through Jesus Christ. All the descriptions of the persons, their names, and the time of their births and deaths provide significant insight into the circumstances surrounding each time period. Furthermore, they play important roles in testifying of the different aspects of Jesus Christ. In this light, these genealogies are the core of redemptive history, and studying them is a definite shortcut to comprehending God's administration.

Just as there are no meaningless sounds in the world, biblical genealogies are also not without meaning; they contain countless treasures to be discovered. Therefore, we must not commit the grave mistake of overlooking them as insignificant enumerations of names. With the guidance of the Holy Spirit, we must discover the rich vein of redemptive history that flows through the genealogies.

2. The Structure and Flow of the Genealogies

God's work in redemptive history is carried out in various ways and forms, but it has one clear purpose and direction—to send the promised seed of the woman, the Messiah, for the redemption of His elect (Gen 3:15; Heb 1:1–2). The Bible is a record of how God carried out this plan. The genealogies, presented in various formats and structures, record this work in the most concise and condensed form.

(1) The structure of the genealogies

First, genealogies can be classified in two linear formats: linear ascending format (listing up from descendants to the ancestors) and linear descending format (listing down from ancestors to descendants). The genealogy in Luke 3 is typical of a genealogy listed in linear ascending order. It traces Jesus Christ's genealogy in ascending order up to Adam and then to God. The genealogy in 1 Chronicles 6:33–47 is a linear ascending genealogy that begins with Heman and traces up to Levi.

On the other hand, in a linear descending genealogy, the main focus is on the last person on the list. For example, the focus in the genealogy of Genesis 5 is on Noah—the tenth generation. The genealogy in Genesis 11 lists Shem and his descendants down to Abraham (tenth generation), and the main focus is on Abraham.

Secondly, genealogies can be categorized as linear or segmented. Genealogies in a linear format record the direct line of offspring. Typical of this linear genealogy format is the genealogy of the line of Cain in Genesis 4 and the genealogy of the line of Seth in Genesis 5.

Genealogies in segmented format simultaneously record the lineages of the different sons of one person. Examples of segmented genealogies are the genealogies of two of Noah's sons, Ham and Japheth (Gen 10:2–20); Nahor's genealogy (Gen 22:20–24); Abraham's sons through Keturah (Gen 25:1–6); Ishmael's sons (Gen 25:12–16); and Esau's sons (Gen 36:1–43).

(2) Two distinct flows of genealogies

Beginning with Cain's act of murder until Herod's conspiracy to kill the infant Jesus, Satan's relentless effort to thwart God's work ran parallel with the progression of redemptive history (Gen 4:1–12; Matt 2:1–13). While Genesis 4 contains the genealogy of Cain's line, which attempted to halt the flow of redemptive history, Genesis 5 contains the genealogy of the patriarchs in the line of Seth (Adam's son) who carried on God's work of redemption. Hence, biblical genealogies are divided into two distinct lines: the genealogy of the faithful who lived to fulfill God's will, and that of the unfaithful whose lives stood against God's will.

The main stem of biblical genealogies are the genealogies of the sons of faith. The most prominent are the genealogies of Adam in Genesis 5 and Shem in Genesis 11, which show the lineage of faith from Adam to Abraham. The genealogy of Boaz in Ruth 4 presents the lineage of faith from Judah's son Perez down to King David. Finally, the genealogy in Matthew 1 explicitly reveals God's work of redemption by showing how

His covenantal work extended throughout the forty-two generations from Abraham to Jesus Christ. Even though there were wicked people in the genealogy of the faithful descendants, they could not hinder God's administration in the history of redemption.

CHAPTER 6

The Genesis Genealogies

The book of Genesis contains ten genealogies. For this reason, Genesis is also called the "book of genealogies" or the "story of lineages." It is the first of the sixty-six books of the Bible and reveals the origin of mankind as well as God's sovereign work and providence over each godly offspring.

The fifty chapters of Genesis cover a span of about 2,300 years of history, from the creation of Adam until the death of Joseph (see Excursus 1: "The Chronology of the Patriarchs"). Since it is impossible to record detailed accounts of God's providence in just fifty chapters, God compressed 2,300 years of history into the genealogies. The chief message of the genealogical accounts in Genesis is that God will accomplish His administration to save mankind through the godly offspring and that He will surely fulfill His promise without the omission of even one iota.

1. The Structure of Genesis

The book of Genesis can be organized into two parts: Part I (chapters 1–11) and Part II (chapters 12–50).

(1) Part I (chapters 1–11)

The theological term for the history outlined in Genesis 1–11 is *primeval history*. These chapters cover a span of 2,023 years, which include the creation of heaven and earth, the creation and fall of Adam and Eve, the story of Cain and Abel, the great flood, the tower of Babel, and the lives of Adam, Noah, and Abraham (see Excursus 1: "The Chronology of the Patriarchs").

God continued His work of salvation despite rebellion against His dominion—rebellion that progressed and climaxed with the attempt to construct the tower of Babel. In the last part of Genesis 11, Abraham departed from Ur of the Chaldeans and migrated to Haran. God's work depicted in Genesis 1–11 comes to an end with Abraham being singled out from among all the descendants of Adam.

(2) Part II (chapters 12–50)

Genesis 12–50 are dedicated to the formative period of the nation of Israel. They record the lives of four patriarchs: Abraham, Isaac, Jacob, and Joseph. Part I (Genesis 1–11) focuses on the creation narrative and Abraham, and Part II (Genesis 12–50) focuses on the personal lives of the four patriarchs (Abraham, Isaac, Jacob, and Joseph). Part II covers a span of about 280 years. This duration of time is only one-seventh the duration of Part I, but the amount of writing dedicated to it is five times longer. Therefore, in comparison, more generations were compressed and stored in the genealogies in Part I of Genesis (Gen 4–5; 10–11).

2. The Ten Genealogies in Genesis

There are ten genealogies (תּוֹלְדוֹת: *toledoth*, Hebrew word for *genealogy*) in the book of Genesis. The first five belong to Part I of Genesis (Gen 1–11) and the last five belong to Part II of Genesis (Gen 12–50).

---

1 – Genealogy of heaven and earth (Gen 1:1–2:4; 2:4–4:26)
Genesis 2:4 This is the account of the heavens and the earth when they were created.

---

2 – Genealogy of Adam's family (Gen 5:1–6:8)
Genesis 5:1 This is the book of the generations of Adam.

---

3 – Genealogy of Noah's family (Gen 6:9–9:29)
Genesis 6:9 These are the records of the generations of Noah.

---

4 – Genealogy of Noah's sons (Gen 10:1–11:9)
Genesis 10:1 Now these are the records of the generations of Shem, Ham, and Japheth, the sons of Noah.

---

5 – Genealogy of Shem (Gen 11:10–26)
Genesis 11:10 These are the records of the generations of Shem.

---

6 – Genealogy of Terah (Abraham) (Gen 11:27–25:11)

Genesis 11:27 Now these are the records of the generations of Terah.

7 – Genealogy of Ishmael (Gen 25:12–18)

Genesis 25:12 Now these are the records of the generations of Ishmael, Abraham's son.

8 – Genealogy of Isaac (Gen 25:19–35:29)

Genesis 25:19 Now these are the records of the generations of Isaac, Abraham's son.

9 – Genealogy of Esau (Gen 36:1–37:1)

Genesis 36:1 Now these are the records of the generations of Esau (that is, Edom).

10 – Genealogy of Jacob (Gen 37:2–50:26)

Genesis 37:2 These are the records of the generations of Jacob.

The word *genealogy* (*toledoth*) is used in the heading of each genealogy either as an introduction or a transition into a new story. This structure in Genesis teaches the following important lessons.

First, the Genesis genealogies narrate the history of creation, the fall, judgment, and the restoration of man. The genealogy in Genesis 5 points to Noah as the central figure who would deliver mankind from the catastrophic judgment of the flood after the fall of Adam. Then, the genealogy in Genesis 11 introduces Abraham as the central figure in the work of salvation. He was singled out by God from among those scattered after challenging God's salvation through the construction of the tower of Babel.

Second, all the genealogies in Genesis focus on Abraham as the chief figure to shoulder the work of redemption. This is why the division within the ten genealogies in Genesis is centered on Abraham—five before him and five after him.

Third, Genesis 1–11 introduces the entire Bible and contains prophecies regarding the beginning and the end of redemptive history. These genealogies of ancient history do not simply list a person's lineage; they are the structural framework of the history of redemption.

3. Sepher Toledoth (Book of the Generations)

✻ Organized and presented for the first time in history

All of the ten genealogies in Genesis begin with the Hebrew word תּוֹלְדֹת (*toledoth*), meaning "account," "book of the generations," "records of the generations," "descendants," or "biography." However, Genesis 5:1 uniquely begins the genealogy by pairing the word *toledoth* with another word, סֵפֶר (*sefer*), which means "book": סֵפֶר תּוֹלְדֹת (*sefer toledoth*).

> **Genesis 5:1** This is the book of the generations of Adam.

Book of the generations in Genesis 5:1 signifies "a record of family history," "lineage dating back to the ancestors," "a record of people's bloodline," and "an order of an academic or philosophical system." The word *sefer* (סֵפֶר, "book") can also be translated as "writing," "letter," or "scroll." Other genealogies are simply *toledoth* (תּוֹלְדֹת), but the genealogy in Genesis 5 is *sefer toledoth* (סֵפֶר תּוֹלְדֹת).

This is a significant difference. Adam's genealogy in Genesis 5 is not a simple list of names. It contains a substantial amount of content—enough to be considered a complete book. From the redemptive-historical perspective, it is God's covenant book that is similar to a legally binding document or treaty.

The term *sepher toledoth*, which appears in the genealogy of the first man Adam (Gen 5:1), appears again (in Greek) in the genealogy of the second man Jesus Christ in Matthew 1 (1 Cor 15:45–47).

> **Matthew 1:1** The book of the genealogy of Jesus Christ, the son of David, the son of Abraham.

Genesis 5:1 Book of the generations – *sefer toledoth* (סֵפֶר תּוֹלְדֹת)

Matthew 1:1 Book of the genealogy – *biblos geneseōs* (βίβλος γενέσεως)

Hence, the term used in Genesis 5:1 is *sepher toledoth* ("book of generations"), not just *toledoth* ("generations"). Likewise, in Matthew 1, it is *biblos geneseos* ("book of genealogies"), not just *genesis* ("genealogy").

The genealogies of the first man (Gen 5:1) and the second man (Matt 1:1) both use the modifying word "book": סֵפֶר (*sefer*) in Hebrew and βίβλος (*biblos*) in Greek. The emphasis on "book" implies that the genealogy in Matthew 1, like the genealogy in Genesis 5, contains enough content to be considered a complete book on its own.

It is important to note that only the most crucial information is compressed into the genealogies. The genealogies replace an immense volume of writings that are otherwise required for a detailed narrative. These narratives would have included all the great works that each patriarch performed in his generation as he battled against the world (Ps 40:5; 71:15–16; 139:16–18; Heb 11:32).

> **John 21:25** And there are also many other things which Jesus did, which if they were written in detail, I suppose that even the world itself would not contain the books that would be written.

What is the common message of these patriarchs (representatives) from each generation? What inspired them to continue their solitary struggle? It was the fulfillment of God's administration to save all mankind. For this purpose, the godly descendants of Seth and Shem continued faithfully to run their respective legs in the course of redemptive history. Eager to pass the baton to the succeeding generations, they endured the tears, the agony, the loneliness, and the pain of being forsaken by the world.

The genealogies are full of traces left behind by the godly descendants who fought the good fight until the coming of the promised seed. As we delve deeper into the study of the Genesis genealogies, we will be able to understand the magnitude of God's abundant grace and feel the loving touch of His hands. Ultimately, His fervent zeal achieved salvation for mankind through the incarnation of Jesus Christ and His atoning work on the cross.

4. The Methodology of the Study of the Genesis Genealogies

The ten genealogies in Genesis are not all recorded in the same format. Some genealogies are recorded twice, and some are written in a simple story format. The genealogy of Seth in Genesis 5 and the genealogy of Shem in Genesis 11 are written in the most typical genealogy format and includes details of the sons' names and ages. In this book, we will study the genealogies of Cain (Genesis 4), Seth (Genesis 5), and Shem (Genesis 11) with an emphasis on the factors listed below.

(1) The meaning of the names

Names distinguish people, places, and things. People's names not only validate their existence (Gen 2:19), but may also allude to their personality and character. The greater significance of names is that they not only follow people throughout their lives, but also remains on the earth after their death. For example, the name *Jacob* (יַעֲקֹב, *yaaqov*) means "one who takes by the heel" or "deceiver," and his new name *Israel* (יִשְׂרָאֵל, *yisrael*) means "striven with God and with men and has prevailed." Israel, Jacob's new name, shows that he had become a new person.

The faith of the parents is the most significant factor that influences the naming process. A name not only describes the child, it reveals the parents' hopes and expectations. It also provides insight into the circumstances of the times. Thus, by studying a person's name, it is possible to obtain an extensive amount of information about that person and the times in which he or she was living.

For the godly patriarchs and men of prayer, the naming process for their sons was a solemn matter. They pondered deeply upon God's desire and will for their generation; this understanding is reflected in the names of their children.

Although there may be many children in a family, the child who brings honor to the parental name becomes the pride of that family and is admired by the succeeding generations. Likewise, the names of the people specially listed in the genealogies of the godly offspring have not faded away even to this day. The names not only reflect the circumstances of their times, but are also compressions of God's work of redemption that penetrates through the ages. Therefore, it is crucial to carefully explore the redemptive significance of the meaning and the origin of the names in Adam's genealogy, especially that of the line of Seth.

(2) Birth and life span

Another basic factor in the study of the genealogies is life span: when the patriarchs were born, how long they lived, and when they died. These are the basic factors that a genealogy addresses. A person's age also reflects the historical circumstances surrounding his or her time. Therefore, it is necessary to examine the religious and social backgrounds during the time of each person's birth and how these factors may have impacted his life span.

(3) Relationships with preceding and succeeding generations

Next, it is important to determine where the years of each patriarch's life falls within the historical timeline. Determining the years of their lives relative to one another helps us understand their relationships with the preceding and succeeding generations. It also aids in determining which patriarchs were contemporaries with one another. Ultimately, we can discover the path and method through which God's administration of redemption was transmitted from the older generations to the younger generations.

Of special importance is the length of time that Adam and Noah—the first and second ancestors of mankind—lived contemporaneously with their direct descendants. This will bring to light many important facts that were previously unknown and will lead us to a better understanding of God's redemptive providence. In summary, understanding the patriarchs' relationship with their preceding and succeeding generations through a close study of their birth years and life spans will confirm that even the years recorded within these genealogies focus on the Messiah who would come as the promised seed of the woman (Gen 3:15).

(4) Progressive revelation of the coming of the Messiah

The Bible progressively reveals Jesus Christ who stands at the center of the entire history of redemption (Heb 1:1–3; Luke 24:27, 44; John 5:39, 45–47). The format of the genealogies and the meanings of the recorded names contain the hope and anticipation of how the redemptive promise to be fulfilled through Jesus Christ would unfold through each successive generation. This discovery will greatly broaden our perspective of the flow of redemptive history. For example, Adam is connected to Noah through Enoch and Methuselah. Noah is connected to Abraham through Shem and Eber. In their respective generations, the lives of Adam, Noah, and Abraham were turning points in the work of redemption to be fulfilled through Jesus Christ.

(5) Additional information about important characters

Some genealogies deviate from the standard format in order to include additional information for certain generations. These additional narratives signal important junctions in the flow of the genealogies and also spotlights Jesus Christ.

For example, additional narratives were included for the following persons:

- In the genealogy of Cain in Genesis 4—Cain and Lamech (sixth generation from Cain)
- In the genealogy of Seth in Genesis 5—Adam, Enoch, Lamech, and Noah
- In the genealogy of Shem in Genesis 10–11—Shem, Eber, Peleg, and Abram

Out of all the persons enumerated in the genealogies, we must pay special attention to the persons listed above.

(6) Placement of the genealogies in the historical timeline

The timing of the emergence of a genealogy in the Bible has great redemptive significance because genealogies are often recorded at crucial turning points or junctions in the history of redemption.

In biblical genealogies, the most important person often appears at the end and becomes the starting point of a new era. Consequently, persons listed either at the beginning or the end of a genealogy hold great redemptive significance. Good examples are Adam, the first person mentioned in the genealogy of the creation; Noah, the last person (tenth generation) in his genealogy (Gen 5:32); Terah and his son, Abraham, the last persons in the genealogy that follow the generation of Noah (Gen 11:26); and Joseph in the account of Jacob's lineage (Gen 37:2–50:26).

The Genesis genealogies are especially meaningful in that they present an overview of God's unfolding work. If we study the genealogies with the aforementioned factors in mind, we will discover the inseparable connection between God's redemptive work and the genealogies.

God's administration, which actively guides the great flow of redemptive history, comes alive in the genealogies. Traces of God's revelations that testify of the coming of Jesus Christ, the Messiah, are also prominent in the genealogies (John 5:39, 45–47; Luke 24:27, 44). With further study of the Genesis genealogies, Moses' words will begin to resonate clearly in your ears: "Remember the days of old, consider the years of all generations" (Deut 32:7).

CHAPTER 7

The Years of the Generations in the Genesis Genealogies

1. Perspective on the Inerrancy of the Bible

An increasing number of modern theologians believe that the Bible contains errors. However, the Bible is the Word of the living God and is therefore 100% inerrant and infallible. This principle of inerrancy applies to the entire Bible. Accordingly, the genealogies in the Bible are also part of the inerrant and infallible Word of God. The records of the persons who appear in each genealogy, including their lives and years, are all without error.

Nonetheless, some genealogies contain omissions. For instance, there are omissions in the genealogy of Jesus Christ in Matthew 1:8. Three kings—Ahaziah (2 Kgs 8:25), Jehoash (2 Kgs 12:1), and Amaziah (2 Kgs 14:1)—were omitted between Joram and Uzziah. In Matthew 1:11, Jehoahaz and Jehoiakim were omitted after Josiah (2 Kgs 23:34; 1 Chr 3:15–16), and Zedekiah was also omitted after Jehoiachin. These omissions imply that the genealogy in the Gospel of Matthew was not written for the purpose of preserving a complete historical record or for calculating the years. Matthew recorded the names of important persons from each era that he deemed necessary for the purpose of the genealogy and omitted the others. He composed three groups of fourteen generations each and recorded a total of forty-two generations. Matthew 1:17 states, "So all the generations from Abraham to David are fourteen generations; from David to the deportation to Babylon, fourteen generations; and from the deportation to Babylon to the Messiah, fourteen generations."

We must not waver in our belief that the biblical genealogies are part of the perfect and inerrant Word of God. Not all genealogies were written for the sake of recording and calculating the years. Certain generations were intentionally omitted in order to communicate God's specific will (Ezra 7:1–3; 1 Chr 6:7–15).

2. Years of the Generations in Genesis 5 and Genesis 11

Together, the genealogies in Genesis 5 and Genesis 11 contain records of twenty generations of patriarchs. The genealogy of the line of Seth, which covers the generations from Adam to Abraham, contains no chronological gaps.

Henry M. Morris, an Old Testament scholar who studied the genealogies in Genesis, based his calculations of the ten generations from Adam to Noah on the years of birth and death. He argued that there are no gaps in these genealogies:

> There is no reason to think there are any "gaps" in this record, or that the years are anything other than normal years (except for the quizzical possibility that the original year was 360 days long, instead of the present 365¼). The record is perfectly natural and straightforward and is obviously intended to give both the necessary genealogical data to denote the promised lineage and also the only reliable chronological framework we have for the antediluvian period of history.[2]

Travis R. Freeman also believes that the genealogies in Genesis 5 and Genesis 11 flow without gaps or disconnections. Freeman states:

> Some modern theologians believe not only that Genesis 5 and 11 contain the names of actual historical figures, but that those names form a continuous (without generational omissions) linear genealogy from Adam to Abraham. While they readily acknowledge fluidity as a fairly common occurrence in ancient genealogies, they reason that the occurrence of fluidity in some genealogies does not prove fluidity in all genealogies. They see the genealogies of Genesis 5 and 11 as two of the many exceptions to the fluidity rule.[3]

In his analysis of early biblical genealogies, Samuel R. Külling began by acknowledging that many biblical genealogies, such as those in Ezra 7 and Matthew 1, contain gaps. He believes that biblical genealogies come in more than one genre. He asserts that the genealogies of Genesis 5 and Genesis 11 are chronological genealogies because of the many numerical notations therein, especially the age of the father at procreation. He claims that there are no gaps or omissions within each of the two genealogies. He emphasizes that the purpose of the passages in Genesis stating Abraham's age at Isaac's birth and Isaac's age at Jacob's birth was to create an accurate chronology.[4]

What, then, is the basis for the belief that the chronological records of the genealogies in Genesis 5 and Genesis 11 are inerrant? There are three arguments.

First, the genealogies in Genesis 5 and Genesis 11 accurately narrate the year of birth, age at procreation, and life span for all twenty generations of patriarchs. Such precise notations of years are not found in other genealogies so they add to the credibility of these records. The narrative of the twenty generations of patriarchs is an actual historical and chronological record. If the purpose was not to record actual accounts, there would be no reason for such a detailed narrative.

Second, the order of the twenty patriarchs in Genesis 5 and Genesis 11 does not contradict any of the other genealogies in the Bible. The order of names in the genealogies in Genesis 5 and Genesis 11 is perfectly consistent with the order of names in the genealogies in 1 Chronicles 1:1–4, 24–27.

(1 Chr 1:1)	Adam, Seth, Enosh
(1 Chr 1:2)	Kenan, Mahalalel, Jared
(1 Chr 1:3)	Enoch, Methuselah, Lamech
(1 Chr 1:4)	Noah, Shem, Ham, and Japheth
(1 Chr 1:24)	Shem, Arpachshad, Shelah
(1 Chr 1:25)	Eber, Peleg, Reu
(1 Chr 1:26)	Serug, Nahor, Terah
(1 Chr 1:27)	Abram (Abraham)

Moreover, the genealogies in Genesis 5 and Genesis 11 are in agreement with the genealogy of Jesus Christ in Luke 3. In Luke 3:34–38, however, there is a difference in the case of one person. Cainan is listed between Arphaxad (Arpachshad) and Shelah in Luke 3, but not in Genesis 11. The insertion of Cainan, however, does not affect the calculation of years (see Excursus 5: "Perspective on Cainan").

Unless there is definite proof that there is a gap in the chronological order of the years, it is far more accurate to base calculations on the Hebrew text than on noncanonical records or assumptions that may be incomplete or inaccurate.

Third, the genealogy in Matthew 1 and the genealogies in Genesis 5 and Genesis 11 are separate genealogies recorded for different purposes. Matthew 1 contains omissions when compared to other historical records in the Bible. This is because the purpose of this genealogy was not to narrate a historical bloodline. By the inspiration of the Holy Spirit, Matthew was calling attention to the fruition of God's plan for redemption.

The genealogy in Matthew contains three groups of fourteen generations of persons who played critical roles in shedding light on God's work of redemption until it reached its zenith with the coming of Jesus Christ (Matt 1:17). It is not an exhaustive list of all the generations in biblical history. Matthew also began the genealogy of Jesus Christ with Abraham so that the Jewish audience may understand that Jesus is their Messiah and accept Him. In this light, the genealogy in Matthew focused on the continuity of faith rather than on the enumeration of the births and lives of every descendant (Rom 9:6–11).

Therefore, skepticism regarding the historicity and accuracy of the genealogies in Genesis 5 and Genesis 11 based on the genealogy in Matthew 1 is unfounded. If we use the records in Genesis 5 and Genesis 11 for our calculations, we will once again realize the astounding inerrancy of the Bible and the profoundness of the spiritual world.

3. A Point of Reference for Calculating the Years

Finding reference points in the Bible is crucial because not every genealogy records the years of birth or death. Selecting precisely recorded dates as reference points and using them to perform calculations forward and backward in time will help to build a complete chronological timeline. One such biblical reference point is the year of the exodus.

(1) The year of the exodus is 1446 BC.

The year of the exodus is an important reference point for calculating the generations of the patriarchs who lived prior to the exodus. The first record that assists in calculating the year of the exodus is found in the records of the kings in 1 Kings 6:1. It states that Solomon began to build the temple in the fourth year of his reign, 480 years after the Israelites came out of Egypt.

> **1 Kings 6:1** Now it came about in the four hundred and eightieth year after the sons of Israel came out of the land of Egypt, in the fourth year of Solomon's reign over Israel, in the month of Ziv which is the second month, that he began to build the house of the LORD.

Furthermore, 2 Chronicles 3:1–2 confirms the specific date that Solomon began to build the house of the Lord: the second day in the second month.

> **2 Chronicles 3:1–2** Then Solomon began to build the house of the LORD in Jerusalem on Mount Moriah, where the LORD had appeared to his father David, at the place that David had prepared on the threshing floor of Ornan the Jebusite. ²He began to build on the second day in the second month of the fourth year of his reign.

It is commonly accepted that Solomon succeeded the throne in 970 BC and began the construction work for the temple in 966 BC, the fourth year of his reign. Thus, calculations show that the year of the exodus was 1446 BC (966 + 480 = 1,446). While there are liberal views that argue that the exodus occurred in thirteenth century BC, the vast majority of conservative theologians agree that 1446 BC is more biblical.

(2) The Israelites were in Egypt for 430 years.
It is clearly recorded in the book of Exodus as follows:

> **Exodus 12:40–41** Now the time that the sons of Israel lived in Egypt was four hundred and thirty years. ⁴¹And at the end of four hundred and thirty years, to the very day, all the hosts of the LORD went out from the land of Egypt.

So if the year of the exodus was 1446 BC, then the year that the Israelites entered Egypt was 1876 BC (1,446 + 430 = 1,876; Gal 3:17).

(3) Israel migrated to Egypt 290 years after the birth of Abraham.
Abraham had Isaac at the age of 100 (Gen 21:5). Isaac had Jacob at the age of 60 (Gen 25:26). Jacob migrated to Egypt at the age of 130 (Gen 47:9). Thus, 290 years passed between Abraham's birth and Jacob's migration to Egypt (100 + 60 + 130 = 290). The sum of 1,446 (year of the exodus), 430 years in Egypt, and 290 years between Abraham's birth and Israel's migration into Egypt, results in the year of Abraham's birth: 2166 BC (1,446 + 430 + 290 = 2,166).[5]

Hence, reference points in the Bible are used as the basis for accurate calculations of dates of events and births unrecorded in the Bible. By building a chronological timeline for the twenty generations of patriarchs from Adam to Abraham, we are able to calculate the birth year of the last person Abraham. By using Abraham's birth year as a reference point, we can also accurately calculate the years of the twenty generations of patriarchs.

From this point, we will continue to examine God's divine administration of redemption as revealed through the genealogies in Genesis 4–5 and Genesis 10–11.

לבר דעת דרך המסעות ארבעים שנה במדבר ׳והרוחב והאורך של ארץ הקדושה מינהו ב׳

עמלק

מדבר צין הוא הקדש

ים המלח
עברים
עמרה
סדום

עתר
מקדה

עיר כרמל

שבט
הצור
ענב
יהד

אלהר
מולדה
שרוחן
רמות

באר שבע
שמעון
בית מירבות
גת
שבט

ארץ פלשתם

מדבר פארן

מדבר שור

מדבר סיני

רעמסס
פתם
שרה
צען

אלכסנדרי

לוח המסעות במדבר
אשר על פי ה׳ יסעו ועל פי ה׳ יחנו

א׳ רעמסס	טו׳ רתמה	כט׳ הרהגדגד
ב׳ סכת	טז׳ רמן פרץ	ל׳ יטבתה
ג׳ אתם	יז׳ לבנה	לא׳ עברנה
ד׳ פיהחירת	יח׳ רסה	לב׳ עציןגבר
ה׳ מרה	יט׳ קהלתה	לג׳ מדברצין
ו׳ אילם	כ׳ הרספר	לד׳ הרההר
ז׳ ים סוף	כא׳ חרדה	לה׳ צלמנה
ח׳ מדברסין	כב׳ מקהלת	לו׳ פונן
ט׳ רפקה	כג׳ התחת	לז׳ אבת
יו׳ אלוש	כד׳ תרח	לח׳ דיבןגד
יא׳ רפידם	כה׳ מתקה	לט׳ עלמןדבלתי
יב׳ מדברסיני	כו׳ הרי עברים	מ׳ הרי עברים
יג׳ קברתהתאוה	כז׳ מסרות	מא׳ ערבהמואב
יד׳ חצרת	כח׳ בני יעקן	

PART THREE

The Genealogy According to the Line of Cain

Genesis 3 is the account of man's original sin and Genesis 4 is a record of subsequent sins committed after the original sin. The impact of Adam's original sin was not limited only to him; its influence spread to all of his descendants. It first manifested through Cain, but this sinfulness was also not confined to Cain. Sin prospered and grew increasingly strong in the people who were unable to restrain its powers through the Word of God. Cain's sinfulness and wickedness became common traits apparent in all the descendants in his lineage. The cycle of sin and violence that began with Cain's act of murder advanced in the succeeding generations and reached its culmination during the generation of Lamech.

The genealogy according to the line of Cain is a genealogy apart from God; any mention of God's name and His works is conspicuously absent.

In this chapter, we will study the genealogy of the line of Cain in Genesis 4 and examine the unfaithful lives of his descendants. We will learn about how unbelief continued to reappear through their lives as they followed after Cain's sinfulness. We will also trace the spiritual root of that unbelief.

CHAPTER 8

The Descendants of Cain

1. Cain (קַיִן): gotten one, received

Adam and Eve had relations and gave birth to their first son Cain by the grace of God (Gen 4:1). He brought great joy to them because he was the first son born to them after they received the promise of the woman's seed in Genesis 3:15.

> **Genesis 4:1** Now the man had relations with his wife Eve, and she conceived and gave birth to Cain, and she said, "I have gotten a manchild with the help of the LORD."

Eve expressed her joy after giving birth to Cain, saying, "I have gotten a manchild with the help of the LORD." The name *Cain* was Eve's confession of faith after receiving the first fruit of mankind. She believed that she had received this son with "the help of the LORD," by His absolute grace and guidance. It is evident that Adam and Eve had great expectations for their first son. They named him with the hope that the lost paradise would be rebuilt through him.

In connection with the birth of her first son, Eve called God by a new name, *Jehovah* (or *Yahweh*), meaning the "Lord of redemption." This was an expression of her faith in the promise of the woman's seed and her hope for salvation (Genesis 3:15).

Eve's gratefulness and praises to God are also apparent in the name *Cain*. The name itself is her prayer of thanksgiving for the grace that delivered her from the pain and dangers of her first childbirth after the curse had fallen on them (Gen 3:16). Her confession indicates that she had repented and lived by faith in God's promise after being banished from the garden of Eden. After many years had passed, both sons, Cain and Abel made offerings to God validating the belief that their parents had nurtured their faith in God. Then, if Cain was born to Adam and

Eve by the grace of God, and if he had been raised in faith, what caused him to kill his brother Abel?

(1) Why Cain became a murderer

The problem began when Cain and Abel made offerings to God. God had regard for Abel and his offering, but for Cain and his offering He had no regard. What was the difference between the two men?

First, Cain had lost his faith.

Hebrews 11:4 states, "By faith Abel offered to God a better sacrifice than Cain, through which he obtained the testimony that he was righteous, God testifying about his gifts, and through faith, though he is dead, he still speaks." The superiority of Abel's offering made in faith was manifested in his offering of the "firstlings" of the flock. In faith, Abel willingly presented to God the best of what he had. God has always consecrated the first of the fruits and the first son (firstborn) as His own. However, there is no mention of "first" with regard to Cain's offering (Gen 4:3–5).

> **Exodus 23:19** You shall bring the choice first fruits of your soil into the house of the LORD your God. You are not to boil a young goat in the milk of its mother.
>
> **Proverbs 3:9** Honor the LORD from your wealth and from the first of all your produce.
>
> **Ezekiel 48:14** Moreover, they shall not sell or exchange any of it, or alienate this choice portion of land; for it is holy to the LORD.

Thus, God accepted faithful Abel and his offering, but He had no regard for faithless Cain and his offering. Although Cain had believed in God at one point, he had already lost his faith by the time he made his offering to God. For this reason, God neither accepted Cain nor was He pleased with his offering.

> **Proverbs 15:8** The sacrifice of the wicked is an abomination to the LORD, but the prayer of the upright is His delight.
>
> **Romans 12:1** Therefore I urge you, brethren, by the mercies of God, to present your bodies a living and holy sacrifice, acceptable to God, which is your spiritual service of worship.

Second, Cain missed the opportunity to repent.

Cain should have realized that he had lost his faith when God rejected him and his offering. Since Abel was a man of faith, Cain should have asked Abel to mediate on his behalf and make another offering to God. Cain's response, however, was an unexpected one. He became very angry before the Lord, and his countenance fell. Becoming angry before God is nothing less than the manifestation of darkness.

> **Genesis 4:5–6** But for Cain and for his offering He had no regard. So Cain became very angry and his countenance fell. ⁶Then the LORD said to Cain, "Why are you angry? And why has your countenance fallen?"

God saw that sin had its desire in Cain and warned him to overcome it (Gen 4:7). Cain, however, did not heed this divine warning and missed the opportunity to turn back and repent. Thus, sin had its way with Cain and he ultimately struck and killed Abel. Nonetheless, in His mercy, God sought out Cain once again and gave him a final chance to repent. He asked Cain, "Where is Abel your brother?" (Gen 4:9). This is similar to how God questioned Adam saying, "Where are you?" (Gen 3:9) after he ate the fruit of the tree of the knowledge of good and evil and hid from God. God asked even though He already knew everything. Just as He knew exactly where Adam was hiding when He questioned him, He also knew what had happened to Abel.

God was waiting for repentance as He questioned Cain. He was really asking, "Should you not have protected your younger brother instead of killing him?" God hoped that Cain would confess that he had sinned by killing Abel and seek forgiveness. God wanted to continue to look after Cain and show him love. Instead of repenting, Cain boldly opposed God, saying, "Am I my brother's keeper?" (Gen 4:9). In the end, Cain not only killed Abel, but also challenged God's Word and missed all the opportunities to repent.

Third, Cain belonged to the wrong side.

What was the main reason Cain failed to guard his faith? The Bible points out that he belonged to the wrong side. First John 3:8–9 states that Cain was "of the devil" and that he was not born of God. Cain did not have "His seed." First John 3:12 reiterates that Cain slew his brother, because Cain was "of the evil one."

By killing his brother, Cain became the first person to blatantly violate the commandment to love one's brother. This is why Apostle John explained that Cain was of the devil's seed (offspring) which belongs to the evil one. Cain committed murder, because he inherently did not have God's seed (1 John 3:9-11).[6]

Cain ended up belonging to the evil one, because he accepted the thoughts of the devil (John 13:2). Cain was born by the grace of God after Adam had relations with Eve. Initially, Cain had faith in God because of his parents' influence; this is evident from his offering to God. However, Satan secretly sowed into Cain thoughts of the devil and thoughts of darkness (Matt 13:25–30).

> **Matthew 13:25–28** But while his men were sleeping, his enemy came and sowed tares among the wheat, and went away. [26]But when the wheat sprouted and bore grain, then the tares became evident also. [27]The slaves of the landowner came and said to him, "Sir, did you not sow good seed in your field? How then does it have tares?" [28]And he said to them, "An enemy has done this!" The slaves said to him, "Do you want us, then, to go and gather them up?"

This is similar to how Satan sowed disbelief into the hearts of the Israelites during the first coming of Jesus Christ. Jesus exposed the true identity of those who claimed to be children of Abraham, saying, "You are of your father the devil" (John 8:44). Although they called themselves children of Abraham, they did not perform the deeds of their father Abraham (John 8:39).

The same people who were born in the land of Israel and boasted of their pure lineage rejected Jesus and crucified Him. This shows that their father was not Abraham, but the devil. As John 8:44 points out, they were not sons of God's kingdom, but sons of the evil one (Matt 13:38). Hence, John the Baptist vehemently rebuked, "You brood of vipers, . . . do not begin to say to yourselves, 'We have Abraham for our father'" (Matt 3:7–9; Luke 3:7–8). This was a sharp rebuke against people who boasted of their elect status. They acted holy, but their hearts were filled with evil intentions. The unrepentant Pharisees and Sadducees asserted that they were children of Abraham, but in truth, they were children of the serpent through whom Satan had deceived and corrupted Adam and Eve in the garden of Eden.[7]

Jesus called Apostle Peter "Satan" when he stood against the will of God, even though Peter was one of His foremost disciples (Matt 16:23).

During the age of the early church, Ananias made an offering, perhaps a large one, but his heart was full of lies and deception. Peter, being full of the Holy Spirit, said of him, "Satan filled [his] heart," (Acts 5:3). False prophets in sheep's clothing may appear righteous and holy, but they are ravenous wolves, full of deceit and lies (Matt 7:15). Today, we must consider whether such characteristics are present in our lives. We must examine our reflection in the mirror of God's Word to see if we are habitually deceitful or have Satan's deceptive characteristics.

(2) Cain, a model of the evil one

Through the parable of the weeds in Matthew 13:24–30, Jesus explained how people become children of darkness from moment to moment without realizing it, and how they become enslaved by Satan like Cain. The main point of the parable is that the master had sown only good seeds, but the enemy came and sowed tares among the wheat and went away (Matt 13:25). Jesus repeated this parable to His disciples and explained to them that the One who sows the good seed is the Son of Man (Matt 13:37), and the enemy who sows the tares is the "evil one" (Matt 13:28, 39). Regarding Judas Iscariot, the Bible states, ". . . the devil having already put into the heart of Judas Iscariot, the son of Simon, to betray Him" (John 13:2, 27; Luke 22:3). This is an example of Satan sowing tares. Jesus further explained that the good seeds represent the "sons of the kingdom," while the tares represent the "sons of the evil one" (Matt 13:38).

Judas heard Jesus' messages about the kingdom of heaven along with the rest of the disciples. Yet, he became a son of the evil one, not a son of heaven. Likewise, Cain belonged to Satan and possessed his traits because he had been more receptive to Satan's thoughts than to the Word of God (1 John 3:12; Gen 4:4, 8; Heb 11:4; Jude 1:11).

The good seed signifies the Word of God (Luke 8:11). Peter also compares the Word of God to a "seed which is . . . imperishable" (1 Pet 1:23). The Word of God is the "good seed," and the sons of the kingdom who receive this seed are also the "good seed" (Matt 13:38; John 6:63). Those who receive the Word of God become sons of the kingdom of heaven, but those who reject the Word of God and accept the thoughts of the devil become sons of the evil one.

The serpent deceived Eve with its craftiness in the garden of Eden and caused her to fall (2 Cor 11:3). What is the identity of this craftiness? According to 2 Corinthians 11:4, it is a different gospel, another Jesus, and a different spirit. Cain belonged to Satan because he had received the devil's seed, a different gospel, another Jesus, and a different spirit.

Furthermore, Cain was like the people described in Romans 8:5–9. He lived according to the flesh with his mind set on the things of the flesh and was, therefore, hostile toward God. He belonged to the devil and was led by the spirit of the devil (Rom 8:12–14). Cain was the first son born to Adam and Eve. The offering that he made to God is evidence that he believed in God. However, Satan planted thoughts of darkness (lies and murder, John 8:44) in him. This is why he killed his brother and reaped tares as his fruit—his title as the first murderer. Cain forsook the God he had first believed in; he abandoned God and became an "offspring of evildoers" who "did not see fit to acknowledge God any longer" (Isa 1:4; Rom 1:28).

It is written in Matthew 7:15–18, "You will know them by their fruits." Cain, who became a murderer, was clearly of the devil and possessed the devil's traits. John 8:44 explains that the sons of the devil follow the desires of the devil who is a murderer and a liar.

> **John 8:44** You are of your father the devil, and you want to do the desires of your father. He was a murderer from the beginning, and does not stand in the truth because there is no truth in him. Whenever he speaks a lie, he speaks from his own nature, for he is a liar, and the father of lies.

Contrary to Eve's expectation and confession made with joy and hope when he was born, Cain belonged to the devil (Gen 4:1).

(3) Desires of sin dwelling in Cain

The identity of the evil seed that dwelt in Cain is vividly described by Paul, the great apostle of the early church, in Romans 7:20, "But if I am doing the very thing I do not want, I am no longer the one doing it, but sin which dwells in me." This verse identifies the seed of darkness that was in Cain as "sin." Sin always involves the whole person, both the inner and the outer person. In Romans 7, Paul repeatedly exposed sin as the cause of the tragic conflict within him. This is similar to God's rebuke to Cain: "If you do well, will not your countenance be lifted up? And if you do not do well, sin is crouching at the door; and its desire is for you, but you must master it" (Gen 4:7).

The Bible warns that there is woe for those who walk in the "way of Cain" (Jude 1:11). Today, we must depart from the "way of Cain" and learn to master sin. The parable of the tares teaches us that no one, including the chosen believer, is exempt from becoming Satan's target. The tares are sown during the night and the results become evident only when they bear fruit later (Matt 13:25).

Therefore, it is important for believers to stay alert and awake at all times so that tares may not be sown in the field of the good seed, the seed of God's Word (Prov 4:23; 16:32; Matt 13:19, 25–27). Otherwise, even believers who have spent years nurturing their faith can become like Cain who had Satan's traits and become his perpetrators.

The Bible says that man is enslaved by what overcomes him (2 Pet 2:19; John 8:34; Rom 6:16; Titus 3:3). We must become God's servants and bear fruit resulting in sanctification (Rom 6:22). We must become a people for His own possession who are zealous to do good deeds (Titus 2:14; Eph 2:10).

(4) Cain settled in the land of Nod

Even after his sin, Cain shamelessly objected to God's punishment, claiming that it was more than he could bear (Gen 4:13–14). There were no traces of repentance or grief in his words over what he had done. His attitude was a direct contrast to that of the repentant psalmist who cried, "Do not cast me away from Your presence, and do not take Your Holy Spirit from me" (Ps 51:11).

What were the curses that fell upon Cain the murderer? The first curse: "When you cultivate the ground, it shall no longer yield its strength to you. . ." (Gen 4:12). This curse was much graver than the one that had fallen upon Adam (Gen 3:17–18), because the land was to reject Cain altogether. Adam had to toil in order to eat the produce of the earth; but for Cain, it would not produce any fruit at all. Regardless of Cain's labor, there would be no harvest. The second curse was that Cain would be cast away from the earth (Gen 4:12). His life as a wanderer had begun and there would no longer be any rest or peace in his life.

Sin keeps us from God. In fact, sin cuts off all our relationships. When our relationship with God becomes distant, our relationship with all creation also becomes distant. The relationships that we have within our communities will also fail and eventually lead us to feelings of isolation and alienation.

After the sons of Cain turned their backs on God, they settled in the land of Nod to the east of Eden (Gen 4:16). The name *Nod* (נוֹד) means "wandering," "vagrant," or "fugitive." This describes the state of mankind after their departure from God—restless wandering without a definite goal or purpose in life. This is a direct contrast to Eden, the land of joy. No sinner, regardless of who he or she is, can escape the curse upon this earth. The only way to break the yoke of this curse and enjoy wealth and prosperity is to believe in Jesus Christ.

Cain built a city as he settled in the land of Nod (Gen 4:17). The Hebrew word used here is *ir* (עִיר), meaning "city" or "town." This construction of the first city (city-state) reveals an underlying desire to dilute God's curse that had cast Adam and Eve out of Eden. It was also the attempt to completely separate themselves from God's intervention through a unified mortal effort to erect a lofty city. The construction of cities by men who have forsaken God comes to a climax with the construction of the tower of Babel in Genesis 11.

Restless wandering began the moment man forsook God to live independently in their man-built cities, apart from His care. Their dwelling place was a land in which they could gather nothing but dust despite their effort and struggle; it was truly the land of "wandering" (Nod). After building the city, Cain named it *Enoch* after his son—evidence that he desired for his descendants to inherit his seedbed of sin and wickedness (Gen 4:17).

2. Enoch (חֲנוֹךְ): dedication,[8] initiated,[9] teacher[10]

Cain's son, Enoch, shares the same name with Enoch, the sixth generation descendant of Seth. However, Enoch from the line of Seth was a godly man who reached the highest peak of faith, whereas Enoch from the line of Cain was an ungodly and corrupt man. Enoch was the first son born to Cain after he departed from God (Gen 4:16–17) and was the first fruit of humanism. It can be inferred that Cain named his son *Enoch*, meaning "dedication," with a hope that he would be dedicated to the success of his humanistic lineage.

The birth of Enoch is described in greater detail than any other person in the line of Cain.

Genesis 4:16–17 Then Cain went out from the presence of the LORD, and settled in the land of Nod, east of Eden. [17]Cain had relations with his wife and she conceived, and gave birth to Enoch; and he built a city, and called the name of the city Enoch, after the name of his son.

The following significant points can be construed from the meanings of the name *Enoch* ("dedication," "initiation," or "teacher"):

1. Cain built a city and named it Enoch after his son. The name Enoch was dedicated to the purpose of flaunting the citadel (city-state) of humanism built by those who had forsaken God.

2. Those who departed from God forsook all the good and beautiful things that they had once enjoyed while they were with God. They initiated a movement to live according to the human will.

3. Enoch became a teacher (beginning, source, ancestor) who instructed rebellion against God through disbelief and betrayal.

In all likelihood, the name *Enoch* became very well-known since Cain's city was named after him. Presumably, the person Enoch was famous throughout the land, but his name will not be remembered by God because he had nothing to do with God.

Enoch was like those described in Revelation 3:1, "you have a name that you are alive, but you are dead," in God's eyes; his existence was meaningless to God. Conversely, the names of the precious saints, although they may appear insignificant in this world, will be written in the book of life and will not be erased (Rev 3:5). Jesus died on the cross to fulfill the will of the Father and God awarded Him with "the name which is above every name" (Phil 2:9). To all those who follow in Jesus' steps, God will also grant the honor of having their names written in the book of life (Phil 4:3); their names will never be blotted out.

Cain and his son Enoch started off without God. Cain named the first son born to him after his independence from God, Enoch. *Enoch* means "dedication," "initiation (start)," and "teacher." Then, he also named the city that they built for themselves, Enoch. Cain and Enoch's humanistic plans and ambitions devoid of God were truly grandiose. They probably aspired to build for themselves a magnificent city, a godless paradise on earth reminiscent of the garden of Eden.

What was the ultimate destiny of these men that had begun their lives without God? They became ideological forefathers of great massacres, all forms of violence, and wickedness. They may have believed that the great city of Enoch was close to becoming paradise on earth.

However, unlike its striking beginning, it became a city of sin, murder, corruption, and injustice.

Many times, we initiate things in our lives without God. We make plans for businesses, marriages, retirements, and even extravagant events outside of God. God is the beginning of all things. Believe that God will guide us from start to finish when we pray to Him, seek answers from the Bible, and turn to His people for advice. He will take responsibility for us until our final goals are achieved.

3. Irad (עִירָד): runner, fleet,[11] boastful[12]

Irad was Enoch's son. He was a braggart, as indicated by the meaning of his name. Presumably, he was the kind of person who fled from God's presence, committing all kinds of sins and saying, "Where is God? God cannot see what I am doing!" He probably had no fear or reservation about committing the grave sin of denying God's existence. The Bible calls this kind of person the most foolish of all.

> **Psalm 10:4** The wicked, in the haughtiness of his countenance, does not seek Him. All his thoughts are, "There is no God."
>
> **Psalm 14:1** The fool has said in his heart, "There is no God." They are corrupt, they have committed abominable deeds; there is no one who does good.

God not only sees our actions, He also searches the depths of our hearts to discover the hidden motives behind those actions (Jer 17:10; Ps 94:9; Prov 5:21). He sees not only the present, but also the past and the future (Ps 139:1–3). We cannot deceive God and nothing can be hidden from Him, for He has seven eyes (Zech 3:9; 4:10; Rev 5:6). He is everywhere in the entire universe and watches over all things like the light of seven days (Isa 30:26). His eyes are like fire, moving to and fro throughout the earth so that no one can flee from them (2 Chr 16:9). Proverbs 15:3 states that His eyes watch "the evil and the good." Psalm 33:13 states, "The LORD looks from heaven; He sees all the sons of men." It continues in verse 14, "From His dwelling place He looks out on all the inhabitants of the earth," and concludes that He understands all their works (Ps 33:13–15). Job 34:21–22 states, "For His eyes are upon the ways of a man, and He sees all his steps. There is no darkness or deep shadow where the workers of iniquity may hide themselves."

They may attempt to hide deeper and run farther away within God-created time and space. Nonetheless, God can command heaven and earth to come to a stop so that He stands exactly in that hiding place at that time (Isa 48:13).

Although none of the Israelites knew that Achan had stolen the mantle, the gold, and the silver, God knew it and exposed his sin (Josh 7:1–26). No one knew that Michal had looked down from her window at King David as he was leaping and dancing and despised him in her heart (2 Sam 6:16). God, however, knew and as a result, she remained childless until the day she died (2 Sam 6:23).

No one other than Ananias' wife knew that Ananias had held back some of the proceeds from the sale of their property. God revealed his evil intention to Peter, and after Peter had rebuked Ananias for his evil deed, Ananias fell and died on the very same day (Acts 5:1–11). Truly, those who try to keep things from God, deceive Him with lies, and run away from Him are foolish!

"Boastful," one of the meanings of the name *Irad*, describes the act of making something appear greater than what it actually is. It refers to the exaggeration of one's current wealth, appearance, power, or honor in order to impress others and comfort oneself. When Nebuchadnezzar, king of Babylon, surveyed the grandeur of his kingdom and boasted of his power and glory, a voice came from heaven even before he had finished speaking. Immediately, King Nebuchadnezzar was reduced to the state of a beast in accordance with the prophecy of the voice (Dan 4:28–37).

God declared that the kingdom of Judah would come to ruin, because King Hezekiah did not speak of God's grace but only boasted of his own strength and power to Berodach-baladan, the king of Babylon (2 Kgs 20:16–19; Isa 39:6–7).

When God is not present in people's hearts, they try to fill the void by adorning themselves with power, honor, and fame. At times, they use the power of wealth, the power of authority, the power of knowledge, and physical strength to hurt and oppress the weak and the poor. For this reason, the Bible advises not to "boast in your arrogance" for "all such boasting is evil" (Jas 4:16). The only boasting that we should do is of Jesus Christ (Gal 6:14).

4. Mehujael (מְחוּיָאֵל): blotted out by God[13]

The name of Irad's son, *Mehujael*, means "blotted out clean by God" (Gen 4:18). The name *Mehujael* is a combination of the root words מָחָה (*mahah*), meaning "to blot" or "to wipe out," and אֵל (*el*), meaning "God." Consequently, the name can be interpreted as "the one whom God wiped out" or "the one whose name God blotted out." This name is a curse and is truly frightening. A name attests to a person's existence, and blotting it out voids that person's existence altogether. This is truly the greatest judgment.

What kind of life did Mehujael live that he should deserve such a cursed name? Although the Bible makes no mention of his deeds or his character, we can make inferences about his life based on other uses of the Hebrew word מָחָה (*mahah*) in the Bible.

The word *mahah*, the root of *mehuh*, was used to describe the act of using a sponge or fabric to absorb and wipe away ink spots from a scroll. When an individual's name, his achievements, or an entire nation is wiped away like ink spots from a scroll, it is a sure sign of fearful judgment. Consequently, this word was mainly used in connection with the punishment and judgment of criminals. In the account of the flood, Genesis 6:7 states, "And the Lord said, 'I will blot out man whom I have created from the face of the land.'" Genesis 7:23 also states, "Thus He blotted out every living thing that was upon the face of the land." The expression "to blot out" is the English translation of the Hebrew word *mahah*. It signifies the wiping away of all things as judgment for sin. However, there are many other usages of this word which can be classified under the following two categories.

First, the word was used in reference to the total annihilation of a city or tribe.

The Bible uses the word *mahah* in reference to cities or tribes that have sinned against God, signifying how they would be removed and made extinct. In the verse, "I will wipe Jerusalem as one wipes a dish" in 2 Kings 21:13, the word *wipe* (*mahah*) connotes God's judgment upon the city.

The word *mahah* was also used in a discussion on how to save the tribe of Benjamin, which was at the verge of extinction. Judges 21:17 asserts, "a tribe may not be blotted out (*mahah*) from Israel." This word was used in connection with judgment upon a city or tribe resulting in destruction so utterly complete that it will be wiped out from people's memories.

Second, this word was used in reference to the act of blotting out a person's name or the memory of the person's existence. A good example is the account of the Amalekites. In Exodus 17:14, God said, "I will utterly blot out the memory of Amalek from under heaven," and in Deuteronomy 9:14, "Let Me alone, that I may destroy them and blot out their name from under heaven." Here, *mahah* signifies the act of blotting out from a person's memory. The Amalekites had attacked the faint and weary stragglers trailing behind at the end of the Israelites' wilderness procession (Deut 25:18; 1 Sam 15:2). God remembered what they had done and commanded the sons of Israel to blot out Amalek's name so that it would not be remembered. The threat to blot out one's name, which is equal to blotting out one's existence, is the proclamation of fearful judgment.

These two examples demonstrate how the word *mahah* was used to describe God's judgment upon nations, tribes, cities, and individuals who stood against His will and committed sin. We can infer from the name *Mehujael* that he had lived his life similar to the ways of the Amalekites who endlessly challenged God and afflicted His people. His life must have resembled that of the people before the flood who were wicked and violent in their purpose.

5. Methushael (מְתוּשָׁאֵל): man of Sheol or man of God[14]

The name of Mehujael's son, *Methushael* (Gen 4:18), has two contradicting meanings.

First, *Methushael* can be rendered as a compound word (name) made up of מַת (*math*), which means "man," and שְׁאוֹל (*sheol*), which means "Sheol" or "hell." Thus, the name means "man of hell." In the Old Testament, "Sheol" usually refers to the grave, hell, or the world of the dead. This implies that Methushael did not walk with God, but that he lived his life seeking to satisfy his worldly greed and personal desires and ultimately fell into Sheol, the world of the dead.

Second, *Methushael* can also be rendered as a compound word made up of *math*, God's name *el*, and *sha*, meaning "of," and means "man of God."

It can be presumed that Mehujael gave his son a name that means "man of God." His own name means "to blot out" and he probably lived a vain life, losing all that he had achieved in one sweep. It is likely that he hoped that his son, Methushael, would become a man of God and be guided by His hands into a life of peace and blessings.

Unfortunately, Methushael's son, Lamech, became a murderer more wicked than Cain (Gen 4:23–24). Thus, we can infer that Methushael's life must have resembled that of a man of hell rather than a man of God.

Like the two meanings of the name *Methushael*, all human beings walk one of the two paths of life. Some live as people of God and follow His will; they are used for His glory to do His great and honorable work. What a glorious honor it is for frail human beings to be called "people of God," to belong to Him, and be used by Him! Moses (Deut 33:1), Samuel (1 Sam 9:8), Elijah (1 Kgs 17:18), Elisha (2 Kgs 4:7; 5:8), King David (Neh 12:24), and other unnamed prophets (1 Sam 2:27; 1 Kgs 13:1) were called "men of God." Paul also called Timothy "man of God" (1 Tim 6:11).

Some people live their lives enslaved by Satan and confined in darkness as children of hell. Jude 1:11–13 describe the lives of people such as Cain, Balaam, and Korah, who stood against God, as "wandering stars, for whom the black darkness has been reserved forever." The "black darkness [that] has been reserved" in this verse refers to hell.

There are always two opposing paths laid out before all people. Moses spoke the words of God, saying, "See, I have set before you today life and prosperity, and death and adversity" (Deut 30:15). He continues, "I have set before you life and death, the blessing and the curse," and then he instructs the people, "So choose life in order that you may live, you and your descendants" (Deut 30:19). We must choose life. We must love God and obey His Word (Deut 30:20). Then, our lives will take shape as lives of the people of God, and the meaning "man of Sheol" will not apply to us.

6. Lamech (לֶמֶךְ): a strong youth,[15] the conqueror[16]

The Bible provides a detailed account of Lamech, the last individual mentioned among the six that appear in the line of Cain (Gen 4:19–24). Sin advanced down the line of Cain after the fall and reached its peak with Lamech the last generation. He yielded the fruit of darkness and wickedness in abundance.

The Hebrew etymology of the name *Lamech* (or *Lamek*) is unclear. In Arabic, it means "strong youth" or "oppressor." John P. Lange interprets it as "strong youth."[17] The meaning of the name suggests that he was an arrogant man who boasted of his strength.

Those who are incomparably stronger and more powerful freely exercise violence against the weak to overpower and control them. Furthermore, they become intoxicated in their own heroism and drift far away from God. Lamech's life manifests the expansion of evil after Adam's fall.

(1) Lamech defiled God's ordained principle of holy matrimony, turning it into a fleshly and hedonistic practice.

Lamech was a lustful man who took for himself two wives. Genesis 4:19 states, "Lamech took to himself two wives." The table below shows that sons were born to Lamech through the two women.

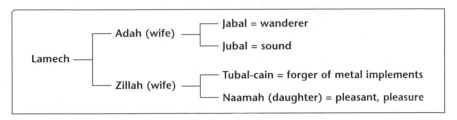

① Adah was Lamech's first wife.

The name *Adah* means "adorn," "decorate," or "glow." It suggests that she beautified herself only for the purpose of seduction, not knowing that beauty also comes from within. Presumably, she was a superficial woman who invested much time in adorning herself and delighting in her own reflection in the mirror. In today's terms, her priority in life was to indulge in fancy clothes, expensive cosmetics, precious jewelry, beautiful houses, and luxurious cars.

② Zillah was Lamech's second wife.

The name *Zillah* means "shade" or "shadow"[18] (possibly implying shady places of sin). It also means "protection" (perhaps alluding to her desire to be protected by any man). The name can also mean "to tinkle," an allusion to the sweet sound of the female voice toward men.[19] She was most likely a lewd woman who whispered flattery into her husband's ears and enticed him to perform even more evil deeds.

Even after committing murder, Lamech returned home and boasted of his strength before his wives without any sense of guilt. With the weapon still in his hand, he sang a song about his gruesome act.

> **Genesis 4:23–24** Lamech said to his wives, "Adah and Zillah, listen to my voice, you wives of Lamech, give heed to my speech, for I have killed a man for wounding me; and a boy for striking me; ²⁴if Cain is avenged sevenfold, then Lamech seventy-sevenfold."

Rather than admonishing their husband for his evil deeds, Lamech's wives most likely praised and applauded him as he sang stories about how he had killed with his sword. Adah was probably preoccupied with beautifying herself to please her husband, while Zillah probably sang along with her husband, spurring him on with the "tinkling" sounds of her voice.

(2) Lamech misused the name of God and murdered for vengeance without any remorse.

Lamech sang, "If Cain is avenged [by God] sevenfold, then Lamech seventy-sevenfold" (Gen 4:24). He sang that God would avenge him as He had avenged Cain, but in actuality Lamech avenged himself. The Bible states, however, that vengeance belongs to God (Deut 32:35; Rom 12:19; Heb 10:30).

In addition, Lamech interpreted God's special favor and mercy toward Cain as divine protection for murderers. He turned the law of compassion into a law of retribution. In Cain's case, God prevented others from taking revenge against him, but Lamech took revenge into his own hands. This was an encroachment upon God's sovereign authority.

In Lamech's poem about his killing, he profaned the name of God Almighty and openly declared that he would take vengeance and kill anyone without mercy. This was a flagrant display of man's arrogance and a blasphemous outburst against God.

(3) Lamech disdained the value of life and humanity.

Lamech boasts in Genesis 4:23, ". . . for I have killed a man for wounding me; and a boy for striking me."

The term *to wound* is פָּצַע (*patsa*) in Hebrew and refers to a light bruise, not a life-threatening injury. Lamech refused to restrain his anger caused by a light wound and mercilessly destroyed a precious life to display his strength and power to others. His actions unfortunately reflected the evil that was prevalent in his time: the exaltation of oneself and the degradation of human life, which should have been held in high esteem because it is the image of God.

(4) Lamech passed down to his children a civilization founded upon strife and murder.

For the descendants of Cain, the purpose of child rearing and education seemed far removed from any desire for the restoration of the intellect, personal character, or the spirituality of a child. They developed their civilization for the purpose of expanding the influence of humanism, and their opposition to God grew stronger with the passage of time.

① Lamech had Jabal and Jubal through his first wife Adah.

> **Genesis 4:20–21** Adah gave birth to Jabal; he was the father of those who dwell in tents and have livestock. [21]His brother's name was Jubal; he was the father of all those who play the lyre and pipe.

The name *Jabal* means "to lead," "to carry," or "to flow" (searching for wet places).[20] He became the father of those who "dwell in tents and have livestock." The word *livestock* here is מִקְנֶה (*miqneh*), and it refers to flocks or herds of animals used for mercantile purposes. Jabal and his descendants were the first nomads dwelling in tents and may have been the first to trade livestock. He was not, however, the first to raise herds; Abel was also a "keeper of flocks" (Gen 4:2).

The name *Jubal* means "sound" or "music." He became the father of all who played the lyre and pipe. Unfortunately, their instruments were not used to praise and worship God. Their music produced sounds of debauchery and licentiousness. The Hebrew word for *pipe*, עוּגָב (*ugav*), is derived from the verb עָגַב (*agav*), which means "to fall into sensual love." Thus, it is certain that Jubal's music was not designed for praising God, but rather for sensual pleasure and entertainment.

② Lamech had Tubal-cain and Naamah through his second wife Zillah.

> **Genesis 4:22** As for Zillah, she also gave birth to Tubal-cain, the forger of all implements of bronze and iron; and the sister of Tubal-cain was Naamah.

Tubal-cain became a forger of all kinds of sharp implements and tools of bronze and iron. He was a blacksmith. The name *Tubal-cain* (תּוּבַל קַיִן) is a compound word made up of תּוּבַל (*tuval*) and קַיִן (*qayin*). The word *tubal* derives its meaning from Arabic roots: "to overflow," "to multiply" (breed), or "to run." Combined with *Cain*, the name reveals Lamech's desire for the future prosperity of the Cainite descendants. The attachment of the name *Cain* (father of this sinful lineage) to the name Tubal-cain suggests that the sinfulness flowing through the lineage was most prominent during his time. Tubal-cain smelted and sharpened metal implements. They were not used as farming or peacemaking tools, but as weapons to kill, like the ones used by his father Lamech.

Lamech's daughter, Naamah, was born of his second wife Zillah (Gen 4:22) and was Tubal-cain's younger sister. Her name means "pleasant," "sweet," or "beautiful (exceptionally)." Naamah was a woman who was adept at arousing sexual desires. Traditionally, women's names are excluded from lists of descendants. Most likely, Naamah's name was recorded in this genealogy, not because she was godly in any way, but because she was extraordinary in her beauty and lust and skilled in giving pleasure.

(5) Lamech deified (heroized) himself.
Metal implements also gave rise to carnage and lawlessness and led to the birth of "heroes" during this period. Naturally, a great band of evil followers formed around these heroes, building enormous strength and challenging God. This was the evil by-product of the advancement of human civilization.

As civilization developed, it headed toward humanism, hedonism, and debauchery. The underlying philosophy was that the development of individual power would allow one to become a supernatural being similar to God. This is an example of Satan at work, always tempting people to disregard God, rebel against Him, and try to gain independence from Him.

Lamech had reached a point where he no longer feared God's wrath. Adam's sin was disobedience to God's command. Cain's sin was rejecting the Word and manifesting his wickedness through murder. Lamech's sin was normalizing the act of murder and heightening the spirit of revenge. Sin lodged deeper into the structure of society, and the world was stained with the blood-shed of revenge. The ungodliness of the Cainite lineage had reached its peak with Lamech, the seventh generation from Adam.

CHAPTER 9

The Descendants of Sin
in the Line of Cain

The descendants of Cain reached their apex in Lamech's time as their civilization flourished and developed, but the genealogy comes to a sudden halt after Lamech. In contrast, the genealogy of Seth continued through Noah, Abraham, David, and eventually to the Messiah.

This is not to say that all the descendants of Cain perished during Lamech's time. Cain's lineage undoubtedly continued through Lamech's three sons, most likely forming a great nation. The Bible, however, discontinues the genealogy of Cain as a warning to its readers. Civilizations may advance and flourish, but they can come to a sudden halt even at its peak if they forge ahead without God.

The Bible testifies that Cain's fleshly genealogy does not stop with Lamech. Rather, Cain's sinful characteristics continue to influence the lives of different people until the end of time. The genealogies that continued through Nimrod (a descendant of Ham who instigated the people to build the tower of Babel), Ishmael, and Esau are prominent examples.

1. The Descendants of Nimrod (נִמְרוֹד) and the Construction of the Tower of Babel

The descendants of Cain in Genesis 4 were pioneers of human civilization. Lamech's three sons became fathers of those who engaged in trading livestock, played musical instruments, and made metal implements. Nimrod became a mighty hunter and warrior on the earth comparable to Cain and Lamech (Gen 10:8–9).

(1) Nimrod, the mighty one on earth

Genesis 10 describes Nimrod as the first mighty one on the earth, a mighty hunter before the Lord, and the father of Babel. The flow of the genealogy of Ham breaks to provide a detailed account of Nimrod's deeds; it was a deliberate attempt to call special attention to him.

First, Nimrod was a "mighty one." The term *mighty one* is defined in the Hebrew lexicon as "hero," "vigorous man," or "influential man." It is also interpreted as "a distinguished man of valor with the ability and wisdom to achieve great works." Although Nimrod was called a mighty one on the earth, he was not a hero in God's sight. Rather, he was fearless and skillful in challenging God and defying His will. He possessed exceptional ability and shrewdness for plundering souls through deception.

The term *mighty one* is נִבּוֹר (*gibbor*) in Hebrew and generally means "one who rules with violence" or "a tyrant." Nimrod was a tyrant who oppressed people and opposed God. He conquered tribes through violence and challenged God by instigating people to build the tower of Babel.

Second, Nimrod was a "mighty hunter." This speaks of his work and relationship with God. The description "mighty hunter" implies that he was a distinctively skillful hunter compared to others. The region where Nimrod dwelled was a fertile land inhabited by numerous beasts of the field (Exod 23:29–30; Deut 7:22). Henry M. Morris comments, "The reference to Nimrod's hunting prowess suggests that wild beasts were thought to be a real source of danger at the time and that Nimrod acquired his heroic reputation by protecting the population against these beasts."[21] Thus, Nimrod gained servile followers and rose to the position of a heroic leader in his time. His power increased as the number of followers multiplied, and he used this power to deify himself. He sat in God's place and opposed Him. He toyed with the people's souls and flaunted his ability to reign over them. Nimrod was a type of the antichrist, robbing the souls of mankind and turning them away from God.

> **Genesis 10:8–9** Cush was also the ancestor of Nimrod, who was the first heroic warrior on earth. [9]Since he was the greatest hunter in the world, his name became proverbial. People would say, "This man is like Nimrod, the greatest hunter in the world." (New Living Translation)

Third, Nimrod the mighty hunter became the founder of Babel (Gen 10:10; 11:4, 9). With the support of his followers, he founded Babel, the atheistic city-state that challenged God's will. Similar in character to that of the Cainite descendants, the kingdom of Babel exalted the names of men rather than God's. Nimrod mobilized the people at the plains of Shinar for the purpose of building the tower of Babel to achieve his great objective.

(2) Constructing the Tower of Babel

The people's desire to build the tower of Babel under Nimrod's leadership originated from their ambition to establish a self-sufficient civilization independent from God. The Bible speaks of three purposes for the construction of the tower of Babel.

The first purpose was to build for themselves a city and a tower whose top would reach heaven (Gen 11:4). This tower was a *ziggurat*, a structure in the form of a terraced pyramid with successively receding stories. At the center of the ziggurat were steps to the top where a small temple or shrine was built. In the ancient world, the purpose of building a tall religious structure that could reach the heavens was to raise a great empire through the unity of human strength. The desire to build a safe and strong nation independent from God was manifested in the construction of the tower of Babel.

This incident occurred not too long after the catastrophic flood that destroyed the entire world. Thus, the construction of the tower of Babel was an expression of the people's discontentment with God's judgment. They had no regard for God's covenant of the rainbow—the promise that He would never again judge the world with water (universal flood, Gen 9:8–17). In defiance, they began to prepare for God's judgment through human strength and ability. How foolish and arrogant it is for men to reject God's protection and attempt to build their own place of refuge! This act is reminiscent of how Cain had disregarded God's sign of protection and went on to build a city for his own protection, naming it after his own son Enoch (Gen 4:15–17). The root of all this is the devil's dark and evil power that opposes God.

Today, similar situations occur not only in the secular world, but also within the church. The congregation of darkness seeks to unify by emphasizing one heart and one will, rather than focusing on the Bible.

Unity outside of the Word of God and gatherings that God does not acknowledge will only lead to conflicts, hurt, a sense of futility, and regret. Furthermore, unified powers outside of God and gatherings for the purpose of enjoyment and convenience are not only lawless, unrighteous, and wicked, but also opposes God's great plan for redemption.

The second purpose for building the tower of Babel was to make a name for themselves (Gen 11:4). Like the descendants of Cain, they sought after their own honor and exaltation rather than the glory of God's name. They used the power of science and civilization to challenge God's authority and reached the peak of human arrogance—the desire to become like God (Isa 14:12–14). However, God destroyed their haughty plans by confusing their language and scattering them throughout the face of the whole earth (Gen 11:7–8).

Adam and Eve were deceived by the serpent's words in the garden of Eden: "For God knows that in the day you eat from it your eyes will be opened, and you will be like God, knowing good and evil" (Gen 3:5). They ate from the tree of the knowledge of good and evil in their proud desire to become like God and were expelled from Eden (Gen 3:23–24). James 4:6 states, "God is opposed to the proud."

The third purpose for building the tower of Babel was to avoid being scattered over the face of the whole earth (Gen 11:4). This was an act of defiance against God's command upon creation. After God created man, the first command He gave to Adam was to "Be fruitful and multiply, and fill the earth, and subdue it" (Gen 1:28). God also gave the same blessing to Noah and his sons after the flood: "Be fruitful and multiply, and fill the earth" (Gen 9:1, 7). This command reveals God's intent to spread His children throughout the world so that they may prosper and turn the kingdom of the world into a kingdom of God's people. In opposition, Nimrod gathered his followers to build the tower of Babel in order to prevent people from being dispersed throughout the face of the whole earth. All this was evil in the eyes of God, and He destroyed all of their plans.

Genesis 11:8–9 So the LORD scattered them abroad from there over the face of the whole earth; and they stopped building the city. ⁹Therefore its name was called Babel, because there the LORD confused the language of the whole earth; and from there the LORD scattered them abroad over the face of the whole earth.

God used the confusion of languages to halt the construction of the tower and scatter the people. Language is more than mere utterances of speech. Unity in language signifies unity in thought and lifestyle. Therefore, the confusion of languages not only leads to differences in beliefs, but also causes chaos in all aspects of life. Differences in pronunciation can result in the breakdown in communication, lead to misunderstandings, and ultimately cause the construction to end. It shows that even the greatest human endeavors can come to naught despite careful planning, detailed coordination, and great investment. Prophet Isaiah declared God's Word to such foolish people: "Surely My hand founded the earth, and My right hand spread out the heavens; when I call to them, they stand together" (Isa 48:13). In 1 Samuel 2:6–10, Hannah, who was barren, gave birth to Samuel by the grace of God. After the birth of Samuel, she realized that all things are part of God's sovereign providence and praised Him, saying, "Those who contend with the LORD will be shattered; against them He will thunder in the heavens" (1 Sam 2:10).

In the promotion of evil schemes, this world is quick to unite, powerfully driven, and grandiose in its dreams. We must examine our lives of faith to see if our plans, our ways, and our goals are devoid of God. Do our plans promote and rely on our abilities? Are our plans human-centered like those of the people who built the tower of Babel? In His sovereign providence God called us for His good purpose. Paul encourages, "Therefore, walk in a manner worthy of the calling with which you have been called" (Eph 4:1). Those who are called according to His purpose will work together for good in order to fulfill what God has planned (Rom 8:28). The times are calling for people of faith who will conduct themselves in "a manner worthy of the gospel of Christ" so that they may be pleasing to God (Phil 1:27).

2. Ishmael (יִשְׁמָעֵאל) and Esau (עֵשָׂו)

The history of the wicked civilization of the descendants of Cain ended after Lamech, but manifested itself again with the attempt to build the tower of Babel. It was unsuccessful because God scattered the people, but the history of the line of Cain did not cease. It continued again through Abraham's son Ishmael and his grandson Esau.

(1) Ishmael, a wild donkey of a man

The Bible states that Abraham's son Ishmael, born of Hagar the maid, would live the life of a "wild donkey." The angel of the Lord spoke of Ishmael in Genesis 16:12, "And he will be a wild donkey of a man, his hand will be against everyone, and everyone's hand will be against him; and he will live to the east of all his brothers." This is a foreboding of the strife between the children of Ishmael and Abraham's promised son Isaac.

His dwelling place will be "to the east." The literal translation of "to the east" is "before the face of." According to the Revised Standard Version, he will dwell "over against" his kinsmen. Hence, the phrase that "he will live to the east of all his brothers" implies that he would become an offspring of sin and wickedness like Nimrod, and stand against God and afflict His people. Nimrod became a mighty hunter and reigned over the people who opposed God. Likewise, Ishmael was like a wild donkey, one that viciously afflicted God's people.

From the verse, "His hand will be against everyone, and everyone's hand will be against him," we can infer that he was the kind of person who stirred up dissension and instigated unnecessary fights wherever he went. He continuously raised his hands to strike God's people and challenge His will. Ishmael's entire life was filled with hostility and animosity toward others. How pitiful would his life eventually become when everyone turns against him (Jer 17:6)!

Ishmael's contention with others started at an early age. He began mocking his younger brother Isaac as soon as he was born (Gen 21:9). Furthermore, he affiliated himself with Nimrod when he took a wife from the land of Egypt (Gen 21:21). In Genesis 10:6, Cush, Mizraim, Put, and Canaan were born to Ham, Noah's son. Mizraim became the father of the Egyptians. Cush became the father of Nimrod. Thus, through his marriage with an Egyptian woman, Ishmael drew closer to Nimrod's line.

(2) Esau, father of the Edomites

Esau, the father of the Edomites, was one of Isaac's twin sons. He ultimately lost his place among God's covenanted people because he took the privileges of his birthright lightly and sold it to his brother Jacob (Gen 25:29–34; Heb 12:16–17). Esau took wives from the daughters of Canaan: Adah the daughter of Elon the Hittite and Oholibamah the daughter of Anah. He also married Basemath the daughter of Ishmael (Gen 36:2–3). Through these marriages he simultaneously connected himself with the line of Canaan (son of Ham) and the line of Ishmael. Thus, the unchosen descendants of Cain not only shared a common philosophy and way of life, but also married their own kind. They stood on the path of unbelief opposing God's will.

One of the most notable persons among the descendants of Esau was Amalek (Gen 36:12). Amalek was born to Eliphaz, Esau's son, through his concubine Timna. Later, the descendants of Amalek attacked the children of Abraham in Rephidim as they journeyed through the wilderness after their exodus from Egypt. God was greatly angered by their attack on His chosen people. As a result, He vowed to wage war against Amalek from generation to generation (Exod 17:16) and commanded Israel to blot out the memory of Amalek from under heaven (Deut 25:17–19). The Amalekites, however, continued to afflict the people of Israel and even allied themselves with neighboring countries to attack Israel ([Ref] Obad 1:1, 2, 10, 18).

There was also a time when Israel came close to being annihilated because of Haman the son of Hammedatha the Agagite (Esth 3:1–15). However, they were miraculously saved from destruction through Queen Esther's sacrificial faith. The Bible introduces Haman as an Agagite, revealing that he was a descendant of Esau (Esth 3:1, 10; 8:5; 9:24). In 1 Samuel 15:8, Agag is described as "the king of the Amalekites"—evidence that Agag was an Amalekite and thus a descendant of Esau. Therefore, Haman was also a descendant of Esau.

Everyone who followed the way of Cain afflicted God's covenanted children and tried to hinder His work of redemption just as Nimrod, Ishmael, and Esau had done (Jude 1:11). Their works of darkness will not cease until the day the work of redemption is complete. Nimrod and the people of Babel inherited Cain's unbelief and it continued through Ishmael and Esau. In the book of Revelation, these descendants of Cain are all together called "Babylon" (Rev 17:5; 18:2).

The name *Babylon* refers to those who are unable to protect the purity of their faith and resist the temptation to partake in the abominable deeds of the "great harlot and the world." They stand against the will of God and rely on and trust only in the civilization that they have built. In the end, these people will be torn into three parts and will perish so that they cannot be restored (Rev 16:19). The genealogies of the un-faithful teach an important lesson. Plans that are devoid of God from the beginning and works whose methods and results oppose Him will collapse even at the height of their success. The genealogy of Cain was suddenly cut off during Lamech's generation, and the construction of the tower of Babel came to an abrupt halt. The Bible testifies that the great city Babylon will also be "fallen, fallen" in the end (Rev 14:8; 18:2).

This was God's sovereign providence and His way of working toward achieving salvation for His chosen people. The line of Cain became a force that attempted to interfere with God's work of redemption and will continue its resistance until the end (1 John 3:12). Although the sinfulness of the line of Cain was great, God's sovereign will was even greater and more fervent. His divine administration of salvation will carry on until the day Satan's head is crushed and made a footstool for God's feet (Ps 110:1; Luke 20:43; Acts 2:35; Heb 1:13; 10:13).

Even as the tides of sin and wickedness swell over the earth, God's work of redemption will continue undaunted, like a great waterway of life that resuscitates the dying ocean. Our present world, completely immersed in all kinds of sin, is evidence that the final segment of the history of redemption is quickly approaching. It is time to prepare the spiritual oil for our lamps (Matt 25:1–13; 24:44). It is now time to wake up from slumber (Rom 13:11; Luke 21:36). The final fulfillment of God's work of redemption is closer now than any other time. It is important for everyone to prepare diligently in faith, strive to achieve godliness, and examine themselves so that they lead lives with no regrets (2 Cor 13:5; 1 Tim 4:7–8; 2 Pet 1:5–8).

PART FOUR

The Genealogy According to the Line of Seth

Genesis 4 sums up the genealogy of those who have forsaken God, and Genesis 5 introduces a new genealogy of faith that begins with Seth. In a world stained by Cain's unbelief and brutal act of murder, the emergence of the line of Seth meant renewed hope and a new beginning for all mankind. There are twenty generations in the genealogy of Seth: ten generations from Adam to Noah and another ten from Noah's son Shem to Abraham.

First, God's administration of redemptive history until the coming of the Messiah flows through this genealogy.

Second, this genealogy introduces Noah (tenth generation from Adam) and Abraham (tenth generation from Shem). These two central figures in the history of redemption are the presages of the Savior who would come to save mankind from judgment (Matt 24:37; Gal 3:16).

Third, the patriarchs in the genealogy are good examples of proper faith for believers who place their hope in the second coming. The God who worked through these twenty patriarchs is also working through us today.

This chapter will introduce the twenty patriarchs through the study of their names, the historical background of their times, and description of their lives of worship and godly faith. In addition, we will examine how God's plan for the redemption of mankind continuously flows through the core of this genealogy.

The Twenty Generations of the Patriarchs

(✶ The chronology of the patriarchs and the correlation of their years organized and presented for the first time in history)

1st אָדָם 'Αδάμ **Adam**	① Adam became the father of Seth at the age of 130. ② He lived 800 more years and had other children. He died at the age of 930 (Gen 5:3–5). ③ Adam lived 56 years contemporaneously with Lamech, his ninth generation.
2nd שֵׁת Σήθ **Seth**	① Seth was born 130 years after Adam. ② He became the father of Enosh at the age of 105. He lived 807 more years and had other children. He died at the age of 912 (1,042 years after Adam, Gen 5:6–8). ③ He lived 800 years contemporaneously with Adam.
3rd אֱנוֹשׁ 'Ενώς **Enosh**	① Enosh was born 235 years after Adam. ② He became the father of Kenan at the age of 90. He lived 815 more years and had other children. He died at the age of 905 (1,140 years after Adam, Gen 5:9–11). ③ He lived 695 years contemporaneously with Adam.
4th קֵינָן Καϊνάμ **Kenan**	① Kenan was born 325 years after Adam. ② He became the father of Mahalalel at the age of 70. He lived 840 more years and had other children. He died at the age of 910 (1,235 years after Adam, Gen 5:12–14). ③ He lived 605 years contemporaneously with Adam.
5th מַהֲלַלְאֵל Μαλελεήλ **Mahalalel**	① Mahalalel was born 395 years after Adam. ② He became the father of Jared at the age of 65. He lived 830 more years and had other children. He died at the age of 895 (1,290 years after Adam, Gen 5:15–17). ③ He lived 535 years contemporaneously with Adam.
6th יֶרֶד 'Ιάρετ **Jared**	① Jared was born 460 years after Adam. ② He became the father of Enoch at the age of 162. He lived 800 more years and had other children. He died at the age of 962 (1,422 years after Adam, Gen 5:18–20). ③ He lived 470 years contemporaneously with Adam.

7th חֲנוֹךְ Ἐνώχ **Enoch**	① Enoch was born 622 years after Adam. ② He became the father of Methuselah at the age of 65. He walked with God for 300 years and had other children. Then, he was transfigured and taken up to heaven without seeing death at the age of 365 (987 years after Adam, Gen 5:21–24; Heb 11:5–6; Jude 1:14–15). ③ He lived 308 years contemporaneously with Adam.
8th מְתוּשֶׁלַח Μαθουσαλά **Methuselah**	① Methuselah was born 687 years after Adam. ② He became the father of Lamech at the age of 187. He lived 782 more years and had other children. He died at the age of 969 (1,656 years after Adam, Gen 5:25–27). ③ He lived 243 years contemporaneously with Adam.
9th לֶמֶךְ Λάμεχ **Lamech**	① Lamech was born 874 years after Adam. ② He became the father of Noah at the age of 182. He lived 595 more years and had other children. He died at the age of 777 (1,651 years after Adam, Gen 5:28–31). ③ He lived 56 years contemporaneously with Adam.
10th נֹחַ Νῶε **Noah**	① Noah was born 1,056 years after Adam. ② He became the father of Shem at the age of 502, and the flood began when he was 600 years old. He lived 350 years after the flood and died at the age of 950 (2,006 years after Adam, Gen 5:32; 9:28–29). Noah did not have additional children after the flood. ③ Noah was born 126 years after Adam's death so the two men did not meet. He lived 58 years contemporaneously with Abraham. ④ The flood occurred 726 years after Adam's death. ⑤ The revelation regarding the flood and instructions for the ark were given after Noah's three sons were married (after Noah was 500 years old, Gen 5:32; 6:10–18). ⑥ Revelation regarding the date of the flood: 1,656 years after Adam (when Noah was 600 years old); 10th day of the 2nd month. ⑦ Date of the flood = 1,656 years after Adam (when Noah was 600 years old); 17th day of the 2nd month (Gen 7:4, 6–12).
11th שֵׁם Σήμ **Shem**	① Shem was born 1,558 years after Adam (before the flood, when Noah was 502 years old). ② He became the father of Arpachshad at the age of 100 (2 years after the flood). He lived 500 more years and had other children. He died at the age of 600 (2,158 years after Adam, Gen 11:10–11). ③ Shem lived 448 years contemporaneously with Noah, his father. ④ Shem lived 35 additional years after Abraham's death, until Isaac was 110 years old and Jacob was 50 years old. ⑤ Shem experienced the flood at the age of 98 and lived a long life, until he was 600 years of age. He had witnessed the world before the flood, after the flood, and even the judgment of Babel. ⑥ He lived contemporaneously with 15 generations of patriarchs (including himself), from Methuselah (8th) to Jacob (22nd).

12th אַרְפַּכְשַׁד Ἀρφαξάδ **Arpachshad**	① Arpachshad was born 1,658 years after Adam. ② He became the father of Shelah at the age of 35. He lived 403 more years and had other children. He died at the age of 438 (2,096 years after Adam, Gen 11:12–13). ③ He lived 348 years contemporaneously with Noah. ④ He lived until Abraham was 148 years old and Isaac was 48 years old.
13th שֶׁלַח Σαλά **Shelah**	① Shelah was born 1,693 years after Adam. ② He became the father of Eber at the age of 30. He lived 403 more years and had other children. He died at the age of 433 (2,126 years after Adam, Gen 11:14–15). ③ He lived 313 years contemporaneously with Noah. ④ Shelah outlived Abraham by 3 years, until Isaac was 78 years old and Jacob was 18 years old.
14th עֵבֶר Ἔβερ **Eber**	① Eber was born 1,723 years after Adam. ② He became the father of Peleg at the age of 34. He lived 430 more years and had other children. He died at the age of 464 (2,187 years after Adam, Gen 11:16–17). ③ He lived 283 years contemporaneously with Noah. ④ Eber outlived Abraham by 64 years, until Isaac was 139 years old and Jacob was 79 years old.
15th פֶּלֶג Φάλεκ **Peleg**	① Peleg was born 1,757 years after Adam. ② He became the father of Reu at the age of 30. He lived 209 more years and had other children. He died at the age of 239 (1,996 years after Adam, Gen 11:18–19). ③ Man's life span was shortened by half after Eber. Thus, Peleg was the first one to die among the 10 generations after the flood. ④ He lived 239 years contemporaneously with Noah.
16th רְעוּ Ῥαγαύ **Reu**	① Reu was born 1,787 years after Adam. ② He became the father of Serug at the age of 32. He lived 207 more years and had other children. He died at the age of 239 (2,026 years after Adam, Gen 11:20–21). ③ He lived 219 years contemporaneously with Noah.
17th שְׂרוּג Σερούχ **Serug**	① Serug was born 1,819 years after Adam. ② He became the father of Nahor at the age of 30. He lived 200 more years and had other children. He died at the age of 230 (2,049 years after Adam, Gen 11:22–23). ③ He lived 187 years contemporaneously with Noah.
18th נָחוֹר Ναχώρ **Nahor**	① Nahor was born 1,849 years after Adam. ② He became the father of Terah at the age of 29. He lived 119 more years and had other children. He died at the age of 148 (1,997 years after Adam, Gen 11:24–25). He lived the shortest life among all 20 generations of patriarchs. ③ He lived 148 years contemporaneously with Noah.

19th תֶּרַח Θάρα **Terah**	① Terah was born 1,878 years after Adam. ② He became the father of Abram at the age of 70. He lived 135 more years and had other children. He died at the age of 205 (2,083 years after Adam, Gen 11:26–32). ③ He lived 128 years contemporaneously with Noah. ④ Although Shem (11th), Shelah (13th), and Eber (14th) outlived Abraham (20th), his father, Terah (19th), died 40 years before Abraham.

20th
 	
אַבְרָהָם
 	
'Αβραάμ
 	
Abraham
	① Abraham was born 1,948 years after Adam.
	② He became the father of Isaac, the covenantal son, at the age of 100. He died at the age of 175 (2,123 years after Adam, Gen 17:1–22; 21:5; 25:7).
	③ He lived 58 years contemporaneously with Noah.
	④ Among the 10 generations after Noah:
	  – Patriarchs who died before Abraham: Arpachshad, Peleg, Reu, Serug, Nahor, Terah.
	  – Patriarchs who died after Abraham's death: Shem (outlived him by 35 years), Shelah (outlived him by 3 years), and Eber (outlived him by 64 years).

Contemporaneous Years

This chart uses the expressions, "He lived [number of] years contemporaneously with Adam" for the prediluvian (before the flood) patriarchs and, "He lived [number of] years contemporaneously with Noah" for the postdiluvian (after the flood) patriarchs. This suggests that there may have been correspondence between the patriarchs, although some may not have lived in the same region or dwelling place.

Adam and Noah, the first and second ancestors of mankind, probably spent their whole lives sharing God's love and the gospel through the historical events they had experienced. Adam lived in the world before sin and in the world after sin. Noah lived through the overtures leading to the flood and the actual flood itself. Since they lived in the same time period as their direct descendants, we can infer that these two ancestors had great influence on the faith of their descendants. Adam lived contemporaneously with Lamech until he was fifty-six years old, and Noah lived contemporaneously with Abraham until he was fifty-eight years old.

CHAPTER 10

The Genealogy from Adam to Noah

The cycle consisting of the fall of man, judgment, and restoration is repeated two times in the genealogy from Adam to Noah. The first cycle begins with Adam's sin and banishment from the garden of Eden and Cain's act of murder and Abel's death. It concludes with the recovery from sin and judgment through Seth. In the second cycle, God sent the flood as judgment against a world that was overflowing with sins committed by the sons of God and the daughters of men. However, He esteemed Noah and established him as the second ancestor of mankind in order to begin a new history.

In the genealogy from Adam to Noah, the most important person is Enoch. Lamech, from the line of Cain, was an important figure whose deeds were recorded in greater detail than others in his line. Likewise, Enoch (seventh generation from Adam) was the focus of attention in the line of Seth. He lived 308 years contemporaneously with Adam and believed in Adam's testimony of the Word of God. Although human beings were doomed to die because of sin, Enoch broke the chains of this wretched fate. By walking with God, he became the first man to be transfigured without seeing death (Gen 5:21–24; Heb 11:5).

In the genealogy from Adam to Noah, there are no additional narratives for the lives of Kenan, Mahalalel, Jared, and Methuselah. Nevertheless, their longevity testifies of their godly lives of faith. Countless passages in the Old and New Testaments emphasize that longevity is God's special blessing bestowed upon those who live godly lives (Deut 4:40; 5:16; 6:2; 11:9; 12:25, 28; 22:7; 30:20; Exod 20:12; 1 Kgs 3:14; Ps 21:4; 55:23; 91:16; Prov 3:1–2, 7–8, 16; 4:10, 20–23; 9:11; 10:27; 16:31; Eccl 7:17; 8:13; Eph 6:1–3). Proverbs 3:1–2 states, "My son, do not forget my teaching, but let your heart keep my commandments; for length of days and years of life, and peace they will add to you." The Bible states, however, that the lives of the wicked will be reduced by half (Ps 55:23).

All the patriarchs from Adam to Noah enjoyed astonishing longevity. Excluding Enoch, who was taken up to heaven without seeing death at the age of 365, the years of the other nine patriarchs in the order of longevity were as follows: Methuselah (969), Jared (962), Noah (950), Adam (930), Seth (912), Kenan (910), Enosh (905), Mahalalel (895), and Lamech (777). Seven patriarchs lived to be over 900 years of age—longevity that is impossible to achieve today. Despite the inevitability of death resulting from sin, longevity was a special privilege awarded to the godly offspring and the greatest blessing for men on earth. In his book, Dr. Kim Eui-Won observes that the blessing of longevity was God's special blessing given to the descendants of Seth, but not to the descendants of Cain.[22] Park Yune-Sun also notes in his commentary on Genesis that there is a close relationship between godliness and longevity. He interprets longevity as the result of God's plan, and also as the result of special reverence for God in each generation.[23]

We will continue to examine the unique structure of the genealogy recorded in Genesis 5, the lives of the ten patriarchs, and the spiritual meaning hidden in their names in order to understand God's sovereign plan and providence.

1. First Generation: Adam

אָדָם (*adam*): man, mankind, human

> Adam became the father of Seth at the age of 130. He lived 800 more years and had other children. He died at the age of 930 (Gen 5:3–5; 1 Chr 1:1).
>
> His name is recorded in the genealogy of Jesus in Luke 3:38 as Ἀδάμ (*Adam*).

The name *Adam* comes from the Assyrian root *adamu*, meaning "to make" or "to create." Man can never be the creator; he is merely the creature. The etymological root of the name Adam is the word *adom* (אָדֹם), which means "red." This means that man was created from red dust (Gen 2:7; 3:19, 23). Adam was formed from the dust (Gen 2:7; 3:19, 23). The term *dust* is עָפָר (*afar*) in Hebrew, meaning "dust" or "ashes," not mud or dirt. Without the breath of God, the essence of man is only dust (Gen 18:27; Job 4:19; 33:6; Ps 103:14; Eccl 3:20; Isa 64:8; 1 Cor 15:47).

(1) Adam lived until Lamech (ninth generation) was fifty-six years old.
✳ Organized and presented for the first time in history

After the fall, Adam and Eve remembered the world before the fall and their blessed lives of close fellowship with God. They probably testified in detail to their descendants about the realities of Eden and their precious faith-life experiences there. All the generations from Seth (second generation) to Lamech (ninth generation) probably received a full account from Adam about the eternal world before the fall, Satan's crafty deception, his fall resulting from disobedience, and the promise of salvation.

As a person who once lived in Eden, Adam received the assured gospel regarding the woman's seed (Gen 3:15). There is no doubt that he preached this gospel to his descendants with tireless diligence, because it was the only ray of hope for him and for all mankind. Immediately after Adam and Eve ate the fruit of the knowledge of good and evil, they made an assortment of excuses for their action and did not repent (Gen 3:7–13). However, by giving Adam the promise regarding the seed of the woman, God made Adam look toward the light of salvation in the midst of the darkness of sin. Adam realized the graveness of his sin and began to earnestly long for the coming of the seed of the woman. This is evident in the name he gave to his wife after they had received the promise in Genesis 3:15. Adam named his wife *Eve*, meaning "life" (Gen 3:20). Through this name, Adam declared that Eve would become the mother of all the living (Gen 3:20). This was the first confession of faith in the promise of the seed and the expression of hope for that day to come—the day when life conquers death. His conviction must have been reinforced each time he called out her name.

God's mercy and compassion shone through as He Himself made the garments of skin to clothe Adam and Eve (Gen 3:21). Adam was a witness to the realities of Eden and the promise that he received there. Furthermore, the garments of skin that God used to clothe Adam and Eve before banishing them from Eden (Gen 3:21) were the assurance of His covenant in Genesis 3:15. For Adam, this was more precious than life itself. The garments made of skin imply that sacrifice is the basic principle of salvation. It also reveals how the redemption of mankind would be accomplished, because a sacrifice of life was necessary to make the garments of skin. This is a foreshadowing of Jesus Christ's sacrifice on the cross.

All through his life, Adam cherished the garments of skin because they were his confirmation of the covenant. He firmly believed that the day would come when the promised seed would bruise the head of the serpent. This is the faith he taught and passed down to his descendants.

(2) Adam testified of the glorious experiences in the garden of Eden

① Adam must have taught his descendants that the garden of Eden was a world without shame, for they were naked but were not ashamed.

Genesis 2:25 And the man and his wife were both naked and were not ashamed.

Before the fall, Adam and Eve were naked, but were not ashamed. After the fall, their eyes were opened to sin and they hid themselves in shame; they used fig leaves as makeshift clothing (Gen 3:7). In Genesis 3:10, Adam says, "I heard the sound of You in the garden, and I was afraid because I was naked; so I hid myself." Their sense of shame brought fear and led them to hide from God's face.

Adam clearly understood the cause of this shame and fear. He probably engraved into the hearts of his descendants images of the world of

Eden where shame did not exist. With God's glory, peace, and love overflowing, there were no mistakes, no guilt, and no condemnation. How could Adam forget such a world?

② Adam must have told them about the days when he heard the voice of God and conversed with Him as He walked through the garden (Gen 2:15–16; 3:9, 10, 11, 17).

The garden of Eden was a garden of happiness and blessings because they heard God's tender voice and conversed with Him (Ps 36:8). However, after they sinned, the same gentle voice caused fear and anguish. When God asked, "Adam, where are you?" he could not answer, "Here I am," as he had previously done. Instead, he hid among the trees from the face of God; ultimately, he was banished from Eden (Gen 3:23). Adam must have testified of God to his descendants without ceasing and with zealous longing for the restoration of Eden where he had once experienced indescribable joy and happiness through fellowship with God.

③ Adam must have told them about how he named all creation with the wisdom God bestowed upon him.

> **Genesis 2:19** Out of the ground the LORD God formed every beast of the field and every bird of the sky, and brought them to the man to see what he would call them; and whatever the man called a living creature, that was its name.

Created in God's own image, Adam possessed great wisdom and creativity. It is humanly impossible to name the countless number of different creatures and living things. It is possible only when God's Spirit is working within. This wisdom is like the wisdom that God bestowed on Solomon who "spoke of trees, from the cedar that is in Lebanon even to the hyssop that grows on the wall ... also of animals and birds and creeping things and fish" (1 Kgs 4:32–34).

Adam must have genuinely enjoyed his sovereign power over all creation as he named them. This wonderful wisdom, however, vanished along with his authority and power over God's creation when he sinned. He was degraded to a being who could hardly sustain himself. Adam most likely shared these experiences with his descendants as well.

(3) Adam died at the age of 930, fifty-seven years before Enoch was taken up to heaven.

Calculation:

987 years after Adam (Enoch's transfiguration)
− 930 years (Adam's age at death)
= 57 years

Adam lived contemporaneously with Enoch for 308 years, but he was not able to witness Enoch's ascension because he died fifty-seven years before Enoch was taken up. Enoch did not walk with God during the first sixty-five years of his life before his son, Methuselah, was born. He only started walking with God at the age of sixty-five after Methuselah was born, and continued to walk with Him for 300 years until the age of 365 (Gen 5:21–24). Thus, Adam witnessed Enoch's walk with God for 243 years (300 − 57 = 243). Adam presumably made great effort to share his testimonies about life before and after his sin and banishment from Eden. Adam's earnest message probably played a critical role in Enoch's walk with God and eventual transfiguration.

Adam lived 930 years and died. Genesis 5:5 states, "So all the days that Adam lived were nine hundred and thirty years, and he died." The Hebrew word for *die* is מוּת (*muth*), and it refers to a natural death. This is the Bible's first reference to natural death since the account of the murder of Abel. The word מוּת (*muth*) is first recorded in the Bible in Genesis 2:17. In this verse, God sternly warns Adam, saying, "But from the tree of the knowledge of good and evil you shall not eat, for in the day that you eat from it you shall surely die." This warning became a reality when Adam died.

God smote the life of Adam into whom He Himself had breathed the breath of life showing the extent of His wrath toward sin. Adam's death was truly tragic because it marks the beginning of death, which all his descendants would ultimately inherit (Rom 5:12, 14–15).

Nevertheless, life propagated through Adam's descendants after his death. This is evident in the phrases "he begot," "he had," "he became the father of," and "after he became the father of," which is יָלַד (*yalad*) in Hebrew. This word appears twenty-eight times in Genesis 5. God's long journey for the redemption of life began when sin brought the curse of death upon all men. God did not abandon man after his tragic failure and fall. Rather, He transformed death into life through His abounding grace and love.

2. Second Generation: Seth

שֵׁת (*sheth*): substitute,[24] granted,[25] appointed one,[26] foundation or grounds[27]

Seth was born 130 years after Adam. He became the father of Enosh at the age of 105. He lived 807 more years and had other children. He died at the age of 912 (1,042 years after Adam, Gen 5:6–8; 1 Chr 1:1). He lived 800 years contemporaneously with Adam and witnessed Enoch's ascension at the age of 857.

His name is recorded in the genealogy of Jesus in Luke 3:38 as Σήθ (*Sēth*).

Adam's second son was Abel (Gen 4:2). In Hebrew, the name *Abel* is הֶבֶל (*hevel*) and means "vain," "emptiness," and "breath (vapor)." This is a foreboding of the abrupt end that his life would encounter. It is a natural parental inclination to give good names to one's children. However, Adam named his second son *Abel*, which hints at his realization of the vanity and futility of man's existence as a result of sin.

Adam and Eve's first son Cain belonged to the evil one; he killed his brother Abel and shattered their hopes for a new life. Furthermore, Cain departed from God's presence and left Adam and Eve grieving (Gen 4:16). Not long after Abel died tragically in Cain's hands, Cain also left the path of faith. Imagine the hearts of the parents who lost two sons at once!

When Jacob heard that his most beloved son Joseph had died, he mourned for him for a long time, refusing to be comforted by his other children. He lamented, "Surely I will go down to Sheol in mourning for my son" (Gen 37:34–35). Jacob's great sorrow is similar to the grief that Adam and Eve experienced after losing both sons.

As immense sorrow and despair enveloped Adam's family, God brought hope and comfort by promising "another seed" in Abel's place. True to the meaning of his name, Abel could not fulfill his years and disappeared like vapor before his life could take root. Seth was then born to Adam at the age of 130. It was an expression of God's abounding grace and a gift that overflows with hope and comfort.

The name *Seth* is derived from שִׁית (*shith*), which means "to put" and "to set." Thus, the hope was for God's work to be wholly established and deeply rooted through Seth.

(1) Seth was a son in Adam's image and likeness.

Adam had a son in his own image and likeness.

> **Genesis 5:3** When Adam had lived one hundred and thirty years, he became the father of a son in his own likeness, according to his image, and named him Seth.

This verse is a declaration that God's image which remained in parts after the fall was being passed down through the line of Seth. Genesis 5:3 states that Adam became the father of "a son in his own likeness." This verse signals that Adam's faith, which was being restored after he received the promise of "the seed of a woman," was passed down to Seth. Thus, Seth, not Cain, was the son bearing Adam's image. God's promise was given to the line of Seth, not to the line of Cain. Seth also inherited the life and the image of God that was given to Adam, although not in its original perfect form because of Adam's sin. The dignity and value of human beings, which distinguishes them from beasts, are based on their creation in God's own image (Gen 1:26-27; 9:6; Jas 3:9). Despite Adam's fall, the image of God continued to be passed down, although this image was not in its original perfect form.

(2) Seth was "another seed" that God granted (Gen 4:25).

As the descendants of Cain continued to corrupt the world through murder and deception, Adam realized that God had granted him "another seed" as an integral part of His redemptive purpose. In response, he gave thanks to God and named his son *Seth*. It is apparent from this name that Adam desired and firmly believed that the path of the promised Savior would be opened up through the line of Seth.

After being plagued by chaos, painful tears, and sorrow, Adam's family was now reestablished through Seth. This is clearly a demonstration of God's determination to bring forth the woman's seed, even if it required granting "another seed."

God's providence for salvation continued until Jesus Christ was born through Mary (Gal 4:4). Jesus was not Joseph's seed; He was "another seed" conceived by the Holy Spirit (Matt 1:18–20). Truly, God's plan is too great for man to comprehend and too immense to measure.

(3) Seth's name contained the hope of securing the path for the coming of the Messiah.

Besides the meaning "another seed," Seth's name also means "to place" and "foundation." From the redemptive-historical perspective, the meaning reveals the hope that Seth, who inherited the image of God, would firmly establish the path for the promised Messiah.

A true church must be established upon the Word of Jesus Christ, the Rock, so that it will neither collapse nor be overcome by the power of darkness (Matt 16:18; 7:24–27). The churches of the end time will also stand firmly upon the foundation of Jesus Christ who came from the line of Seth.

(4) Seth witnessed Adam's death and Enoch's ascension.

Chronologically, Seth died 112 years after Adam's death and fifty-five years after he witnessed Enoch's ascension. Noah (Adam's tenth generation), a type of the Savior, was born fourteen years after Seth's death.

> **Calculation:** Year of Seth's death (1,042 years after Adam)
> – Year of Adam's death (930)
> = 112 years
>
> Year of Seth's death (1,042 years after Adam)
> – Year of Enoch's ascension (987)
> = 55 years
>
> Year of Noah's birth (1,056 years after Adam)
> – Year of Seth's death (1,042)
> = 14 years

3. Third Generation: Enosh

אֱנוֹשׁ (enosh): man, mortal frailty[28]

Enosh was born to Seth at the age of 105 (Gen 5:6; 1 Chr 1:1), which was 235 years after Adam. Enosh became the father of Kenan at the age of 90. He lived 815 more years and had other children. He died at the age of 905 (1,140 years after Adam, Gen 5:9–11). He lived 695 years contemporaneously with Adam and 84 years with Noah. He witnessed Enoch's ascension at the age of 752.

His name is recorded in the genealogy of Jesus in Luke 3:38 as Ἐνώς (Enōs).

The name *Enosh* is derived from אָנַשׁ (anash), which means "incurable" and "very sick." The name communicates man's total helplessness and predestined frailty. It likens the state of sinful man to the condition of one groaning in sickness and affliction or the state of one suffering from an incurable illness (Jer 15:18; Mic 1:9). Enosh's father, Seth, realized that without God man is too frail to overcome the temptations of sin that sweeps ferociously over the world. Like the name Adam, *Enosh* can be used either as a proper noun or as a common noun meaning "man."[29] The name *Enosh* was a confession of faith from the mouth of Seth who began to call upon the name of God. Through the name *Enosh*, we can better understand the mindset and the spirit of that time.

(1) People began to call on the name of the Lord (Jehovah) during Enosh's time.

The Bible states that around the time Seth named his son *Enosh*, men began to call upon the name of the Lord (Jehovah).

> **Genesis 4:26** To Seth, to him also a son was born; and he called his name Enosh. Then men began to call upon the name of the LORD.

The phrase, "call upon the name of the LORD," emphasizes that people began to develop personal relationships with God. Even in human relationships, addressing someone by name rather than by title indicates a more familiar and closer relationship. The Bible connects the significant act of men calling upon the name of the Lord directly to the issue of salvation.

> **Acts 2:21** And it shall be that everyone who calls on the name of the LORD will be saved.

> **Romans 10:13** For "Whoever will call on the name of the LORD will be saved."

A proactive relationship between God and men had begun when men began to call upon the name of the Lord. The word *call* (קָרָא, *qara*) used here means "to proclaim" and "to cry out." It signifies that the name of the Lord had been proclaimed even to the far regions. We can infer that the practice of true worship was well established during Enosh's time and the gospel began to reach larger groups of people.

(2) Proper worship and development of faith in God began during Enosh's time.

The statement in Genesis 4:26 that men began to call upon the name of the Lord means that formal worship had begun. The New Living Translation of Genesis 4:26 renders it as an act of worship: "When Seth grew up, he had a son and named him Enosh. At that time people first began to worship the LORD by name." However, this worship was not the first offering of sacrifices in the 235 years after the fall of Adam. Since Cain and Abel offered sacrifices to God, we can infer that people had begun offering sacrifices long before. Thus, the phrase, "men began to call upon the name of the LORD," refers to formal and proper worship services. Theologians concur that the fundamental philosophy and attitude of worship that call for the presence of God was established during the time of Enosh. It was an expression of people's desire to surrender their will in order to fully commit to God's sovereign rule. At the same time, it was a dire cry to God for deliverance from a pervasively sinful world.

Whereas the descendants of Cain were arrogant and relied on their own strength in all aspects of life, the godly descendants of Seth stood humbly before God and established a life of worship and fellowship with Him.

(3) Enosh represents all mankind that is frail and unable to attain salvation on its own.

When we acknowledge that we are frail beings (like the meaning of *Enosh*) who are unable to escape death, we can properly present ourselves as a living and holy sacrifice acceptable to God. This is true spiritual worship (Rom 12:1). Furthermore, we receive the gift of salvation when we call upon the name of the Lord with a heart of true worship (Acts 2:21; Rom 10:13).

Apostle Paul cried out, "Wretched man that I am!" (Rom 7:24). Realizing that he was a weak being (like Enosh) who cannot overcome death by his own strength, he confessed, "For the law of the Spirit of life in Christ Jesus has set you free from the law of sin and of death" (Rom 8:1–2). Furthermore, Paul heard the voice of God telling him, "My grace is sufficient for you, for power is perfected in weakness." Thus, he rejoiced in his own weakness, saying, "Most gladly, therefore, I will rather boast about my weaknesses" (2 Cor 12:9). He was able to make this confession because he came to understand the profound truth that the power of Christ dwells in those who call upon the name of the Lord in their weakness.

As the meaning of the name *Enosh* ("weak man") points out, human beings are weak, powerless before sin, and easily susceptible to temptations; they are destined to die in sin. Hence, people who lived during Enosh's time wholeheartedly confessed that they were helpless beings overpowered by the burden of sin and death; they were unable to save themselves and thus awaited the coming of the seed of the woman. They devoted their hearts and souls to worshiping God and calling upon His name. There is an earnest call today for people who sincerely anticipate God's eternal reign to confess that they are like Enosh (i.e., weak) and revive true worship.

4. Fourth Generation: Kenan

קֵינָן (qenan): a child, one begotten,[30] possession[31]

Kenan was born to Enosh at the age of 90 (1 Chr 1:1–2). He was born 325 years after Adam. He became the father of Mahalalel at the age of 70. He lived 840 more years and had other children. He died at the age of 910 (1,235 years after Adam, Gen 5:12–14). He lived 605 years contemporaneously with Adam and 179 years with Noah. He witnessed Enoch's ascension at the age of 662.

His name is recorded in the genealogy of Jesus in Luke 3:37 as Καϊνάν (Kainan).

The name *Kenan* is קֵינָן (qenan) in Hebrew and shares the same root as קֵן (qen), which means "nest," and קִנֵּן (qinnen), which means "to build a nest." The descendants of Seth realized that human beings are weak and powerless and began a movement to revive their faith by calling upon the name of the Lord in true repentance. However, Kenan's name suggests that it was during his time that the people finally built a nest of faith.

(1) *Kenan* means "unexpectedly found mercy."

Kenan was probably an unexpected gift from God, a son of great joy born through His providence. In His mercy, God gave a great gift called Jesus Christ. Why is Jesus Christ an unexpected gift to mankind?

First, the love and grace of salvation through Jesus Christ are unexpected gifts because they are too great, too high, and too deep for man to fathom. However, anyone can receive this gift and it is a gift of great joy.

Second, it is unexpected because we do not possess any merit to receive salvation; it is granted entirely by grace and not due to any virtue or friendship. It is truly a gift of joy, a gift of glory, and the greatest possible gift that mankind could ever receive.

> **Ephesians 2:8–9** For by grace you have been saved through faith; and that not of yourselves, it is the gift of God; [9]not as a result of works, so that no one may boast.

Mary's conception of Jesus Christ through the Holy Spirit is also an unexpected gift. The conception of Jesus Christ was the foremost and greatest blessing for Mary.

> **Luke 1:28–30** And coming in, he said to her, "Greetings, favored one! The LORD is with you." [29]But she was very perplexed at this statement, and kept pondering what kind of salutation this was. [30]The angel said to her, "Do not be afraid, Mary; for you have found favor with God."

The unexpected news about Jesus Christ's birth was "good news of great joy" to the shepherds who were tending their sheep at night (Luke 2:10).

Jesus came in the fullness of time (Gal 4:4) and was an unexpected gift and the true gospel to sinners without hope (John 1:14, 16; 3:16; Rom 5:15; 2 Cor 9:15).

(2) *Kenan* means "vast possession."

Enosh, his father, hoped to enlarge the borders of faith and further recover the lost sovereignty, which man had in Eden, through his unexpectedly begotten son Kenan. The meaning of Kenan's name, "vast possession," hints at the hope of recovering the lost work of creation (Luke 4:5–7; Matt 4:9), the lost dominion over creation, and the lost sovereignty (Gen 1:28; 2:15, 19). From the redemptive-historical perspective, the name *Kenan* foreshadows Jesus who would bring the good news to this world, save all mankind, and completely restore all creation.

The confession of the descendants of Seth hints that they had expanded their spiritual territory through greater faith in the awesome God, the Lord and Creator of the vast universe.

Today, we must obey God's command to "subdue the earth" (Gen 1:28) and Jesus' command to "make disciples of all the nations" (Matt 28:18–20) by conquering this world with the gospel and turning it into God's vast possession.

5. Fifth Generation: Mahalalel

מַהֲלַלְאֵל (*mahalalel*): praise of God,[32] God be praised, glory to God

> Mahalalel was born to Kenan at the age of 70 (Gen 5:12; 1 Chr 1:2). He was born 395 years after Adam. He became the father of Jared at the age of 65. He lived 830 more years and had other children. He died at the age of 895 (1,290 years after Adam, Gen 5:15–17). Mahalalel lived contemporaneously with Adam for 535 years and with Noah for 234 years. He witnessed Enoch's ascension at the age of 592.
>
> His name is recorded in the genealogy of Jesus in Luke 3:37 as Μαλελεήλ (*Maleleēl*).

The name *Mahalalel* is a compound word made up of a Hebrew noun that means "praise" (מַהֲלָל, *mahalal*), which originates from the verb *to praise* (הָלַל, *halal*), and the name of God אֵל (*el*). Together, it means "praise to God" or "praise of God."

To praise is to sing of God's wonderful virtues through lyrics and music. It is the greatest form of exaltation for the wonders of nature and people of distinction. However, only God who governs all history is worthy to receive true praise and worship (Rev 5:12; 19:1–5).

The act of praising God is emphasized in this name. It suggests that an explosive spiritual revival and growth in faith had led the people significantly closer to God. Formal worship that started at the time of Enosh evolved and formed a nest of holy believers during the time of Kenan. Now, in the days of Mahalalel, God dwelled in praise-filled worship and received glory.

(1) Only God is worthy to be praised (Rev 5:12).

It is only right that God's creatures praise Him for who He is (Isa 43:7, 21; Ps 79:13; 105:1–4; Eph 1:6, 12, 14). Singing praises is exalting God through music. The psalmist sings, "Let everything that has breath praise the LORD. Praise the LORD!" (Ps 150:6). Here, the phrase "praise the LORD" is a rendering of the Hebrew expression "Hallelujah." Augustine said that a hymn is a song that is sung to the praise of God.[33]

Like the meaning of the name *Mahalalel*, we must also glorify God by living lives that praise Him.

(2) Praise is a force that unleashes God's power.

The sound of powerful praises brought down the wall of Jericho (Josh 6:16–20), drove out the evil spirit in Saul (1 Sam 16:23), and caused a violent earthquake that opened the prison gates and unfastened the chains (Acts 16:25–26). Armies were victorious in battles when people singing God's praises marched before them (2 Chr 20:20–23). These amazing works were possible because God is enthroned upon praises (Ps 22:3).

After King Solomon completed the construction of the temple, God's presence was upon the temple when a choir clothed in fine linen praised the Lord with cymbals, harps, and lyres, along with 120 priests blowing trumpets (2 Chr 5:12). God manifested His presence when they praised Him in unison with singing and music (2 Chr 5:13). The cloud of God's glory filled the temple so that the priests could not minister because of it (2 Chr 5:14). Thus, praise is the holy aroma that draws God close and reveals His powerful and amazing works that are unimaginable for man.

(3) Praise is an inspired confession of grace received.

The godly descendants of Seth engaged in fierce and ongoing spiritual battles against sin and wickedness, but they were victorious through God's help (Deut 1:30; 20:4; Josh 10:14, 42; 23:1; Neh 4:20). Kenan must have named his son *Mahalalel* to commemorate the grace that he had received. He did this to glorify God and to testify to many that God is alive. Those who have experienced God's grace cannot help but sing praises and testify of His grace (Acts 9:22; 18:5, 28; John 1:41).

Judah, the name of one of the twelve tribes of Israel, means "praise the LORD" (Gen 29:35). Each time Israel went to battle, the tribe of Judah marched at the forefront and they always returned victorious (Judg 1:1–10; 20:18). From the redemptive-historical perspective, Mahalalel is a type of the Messiah, who was to come from the tribe of Judah to save all mankind through the cross, obtain victory through the resurrection, and be enthroned in praises (Ps 78:68–70; Heb 7:14; Rev 5:5). Truly, only the Lord Jesus deserves our worship and praise, for He came and granted salvation to sinful mankind that is helplessly frail and deserving of death.

6. Sixth Generation: Jared

יֶרֶד (*yered*): descent or descendant,[34] to go or come down (from a higher place)[35]

> Jared was born to Mahalalel at the age of 65 (Gen 5:15; 1 Chr 1:2). He was born 460 years after Adam. He became the father of Enoch at the age of 162. He lived 800 more years and had other children. He died at the age of 962 (1,422 years after Adam, Gen 5:18–20). He lived 470 years contemporaneously with Adam and 366 years with Noah. He witnessed Enoch's ascension at the age of 527.
>
> His name is recorded in the genealogy of Jesus in Luke 3:37 as Ἰάρετ (*Iaret*).

The name *Jared* originates from the Hebrew word יָרַד (*yarad*), which means "to carry down," "to transport," or "to put down."

This is an indication that the spiritual movement to praise God was not limited to a few, but was widespread among the people at that time. It also suggests that the practice of worship had been successfully passed down through the generations. Enosh, Kenan, and Mahalalel had established the foundation of faith. The meaning of the name *Jared* hints at the hope that this God who is worthy to be praised would come down to the world and save them. There was simply no way for mankind, who cannot break free from the cycle of sickness and death, to recover the lost kingdom of heaven. The people of that time realized that they could not neutralize the serpent's lethal venom on their own.

Their sincere longing for the woman's seed (Gen 3:15) is also evident from the alternative meaning of the name *Jared*: "descendant." As the fulfillment of this hope, Jesus Christ, the Word incarnate, came into this world and dwelt among the people (John 1:14).

(1) Jared lived longer than the preceding patriarchs and lived the second longest life in primeval history.

Jared lived 962 years and thus lived the longest among the patriarchs from Adam to Jared. He lived thirty-two years longer than Adam. Only his grandson, Methuselah, lived longer than Jared by seven years and set the record for longevity with 969 years. Thus, Jared lived the second-longest life in primeval history. Longevity was a special privilege and the greatest blessing on this earth from God to the godly descendants.

Regarding Jared, Suh Chul-Won states in his exegesis of Genesis, "He received this blessing because he was godly. He had entrusted everything to God and educated his children well so that they were righteous, and evil did not thrive among them."[36]

Those who do not share the same beliefs in God's blessing of longevity assert a negative interpretation of the name's origin. They believe that the meaning of the name, "to go down" or "to descend," suggests that Jared had fallen into sin. However, their argument is unconvincing since Jared was blessed with the longest life among the first five generations in the line of Seth and the second-longest in primeval history.

(2) Jesus Christ humbled Himself and came down in the lowest and humblest form (Phil 2:6–8).

Similar to the meaning of the name *Jared*, Jesus rejected the glory of His throne in heaven and came down to this lowly world (John 3:13; 6:41). The moment Jesus was born, He was laid in a manger and the smell of animal excrement blanketed Him (Luke 2:7). He grew up in a poor carpenter's family (Matt 13:55; Mark 6:3) and His own brothers looked down on Him (John 7:5). Religious leaders treated Him with contempt because He had not received a proper education (John 7:15). He came unto His own people, but He spent thirty-three years of His life in sorrow because they did not receive Him (John 1:11).

Nevertheless, Jesus, the Son of Man who descended from heaven (John 3:13), completely obeyed the command of the Father who had sent Him (John 8:42; 16:28). Throughout His life, He sought to glorify the Father (John 7:18), praying in tears and working to fulfill the will of the Father (Luke 22:42). He did only what was pleasing to the Father (John 8:29). He spoke what the Father taught Him and acted according to what the Father showed Him (John 5:19; 7:16; 8:28, 38; 12:49). The Father's command was eternal life (John 12:50) and He was obedient even to the point of death on the cross (Phil 2:8). This is why God was always with Jesus—"Immanuel" (John 8:29).

Let us examine ourselves to see if we are bearing the fruit of obedience to the Father's will and sincerely repent so that we may also meet with God, Immanuel.

(3) Enoch was Jared's fruit of faith.

As the meaning of his name suggests, Jared probably lowered himself before God and was always humble. This is also apparent in the name of his son Enoch. The name *Enoch* means "dedicated" or "offered," hinting that Jared wanted to wholly dedicate his son to God. Enoch later fulfilled Jared's cherished desire in faith: he reached the peak of godly faith by overcoming death and ascending into heaven. Enoch was truly Jared's fruit of faith.

Moreover, the meaning of the name *Enoch* clearly demonstrates Jared's devoted faith. One cannot possibly name his child "dedicated" before God if he himself were not dedicated in faith. Hannah had offered Samuel to God's temple (1 Sam 1:22) and Abraham had offered Isaac to God on a mount in Moriah (Gen 22:2). Likewise, Jared offered his son to God because he had realized that his son ultimately belonged to Him even though he was God's gift (Ps 127:3). He acknowledged that the ownership of his son belonged totally to God, and he wished for his son to be used according to His will.

Jared possessed a true understanding of the corruption of his time. In his desire to set the standard for righteousness and truth, he dedicated his son to God. Jared possessed a mature faith. Instead of blaming others or the social decay of the times, he prayed to God. He was a father of faith who joyfully consecrated his son apart from the sinful world and willingly offered him to God so that he might live as a public figure dedicated to the nation and to the times.

7. Seventh Generation: Enoch

חֲנוֹךְ (*hanokh*): dedicated (offered),[37] begin or initiated,[38] teacher

> Enoch was born to Jared at the age of 162 (Gen 5:18; 1 Chr 1:2–3). He was born 622 years after Adam. He became the father of Methuselah at the age of 65 and walked with God for 300 years, had other children, and ascended to heaven without seeing death at the age of 365 (987 years after Adam, Gen 5:21–24; Heb 11:5–6; Jude 1:14–15). He lived 308 years contemporaneously with Adam. Noah was born 69 years after Enoch's ascension so the two men did not meet.
>
> 1,056 years after Adam (Noah's birth)
> – 987 years after Adam (Enoch's ascension)
> = 69 years
>
> His name is recorded in the genealogy of Jesus in Luke 3:37 as Ἐνώχ (*Henōch*).

In Hebrew, the name *Enoch* is חֲנוֹךְ (*hanokh*). It is the noun form of the verb meaning "to offer," and the most common rendering is "offered" and "dedicated one." The root of this name is חָנַךְ (*hanakh*), which means "to inspire" or "to teach." Thus, the noun form would be rendered as "teacher." Jared must have named his son "dedicated (offered)" out of the desire to fully dedicate his son to God as the first fruit of his godly life. Enoch presumably lived out God's teachings in his life and deeply inspired many people. As suggested by the meaning of his name, Enoch was a foreshadowing of Jesus Christ, the Lamb who was fully dedicated before God to die on the cross as an atoning sacrifice for the sins of all mankind (John 1:29; 1 Cor 5:7).

Until Enoch, every generation in the genealogy concluded with the inevitable phrase "and he died," as though death were the natural path to the end. The phrase, "and he died," appears eight times in Genesis 5 (Gen 5:5, 8, 11, 14, 17, 20, 27, 31). However, there was one person whom death could not conquer: Enoch, the seventh generation from Adam. He was like the morning star shining brightly in the dark night sky. He walked with God and attained eternal life without seeing death; his life and ascension attests to the apex of godly life. Truly, the mystery of overcoming death, which had never been witnessed until then, was the ultimate blessing.

There is only one record of Enoch's deeds on this earth (Jude 1:14–15). He prophesied about God's judgment against the "ungodly deeds" and the "ungodly speech" prevalent during his time. Enoch lived up to his father's expectations by dedicating his life to God as a true prophet of his age.

(1) Enoch was a teacher who taught an important redemptive-historical lesson to all mankind.

Besides the meaning "dedicated" or "offered," Enoch's name also means "successor," "beginning," and "teacher." The following conclusions can be drawn regarding Enoch's ministry from the redemptive-historical perspective:

① Enoch earned God's trust by walking with Him and pleasing Him (Heb 11:5).

② Enoch was a teacher to all mankind and he demonstrated for the first time that whoever walks with God in faith will obtain eternal life (Gen 5:21–24). He taught that there was a way to reach heaven without seeing death: transfiguration and ascension into heaven.

(2) Enoch walked with God and was taken up by God.

God did not take Enoch in death. The phrase *to take* in Genesis 5:24 is לָקַח (*laqah*) in Hebrew. Its usage here connotes the act of "snatching (taking) away" alive to a place different from this world, the kingdom of God. Hebrews 11:5 expresses this as, "By faith Enoch was taken up so that he would not see death." This signifies that God had transfigured Enoch into a spiritual body while he was living on the earth. He took Enoch up to heaven to Himself without allowing him to experience death. Elijah was the other person in the Bible who was transfigured. He was taken up to heaven by a whirlwind, and the word לָקַח (*laqah*) was also used in his case (2 Kgs 2:10–11). The usage of this word teaches us that death, an impassable obstacle for man, kneels before the power of God Almighty.

What is the secret to Enoch's ascension in a spiritual form? Genesis 5:24 explains that Enoch was taken because he walked with God. The

Hebrew word for *walk* in Genesis 5:24 is יִתְהַלֶּךְ (*yithhallekh*), the reflexive form of the verb הָלַךְ (*halakh*), and means "to subject oneself to another person's will and follow." According to this meaning, walking with God is more than just a journey with Him. It refers to taking each step in accordance with His will and abandoning one's own thoughts. Strictly speaking, walking with God is to become one with Him, as if there are two bodies but one being.

There was no change of heart in Enoch during his 300-year walk with God. He willingly and joyfully followed God and embraced His will in his heart; this pleased God and compelled Him to grant Enoch the glory of ascension into heaven without seeing death (Heb 11:5). We, too, can be liberated from the reign of death over our lives if we hold God's hand and walk with Him wholly.

Therefore, before we ask the question, "Would it be possible for me to be transfigured now without seeing death?" we must ask ourselves, "Am I truly walking with God?" The Hebrew word הָלַךְ (*halakh*) for *walk* appears in Deuteronomy 30:16 and is associated with life, meaning that walking with God is the secret to the transition from death to life. The Bible promises that reconciliation and close fellowship with God overcome sin, liberate us from death, and grant us eternal life.

(3) Enoch lived contemporaneously with Adam for 308 years and ascended into heaven fifty-seven years after Adam died at the age of 930.

❋ Organized and presented for the first time in history

Calculation:

987 years after Adam (year of Enoch's ascension)
– 930 (Adam's age at death)
= 57 years

God's greatest gift, the light of life that allows us to be transfigured without seeing death, was slowly being forgotten after the fall. Yet, Enoch's ascension was a special event that illuminated this light of life, the immortal light. Enoch's transfiguration sowed conviction in life's victory over death. This is great encouragement and hope for the righteous who thirst for the good news of eternal life while living under the shadows of sin and death.

After his judgment from God for his disobedience, Adam also received the firm promise that Eden would be restored by the seed of the woman (Gen 3:15). Because he had experienced Eden firsthand, he must have testified of the blessed world to his descendants through vivid accounts. He probably emphasized to them that the most significant issue that mankind needed to resolve was the issue of death. Furthermore, he most likely testified in detail about the world before and after sin. Adam's desire, born in faith, finally materialized and yielded fruit through Enoch. There were godly descendants after Adam who also believed in God. However, only Enoch yielded the fruit of transfiguration because he had reverence for the Word of God, which he learned through Adam during their 308 years together. Among Adam's numerous descendants, only Enoch followed the Word fully. As a result, when he had walked with God for 300 years, God took him. He had no reason to keep Enoch on the earth.

Enoch was not excluded from the curse of death resulting from the fall; he was to die just as Adam had died fifty-seven years earlier. However, God granted him the special privilege of overcoming death and directly entering into eternal life. His life testifies to the ultimate fate of those who live godly lives when ungodliness is at its peak.

(4) There were seven witnesses to Enoch's deeds, transfiguration, and ascension.

All the patriarchs of primeval history were alive at the time of Enoch's ascension except for Adam, who had died fifty-seven years earlier, and Noah, who was born sixty-nine years later.[39] These seven patriarchs were Seth, Enosh, Kenan, Mahalalel, Jared, Methuselah, and Lamech.

When Enoch was taken up to heaven, Seth was 857 years old, Enosh 752, Kenan 662, Mahalalel 592, Enoch's father Jared 527, Methuselah 300, and Lamech 113. They witnessed Enoch preaching fearlessly the Word of God and His judgment against the ungodly world (Jude 1:14–15). They observed his perfect walk with God, his ability to preserve his godliness while raising a family, and his final transfiguration and ascension. His ascension confirmed Adam's teachings about the garden of Eden and that the world of eternal life without death is real.

(5) The birth of Enoch's son, Methuselah, was a sign of the judgment by flood.

When Enoch fathered Methuselah, he received a revelation from God regarding the judgment of the flood upon the pervasively wicked world.

① Enoch fathered a son at the age of 65 and began to walk with God. He named this son Methuselah (when he dies, judgment).

② Methuselah died in his 969th year, which coincides precisely with the year of the flood (Gen 5:27–32; 7:6; 11:10).

> **Calculation:**
>
> Methuselah was 187 years old when he fathered Lamech;
> Lamech was 182 years old when he fathered Noah;
> the flood occurred when Noah was 600 years old:
> 187 + 182 + 600 = 969

Therefore, Methuselah's birth was God's revelation and sign of the judgment by flood.

(6) Enoch showed that Adam could have enjoyed eternal life if he had not fallen.

Enoch was the true image of Adam. The eternal life that Enoch received after walking with God showed the world that Adam could have possessed eternal life if he had not sinned. Enoch's walk with God—the secret to his transfiguration—revealed the kind of life that God had wanted and expected from Adam when He created him. God wanted Adam to be of one heart and will with Him; He wanted Adam to eat and live before Him. However, Adam disregarded God's command and listened to Eve's words. In his arrogance, he made the decision to eat the fruit from the tree of knowledge of good and evil without asking God (Gen 3:6). As a result, Adam strayed away, prompting God to remind him of his place and state by asking, "Where are you?" (Gen 3:9).

Close examination of the ten generations between Adam and Noah reveals that even though Enoch was Adam's seventh generation descendant, all of Adam's direct descendants were alive at Enoch's ascension except for Adam. Among the ten generations from Adam to Noah, Adam was the first to die at the age of 930 years. Enoch was the second patriarch to conclude his life on this earth, but without seeing death (see Excursus 1: "Chronology of the Patriarchs").

Enoch's ascension teaches all mankind an important lesson. Through the death of the first man, Adam, God clearly demonstrated that the wages of sin is death (Rom 6:23). Immediately after Adam's death, God revealed the way to overcome the power of death through Enoch.

This is the hope for all: mankind can sufficiently overcome death if they restore fellowship with God and walk with Him the way Enoch had done. Enoch's ascension is a revelation to all generations to come that only faith has the power to overcome death.

About 2,200 years after Enoch, Prophet Elijah was also taken up to heaven without seeing death (2 Kgs 2:10–11). Enoch prophesied during the period between Adam and Abraham, while Elijah prophesied during the period between Abraham and Christ.

(7) Enoch foreshadows three events in the history of redemption.

① Enoch's walk with God pleased Him. This foreshadows how Jesus Christ's walk with God will also please Him (John 8:29). Additionally, Enoch's ascension foreshadowed Jesus Christ's triumph over the powers of Satan, the eternal destruction of death, and the assurance of salvation for mankind through His resurrection and ascension.

② Enoch's life points to the precious truth that although all mankind is under condemnation through Adam, by the grace of God, there is life for all men through His only begotten Son, Jesus Christ (Rom 5:18–21; 1 Cor 15:22).

③ Enoch's life prefigures the saints' glorious transfiguration at the second coming of Jesus Christ, when suffering and rebellion will reach their culmination (Matt 24:40; John 8:51; 11:25–26; 1 Cor 15:50–54; 1 Thess 4:16–17; Phil 3:21). Matthew Henry states, "Enoch's translation was ... an evidence to faith of the reality of a future state, and of the possibility of the body's existing in glory in that state."[40]

Enoch's life became the foremost testimony of eternal life as he leaped over the great obstacle of death that stood between God and man. Enoch received special grace and blessings as a result of his faith in God's Word taught by Adam and his walk with God in obedience to the Word. It is our sincere hope that we will also receive the Word of God and believe in it without doubting so that we may also triumph over the power of death and be transfigured into a spiritual body at the second coming of Jesus Christ.

1 Corinthians 15:51–54 Behold, I tell you a mystery; we will not all sleep, but we will all be changed, [52]in a moment, in the twinkling of an eye, at the last trumpet; for the trumpet will sound, and the dead will be raised imperishable, and we will be changed. [53]For this perishable must put on the imperishable, and this mortal must put on immortality. [54]But when this perishable will have put on the imperishable, and this mortal will have put on immortality, then will come about the saying that is written, "Death is swallowed up in victory."

8. Eighth Generation: Methuselah

מְתוּשֶׁלַח (*methushelaḥ*): when he dies, judgment,[41] man of dart

> Methuselah was born to Enoch at the age of 65 (Gen 5:21; 1 Chr 1:3). He was born 687 years after Adam. He became the father of Lamech at the age of 187. He lived 782 more years and had other children. He died at the age of 969 (1,656 years after Adam). Amazingly, the year of his death and the year of the flood coincides (Gen 5:25–27). He lived contemporaneously with Adam for 243 years, with Enoch 300 years, and with Noah 600 years.
>
> His name is recorded in the genealogy of Jesus in Luke 3:37 as Μαθουσαλά (*Mathousala*).

Methuselah was the son of Enoch who was taken up to heaven without seeing death. The name *Methuselah* means "when he dies, the world will end." Enoch must have received a special revelation at the time of Methuselah's birth regarding the fate of his child. The name is composed of two words מַת (*math*), meaning "man" or "male," and שֶׁלַח (*shelah*), meaning "missile" or "weapon." In this case, his name would be translated as "man of the weapon" or "man of the javelin (dart)." Alternatively, the name can be interpreted as being a combination of the words מוּת (*muth*), meaning "die" or "kill," and שָׁלַח (*shalah*), meaning "sent," "sent away," or "let go." In this case, *Methuselah* would mean "when he is dead, it shall come (be sent)."[42] According to a tale from the ancient Near East, every village had a guard who, with a spear in hand, protected the village. If this guard died, the village would be vulnerable to attacks from outside forces and face the threat of destruction. Perhaps, *Methuselah* was named with this narrative in mind.

James M. Boice states, "Simply that Enoch had a revelation at the time of Methuselah's birth of the destruction to come on the earth by flood. God said that the flood was to come after the death of that son. So either at God's explicit direction or as an act of his own faith, Enoch named the child Methuselah—'when he is dead, it shall come.' While Methuselah lived, the flood would be held back. But when he died, it would come."[43]

What kind of parent would choose a name with such a dreadful eschatological meaning? Enoch spread the message regarding the coming judgment and named his son according to the Word in order to prepare faith that is fortified for the end time.

Finally, the long-prophesied flood came upon the earth 1,656 years after Adam, on the seventeenth day of the second month of the year that Noah turned 600 years old. This was the year of Methuselah's death at the age of 969 (Gen 5:27; 7:11).

(1) Through Methuselah, Enoch came to a thorough awareness of the end.

Enoch experienced a turning point in his life with the birth of Methuselah when he was sixty-five years old and began to walk with God. The Bible emphasizes that Enoch began his walk with God after the birth of Methuselah (Gen 5:21–22). This means that there was a direct correlation between Enoch's walk with God and Methuselah's birth. Since the meaning of Methuselah's name is, "when he is dead, the end of the world shall come," each time Enoch called out to his son, he was reminded of the impending judgment. This impelled Enoch to prepare his faith for the end.

Enoch did not withdraw from the world to live in seclusion. He lived among his fellow men. He fathered children, raised and educated them, and labored to support his family. Undoubtedly, it is difficult to walk with God during dark times governed by the sinful cultures of the secular world. Yet, Enoch's awareness of the impending judgment and his consciousness of the end made the walk possible (Luke 21:32–36).

Jude 1:14–15 supports the notion of Enoch's eschatological faith. He lived his life prophesying about God's impending judgment against ungodly deeds and ungodly words.

(2) Methuselah enjoyed the greatest longevity in all human history.

Excluding Enoch, who was taken up to heaven, the life spans of the descendants of Adam in Genesis 5 ranged from 777 years to 969 years (average of 912 years). This long life span is unimaginable today. Life spans that last almost 1,000 years testify that mankind was originally created for eternity. This gives us hope that in the future mankind will live eternally in a spiritual body (1 John 2:25; Rev 22:5). At the same time, it is a demonstration of God's mercy toward mankind. God planned judgment when He saw that sins of all sorts had invaded every corner of the earth, but He delayed judgment for the 969 years of Methuselah's life. Even after Noah's ark had been built, God granted one last chance for repentance by giving notice of the impending judgment seven days prior to the flood. In essence, Methuselah's longevity represents God's patience and His great mercy and compassion for mankind (1 Tim 2:4; 2 Pet 3:9).

(3) Methuselah enjoyed the special privilege of witnessing God's amazing providence of salvation.

Methuselah was a witness to the entire redemptive work until the flood. His long life allowed him to witness the following key events in redemptive history.

① He heard Adam's account of the garden of Eden for 243 years.
② He witnessed his father Enoch's walk with God for 300 years and saw him being taken up to heaven alive.
③ He also saw the birth of Noah, his grandson. As his son Lamech had hoped, Noah was a type of the Savior during a time of overflowing sin and wickedness. He lived contemporaneously with Noah for 600 years.
④ He helped with the construction of Noah's ark from the beginning until the end. He was presumably the greatest source of strength, courage, and hope for Noah. It is most likely that Methuselah understood the ominous meaning of his name—God's judgment would come upon his death. Consequently, he lived a godly life with keen sensitivity regarding the end time until the very last day of his life and presumably expended all his efforts in testifying that God's judgment was near. As prophesied, he died at the age of 969 in the year of the flood.
⑤ He witnessed the birth of Shem, Noah's eldest son, who would carry on the godly lineage after the great flood. He lived contemporaneously with Shem for ninety-eight years (Gen 5:32; 7:6; 11:10).

9. Ninth Generation: Lamech

לֶמֶךְ (*lemekh*): strong youth[44]

> Lamech was born to Methuselah at the age of 187 (Gen 5:25; 1 Chr 1:3–4). He was born 874 years after Adam. He became the father of Noah at the age of 182. He lived 595 more years and had other children. He died at the age of 777 (1,651 years after Adam), five years before the flood (Gen 5:28–31). He lived 113 years contemporaneously with Enoch, 595 years with Noah, and 56 years with Adam. The tenth generation Noah, however, did not meet Adam because he was born 126 years after Adam's death.
>
> His name is recorded in the genealogy of Jesus in Luke 3:36 as Λάμεχ (*Lamech*).

Enoch was sixty-five years old when he became the father of Methuselah and 252 years old when he became the grandfather of Lamech. Lamech must have been about 113 years old when Enoch was taken up to heaven. Thus, both Methuselah and Lamech witnessed Enoch's godly life and walk with God. Surely, both Enoch's son and grandson were raised under his godly influence.[45]

Two sets of people with the same names appear in Genesis 4 and Genesis 5. They are Enoch (Gen 4:17) and Lamech (Gen 4:18) from the line of Cain, and a different Enoch (Gen 5:21) and Lamech (Gen 5:28) from the line of Seth. In the genealogy, these two groups of people are differentiated by additional narratives in the Bible. Lamech from Cain's line was a man of grief and despair, while Lamech from Seth's line was a man of hope. They undoubtedly took two opposite paths in life.

In addition, the meaning of the name *Lamech* from the line of Cain is understood as "conqueror" or "strong one in confronting God." These meanings are derived from the Arabic origin of his name, which means "oppressor" or "strong one." He deserted God and boasted of his own strength. He wanted to conquer the world with evil and challenged God's will. Although they share the same name, the meaning "conqueror" or "strong one" is befitting for Lamech (Methushael's son) from the line of Cain, but not for Lamech (Methuselah's son) from the line of Seth.

The meaning "powerful one" and "a man of prayer"[46] are other denotations of the name Lamech. Both these meanings are appropriate for the Lamech in the line of Seth since only through prayer can one attain the power of faith that can cast out demons and defeat the forces of evil (Mark 9:29). May you all become people of prayer and powerful believers who can defeat the forces of evil.

In the genealogy in Genesis 5, the narrative on Lamech moves away from the traditional genealogical structure with additional accounts that underscore the importance of his son. In other words, more attention is focused on his son rather than on Lamech himself.

(1) Lamech had a son and named him Noah ("comforter" or "giver of peace").

The name *Noah* was Lamech's confession of faith and his desire for the will of God.

> **Genesis 5:28–29** Lamech lived one hundred and eighty-two years, and became the father of a son. [29]Now he called his name Noah, saying, "This one will give us rest from our work and from the toil of our hands arising from the ground which the LORD has cursed."

This passage contains Lamech's anguished cry regarding the fragility of mankind that he acutely understood through his own deep suffering on this earth. He acknowledged man's inability to overcome suffering. He recognized that suffering and sadness in life were the result of the fall of man and God's subsequent curse. Thus, he did not rebel against God or give up under the duress of suffering and affliction; rather, these things motivated his faith. He trusted solely in God and hoped that the curse would be lifted through his son (Gen 5:29).

Only those who sincerely repent, acknowledging that the evil of the times is the result of their own sins, can possess true faith to conquer this world.[47]

(2) Lamech earnestly anticipated the coming of the Messiah.

Lamech longed for the sorrowful state of fallen men to end and for Eden to be restored. He hoped that someone would lift the death sentence pronounced upon man (Gen 3:24; 4:16) and open the path for recovery to the original state of man before the fall. He understood all too keenly the anguish associated with life and the frailty of mankind and hoped that true peace and consolation from God would come with the birth of his son. Accordingly, Genesis 5:29 expresses Lamech's sincere longing for the coming of the Messiah, the "seed of the woman" promised in Genesis 3:15, and how it will bring joyful news and great comfort for all mankind. His hope was similar to that of Apostle Paul expressed in 2 Corinthians 1:5: "For just as the sufferings of Christ are ours in abundance, so also our comfort is abundant through Christ."

Lamech's son Noah promised a new beginning for mankind; he was a gift from the "God of all comfort" (2 Cor 1:3–7). He was a type (foreshadow) of Jesus Christ whom God had sent. Jesus Christ is the one who gives true comfort and rest to this earth (Isa 9:6; John 14:27).

(3) Lamech lived the shortest life (777 years) among the ten generations since Adam.

Lamech lived the shortest life among the first ten patriarchs from Adam to Noah. Considering that the number *seven* represents completion, however, it is plausible that he completed all his tasks in life during the 777 years. He helped his son Noah build the ark since he longed to see the day of the fulfillment of the revelation he received. Lamech's entire life was perfect in that he did his best for the fulfillment of God's will. Thus, God took Lamech promptly five years before the flood—before calamity and evil came (Isa 57:1).

(4) Like other patriarchs, Lamech had many children besides Noah until he was 777 years old.

> **Genesis 5:30** Then Lamech lived five hundred and ninety-five years after he became the father of Noah, and he had other sons and daughters.

Lamech's children were Noah's biological siblings. They were all loved, raised, and trained in the Word by the same godly father. However, none of Noah's many siblings were to be found at the time of the flood; only the eight members of Noah's immediate family were saved (1 Pet 3:20; 2 Pet 2:5). All the other children born to Lamech had rejected their father's teachings and refused to listen to the Word of God. They followed after the wickedness of the times. Noah's siblings probably received more pleas than others to enter the ark, but they rejected them all.

They enjoyed life in the world, yielded to their own desires, and did not help with the building of the ark. Even though they were so close to the actual builder of the ark, all of Noah's siblings were swept away by the waters of judgment. "They did not understand until the flood came and took them all away" (Matt 24:39). They had the gateway to salvation so close to them, but they could not be saved because they did not believe.[48]

In Matthew 24:37 it is written, "For the coming of the Son of Man will be just like the days of Noah." We must not be so foolish as to disregard the Word of God and miss the ark of salvation like Noah's siblings.

10. Tenth Generation: Noah

נֹחַ (*noah*): rest, comfort

> Noah was born to Lamech at the age of 182 (Gen 5:28; 1 Chr 1:4). He was born 1,056 years after Adam. He became the father of Shem at the age of 502 and later of Ham and Japheth. He lived 350 years after the flood, but he did not have any other children. He died at the age of 950 (2,006 years after Adam, Gen 5:32; 9:28–29; 11:10).
>
> His name is recorded in the genealogy of Jesus in Luke 3:36 as Νῶε (*Nōe*).

The name *Noah* is derived from the Hebrew word נוּחַ (*nuah*), which means "to settle down," "appease," or "rest" (Deut 5:14; 2 Kgs 2:15; Lam 5:5). The derived meanings from this word are "Sabbath," "rest," and "comfort."

The godly descendants who lived in the world overflowing with iniquity longed earnestly for God's comfort through the birth of this son (Gen 6:5). Genesis 5:29 states, "Now he called his name Noah, saying, 'This one will give us rest from our work . . . .'" Here, the Hebrew verb *give rest* is in the Piel stem, stressing the notion that rest would *surely* be brought. This points to the godly descendants' desire to be consoled by God.

It was not Lamech's personal desire or insight that compelled him to name his son Noah. This name has the messianic meaning, "comfort" and "consolation," because a revelation from God had revealed a new providence of redemption.[49] The end to the long period of suffering had come; it was now time for God's comfort and rest. In his commentary on Genesis, Park Yune-Sun notes on Genesis 5:29 that Lamech had named his son "rest," because he mistook this child to be the Messiah. In other words, he suggests that Lamech thought that this child was the Savior who was to come and deliver all mankind from the curse of sin. Park deduces that people of the early times must have placed their hope in the coming of the Messiah according to the promise of God (Gen 3:15).[50]

The Bible states that Noah's time was so wicked that God was sorry that He had made man (Gen 6:5–7). Accordingly, the verse, "But Noah found favor in the eyes of the LORD" (Gen 6:8), emphasizes that Noah was God's bright lamp during that dark and wicked time. It shows a totally depraved world where there are no godly persons except for Noah and the seven members of his family. Second Peter 2:5 states, "And [God] did not spare the ancient world, but preserved Noah, a preacher of righteousness, with seven others, when He brought a flood upon the world of the ungodly."

Noah's time was so ungodly that there was not one person who received Noah's message of warning as the truth or in any way attempted to understand it until all were destroyed by the flood (Matt 24:38–39). However, God will seek out the godly during the ungodly end times. Like Noah, we must also find favor in God's eyes so that we may stand before the Son of Man (Ps 12:1; Mic 7:2; Luke 21:36).

(1) Lamech fathered a son at the age of 182 (Gen 5:28).

> **Genesis 5:28** Lamech lived one hundred and eighty-two years, and became the father of a son.

This verse deviates from the usual repetitive structure of the genealogy. For the previous patriarchs, it was written "became the father of" followed by the son's name. For Lamech, however, it was written "became the father of a son" with no mention of the son's name. This son is mentioned again in the next verse (Genesis 5:29).

> **Genesis 5:29** Now he called his name Noah, saying, "This one will give us rest from our work and from the toil of our hands arising from the ground which the LORD has cursed."

The word *son* is used distinctively in Genesis 5:28. The author makes a deliberate effort to suggest that this was not just another son among many, but rather, a *unique son* much like the "only begotten Son" (John 1:14, 18; 3:16, 18; 1 John 4:9). Eve had rejoiced after giving birth to her first son, saying, "I have gotten a manchild with the help of the LORD" (Gen 4:1). In the same way, Noah's birth stirred up special expectations, special joy, and special meaning, because this son was a type of Jesus Christ who was to come as the only begotten Son.

The name *Noah* foreshadows Jesus Christ, who would come to save this world and give true rest and comfort. In obedience to God's Word, Noah prepared the ark and saved his family from God's judgment that destroyed the fallen world and gave them rest. Jesus is the Comforter who came in the flesh to the fallen world to proclaim true rest (John 14:27). In the second coming, Christ arrives to judge the world by fire. He will once again save His chosen people and lead them to heaven, the kingdom of true rest.

(2) Noah lived at the junction of two ages.

There is no mention of Noah's age or the remaining years of his life in Genesis 5. This shows God's holy will to establish a new work of redemption through Noah (Gen 5:32). Primeval history was to end with Noah, and a new world was to commence after the flood with the emergence of Abraham (Gen 12:1–3). Noah lived contemporaneously with Abraham for fifty-eight years.

> **Calculation:**
> Year of Noah's death (2,006 years after Adam)
> – Year of Abraham's birth (1,948)
> = 58 years

Noah met with all but three (Adam, Seth, and Enoch) of the ten generations of patriarchs before the flood. Among the ten generations after Adam, he lived the third-longest life until the age of 950 (Gen 9:28–29). He also lived to see all ten generations after the flood down to Abraham; Noah lived contemporaneously with seventeen generations of patriarchs, including himself.

The following are facts related to Noah's birth:
① Noah was born 126 years after Adam's death.

> **Calculation:**
> Year of Noah's birth (1,056 years after Adam)
> – Year of Adam's death (930)
> = 126 years

② Noah was born 69 years after Enoch's ascension.

> **Calculation:**
> Year of Noah's birth (1,056 years after Adam)
> – Year of Enoch's ascension (987)
> = 69 years

③ Noah was born 14 years after Seth's death.

Calculation:
Year of Noah's birth (1,056 years after Adam)
− Year of Seth's death (1,042)
= 14 years

(3) Noah did not meet Adam and Seth.

Although Noah did not meet Adam, there were people who bridged the longtime gap between Adam and Noah. They were Adam's grandson Enosh and the succeeding generations: Kenan, Mahalalel, Jared, Methuselah, and Lamech. These six patriarchs saw Adam during the first half of their lives and met Noah during the second half. These men played crucial roles in passing down their faith so that the history of redemption would not come to a halt. They inherited their faith through their time with Adam and passed this faith down to their descendant Noah so that God's work of redemption continued.

Enosh lived 695 years contemporaneously with Adam and passed down the faith that he had inherited to Noah for eighty-four years.

Kenan lived 605 years contemporaneously with Adam and passed down the faith that he had inherited to Noah for 179 years.

Mahalalel lived 535 years contemporaneously with Adam and passed down the faith that he had inherited to Noah for 234 years.

Jared lived 470 years contemporaneously with Adam and passed down the faith that he had inherited to Noah for 366 years.

Methuselah lived 243 years contemporaneously with Adam and passed down the faith that he had inherited to Noah for 600 years.

Lamech lived fifty-six years contemporaneously with Adam and passed down the faith that he had inherited to Noah for 595 years.

Noah never met Adam, but he received the true inheritance of the covenant faith from the six patriarchs who had inherited their faith directly from Adam. Noah inherited Adam's faith from Enosh (third generation) and the process continued on with every generation until Lamech (ninth generation).

(4) During the 136-year period between the death of Jared (sixth generation) and the birth of Shem (eleventh generation), all the patriarchs in the line of Seth had died except for Methuselah, Lamech, and Noah who were alive and working.

Calculation:
Year of Shem's birth (1,558 years after Adam)
− Year of Jared's death (1,422)
= 136 years

Noah was 502 years old when he became the father of Shem. During the 136 years between the death of Jared and the birth of Shem, only three patriarchs in the line of Seth were alive. After Shem, Ham and Japheth were also born to Noah (Gen 5:32; 6:10). God appeared to Noah and gave him precise instructions for the construction of the ark only after all three of his sons had married (Gen 6:14–18).

(5) The prediluvian world in which Noah lived was completely corrupt. Genesis 6:2 states, "The sons of God saw that the daughters of men were beautiful; and they took wives for themselves, whomever they chose." This refers to how the godly descendants of Seth (Gen 5) intermarried with the corrupt descendants of Cain (Gen 4), deserted God, and became men of the flesh (Gen 6:3). Consequently, God declared, "My Spirit shall not strive with man forever" (Gen 6:3).

During Noah's time, the wickedness of the world had accelerated and the earth abounded with all types of sin, and no place was left uncorrupted (Gen 6:5). Here, "the wickedness of man was great on the earth" implies that sin had seeped into every corner of the human heart and wickedness had sprung forth and overflowed. All the intents behind people's thoughts and plans were continually against faith; they were evil from the beginning to the end. They completely rejected God's rule and involvement (Gen 6:5).

Genesis 6:11 describes the extent of the corruption: "Now the earth was corrupt in the sight of God, and the earth was filled with violence." The English word *corrupt* comes from the Latin word *corruptus*, past participle of *corrumpere*, from *com* and *rumpere* ("to break"), meaning "to change from good to bad in terms of morals, manners, or actions," or "to degrade with unsound principles or moral values." Violence is the exertion of physical force so as to injure or abuse (as in warfare, or effecting illegal entry into a house).[51] Thus, the phrase "the earth was corrupt and filled with violence" means inflicting harm to take from others, robbery, rape, murder, and the use of brutal force were rampant. This is why God said, "The end of all flesh has come before Me" (Gen 6:13), declaring that evil was at its peak just before the flood and judgment was inevitable.

The world just before the flood was so exceedingly corrupt that God grieved in His heart (Gen 6:6). This is surely a shocking statement. The flood was God's fearful punishment against the dissipated world that did not have God in its heart. Noah, however, found favor in the eyes of God despite the corruption of the times (Gen 6:8). Genesis 6:9 explains, "Noah was a righteous man, blameless in his time; Noah walked with God."

This age in which we are living is also rapidly following the same path; it has become a world filled with extreme violence and is corrupt in God's sight. Jesus said that the time of the Son of Man would be like the days of Noah (Matt 24:37; Luke 17:26). Noah found favor in the eyes of the LORD (Gen 6:8) and he built the ark as God had commanded (Gen 6:22; 7:5), and as a result God said, "You alone I have seen to be righteous before Me in this time" (Gen 7:1).

We also need to receive God's grace just as Noah did. First Peter 1:13 urges us, "Therefore, prepare your minds for action, keep sober in spirit, fix your hope completely on the grace to be brought to you at the revelation of Jesus Christ." We also need to receive this grace in order to prepare the ark of faith (Heb 11:7) and stand in the order of those who are saved when He comes to judge by fire in the end (2 Pet 3:7, 12).

(6) There are three unique characteristics regarding the birth of Noah's sons.

① Until Noah, the patriarchs' average age at procreation was 118 (Gen 5). Noah was unique in that he fathered his sons after the age of 500 (Gen 5:32). Among the three sons, the Bible gives the exact year of Shem's birth. He was born ninety-eight years before the flood, when Noah was 502 years old.

> **Genesis 11:10** These are the records of the generations of Shem. Shem was one hundred years old, and became the father of Arpachshad two years after the flood.

Noah lived until he was 950 years old. He lived almost 400 years after he fathered his three sons (Gen 5:32), which was long enough to witness the births of about six generations. Jared, the sixth generation from Adam, was born 460 years after Adam.

② Unlike the other patriarchs who fathered children until they died, there is no record of Noah having additional children after he had his three sons. It is only recorded that he lived another 350 years (after he was 600 years old), for a total of 950 years, and then died (Gen 5:32; 6:10; 9:28–29). This pattern repeats once again with Terah (nineteenth generation from Adam; Gen 11:26). He had Abraham, Nahor, and Haran at the age of seventy and did not have additional children.

③ Noah's three sons were married before the flood, but did not have any children until they entered the ark and the flood came.

> **Genesis 6:18** But I will establish My covenant with you; and you shall enter the ark—you and your sons and your wife, and your sons' wives with you.

Only eight people entered the ark (Gen 7:7, 13; 8:18; 1 Pet 3:20; 2 Pet 2:5). The Bible states that Noah's three daughters-in-law gave birth to sons after the flood.

> **Genesis 10:1** Now these are the records of the generations of Shem, Ham, and Japheth, the sons of Noah; and sons were born to them after the flood.

Moses (author of Genesis) meticulously recorded the ages in which each patriarch fathered his firstborn in the godly genealogy of faith because they are significant. These details reveal the patriarch's godly lives and the circumstances of their times.

Noah had children at an old age (after he was 500 years old, Gen 5:32) and did not have additional children after the three sons that God had given to him. His sons began to have children only after the flood. These facts reveal that they had wholeheartedly believed in God's message of judgment to Noah and fully participated in the preparation work. This is also evident in the verse, "Thus Noah did; according to all that the LORD had commanded him" (Gen 6:22; 7:5). God was bringing the corrupt age to a close; its end was near.

Genesis 6:13 Then God said to Noah, "The end of all flesh has come before Me; for the earth is filled with violence because of them; and behold, I am about to destroy them with the earth."

(7) Noah built the ark with reverence for God.

God directed Noah to build the ark (Gen 6:14–16) after He warned Noah about the corruption of his time (Gen 6:1–8). Of course, God Himself supplied Noah with the precise instructions and design for the ark. The Bible testifies that Noah built the ark according to the plan that God had given to him (Gen 6:22; 7:5). How was Noah able to completely obey when God only appeared to him one time with the command?

Hebrews 11:7 states, "In reverence [he] prepared an ark." The word *reverence* describes a heart that strives, with fear and trembling, to obey God's Word—spoken only once—until the very end. Noah did not envy the prosperity of the wicked. He believed it was man's rightful duty to revere God (Prov 23:17; Eccl 12:13). The more he revered God, the more God poured His wisdom upon Noah, so that he could complete the ark. The fear of God is the beginning of wisdom (Job 28:28; Ps 111:10; Prov 1:7; 9:10; 15:33). In truth, the ark was the perfect manifestation of Noah's faith and reverence for God.

Noah's ability to spend such an extended period of time building the ark without a change of heart is proof of his reverence and firm belief in God's promise. While Noah was building the ark, people merely watched, ridiculing him and pointing their fingers at him in reproach. One can only imagine Noah's heartache and his physical exhaustion during the long and arduous construction period.

Observing how Noah had quietly built the ark through all those years, God said, "For you alone I have seen to be righteous before Me in this time" (Gen 7:1). God's praise must have felt like a long-awaited rainfall during a drought. Faith is not about words, but about deeds, like Noah's act of building the ark. The greater the faith, the better the preparation. Jesus also commanded, "For this reason you also must be ready" (Matt 24:44). Those who are ready can enter the wedding feast (Matt 25:10). Let us stay alert and prepare the lamp and the oil to welcome the bridegroom (Matt 25:1–13). There is no other way for believers to stand before the Son of Man in the end except by being alert in prayer (Luke 21:36).

(8) After the flood, God made a covenant with Noah, the second ancestor of mankind after Adam.

God completely tore down the structure of the entire wicked world through the flood to make ready His second work of creation. The flood did not bring an end to the world. Although God knew that the evil heart of man remained even after the flood (Gen 8:21), in His absolute grace and mercy He established the eternal covenant of the rainbow, vowing that He would never again destroy the earth by flood (Gen 9:9–17).

Thus, history will be preserved by the grace of God until the end predetermined by God and until salvation is perfected through Jesus Christ. God blessed Noah and his sons to be fruitful, to multiply, and to fill the earth (Gen 9:1, 7) just as He had blessed Adam (Gen 1:28; 2:15). The *blessing of the beginning*, "be fruitful and multiply," was renewed in Noah's time and remained effective in the new world after the flood.

Excursus 3

The Duration of the Construction of the Ark

(✻ Organized and presented for the first time in history)

In general, commentaries and expositions on the book of Genesis assert that the construction of Noah's ark took 120 years. The following is a collection of excerpts in support of the view that the duration of the construction of the ark was 120 years.

"One hundred and twenty years were sufficient time for constructing the ark."

The Grand Bible Commentary: With Comprehensive and Synthetic Exegetical Study Methods. Edited by Disciples Publishing House (Seoul: Bible Study Material Publisher, 1991), 1:400

"For about 120 years (Gen 6:3) . . . Noah and his sons followed God's instructions and were building a great ship."

C. H. Kang and Ethel R. Nelson, *Discovery of Genesis: How the Truths of Genesis Were Found Hidden in the Chinese Language* (St. Louis: Concordia, 1998), 113

"One hundred and twenty years is the time in which Noah built the ark by persistently following the Word of God through unchanging faith. . . ."

Lee Byung-Don, *Genesis Exegetical Postil* (Seoul: Yechansa, 1985), 48

"Noah built the ark for 120 years according to God's command" [Gen 6:3].

Suk Won-Tae, *Complete Sermon Collection*, vol. 2 (Seoul: Kyunghyang, 1985), 350

"...said, 'prepared an ark. . . .' He prepared the ark for about 120 years."

Suk Won-Tae, *Anthology 4: Revealed Theology* (Seoul: Kyunghyang, 1991) , 113

"During the long period of 120 years, all eight members of Noah's family (Gen 7:7–13) put their strengths together to complete the ark, the great vessel, according to God's blueprint. . . . They built the ark for 120 years according to God's command."

David Yonggi Cho, *Commentary on the Genesis I* (Seoul: Seoul Logos, 1996), 111

"A ship is not something that can be built in 1 or 2 years. I would think that it took all 120 years."

Kim Suh-Taek, *The Great Flood and the Covenant of the Rainbow* (Seoul: Hong Sung Sa, 1997), 207

Despite arguments presented by many scholars, it is clear that Noah did not spend 120 years building the ark. This is a critical issue since nothing should be added or taken away from the Word of God recorded in the Bible (Rev 22:18–19). For instance, how erroneous would it be to say that Jesus lived on this earth for thirty-five years when He actually lived here for thirty-three years?

When God mentioned the "one hundred and twenty years" in Genesis 6:3, it was His warning against the corruption of mankind—living only for the desires of the flesh. It was also a warning regarding the impending judgment (Gen 6:7), but God did not give a revelation about the ark at this time.

After time had passed, Noah became the father of three sons (Gen 6:10). Later, his sons married and Noah had three daughters-in-law. It was only after this that God commanded Noah, "Make for yourself an ark" (Gen 6:14), and gave him detailed instructions for the ark (Gen 6:15–16). Then He declared, "And behold, I, even I am bringing the flood of water upon the earth" (Gen 6:17). However, 120 years before the flood, Noah was 480 years old and that was twenty-two years before he had Shem, his first son (Gen 5:32; 7:7, 11; 11:10).

Calculation of the duration of the construction:

---

1. **Noah was 600 years old when the judgment of the flood occurred (Gen 7:6, 11). Noah gave birth to his three sons after he was 500 years old (Gen 5:32).**

2. **God commanded Noah to build the ark after his three sons were born.**

Genesis 6:10 states, "And Noah became the father of three sons: Shem, Ham, and Japheth." Later, in Genesis 6:14, Noah received a revelation to build the ark. God, then, gave him detailed instructions on how to construct the ark and pronounced destruction upon all living things on the earth through the flood (Gen 6:17).

Noah fathered his three sons after he was 500 years old. He built the ark after his sons were born until he was 600 years old when the flood occurred. This means that the ark was actually built in less than 100 years.

---

3. **Noah's sons were born to him after he turned 500 years old and were already grown and married when God commanded Noah to build the ark (Gen 6:18).**

The New Revised Standard Version of Genesis 5:32 states, "After Noah was five hundred years old, Noah became the father of Shem, Ham, and Japheth." According to Genesis 11:10, Noah was 502 years old when he became the father of Shem. The Bible states that Noah received the revelation about the flood after his sons grew up and were married (Gen 6:18; [Ref] Gen 7:13). This is when Noah began to build the ark according to God's instructions (Gen 6:22).

---

4. **Since Noah had Shem at the age of 502, we can conclude that it took Noah less than 98 years to build the ark (Noah's age 600 – 502 = 98). When you take into account Shem's age at marriage, the number of years to build the ark will decrease further.**

Noah gave birth to his first son Shem at the age of 502 (Gen 11:10). Even if Noah had all three sons consecutively, it would have taken him at least two years from the age of 502. If Noah had the remaining two sons every two years after Shem, then it would have taken him another four years to have all his children. If Noah had the remaining two sons every three years after Shem, then it would have taken him another six years to have all his children. Then, the time that Noah spent on building the ark would be much shorter than ninety-eight years. Furthermore, his sons would have been at least fifteen years of age when they married. Considering this, the period for building the ark can be estimated to have been approximately seventy to eighty years. Therefore, the view that it took Noah 120 years to build the ark is erroneous.

The Meaning of the 120 Years in Genesis 6:3

Genesis 6:3 Then the LORD said, "My Spirit shall not strive with man forever, because he also is flesh; nevertheless his days shall be one hundred and twenty years."

וַיֹּאמֶר יְהֹוָה לֹא־יָדוֹן רוּחִי בָאָדָם לְעֹלָם בְּשַׁגַּם הוּא בָשָׂר

וְהָיוּ יָמָיו מֵאָה וְעֶשְׂרִים שָׁנָה

People generally believe that it took 120 years to build the ark. Where did this number come from? The assertion that Noah built the ark for 120 years seems to be based on Genesis 6:3. However, as noted in Excursus 3, the 120 years mentioned in Genesis 6:3 clearly does not refer to the number of years that it took Noah to build the ark.

What, then, do the 120 years in Genesis 6:3 refer to? There are two differing views among theologians regarding this time period.

I. The View That the 120 Years Refers to the Shortened Life Span

The following is a collection of excerpts from scholars who interpret the 120 years as the maximum life span granted to mankind as a result of sin.

"On the other hand, according to 5:32, Noah was 500 years old when he fathered Ham, Shem, and Japhet, and 600 years old when the Flood began (7:6), so some commentators (e.g., Heil, Konig, Kidner) have suggested that 120 years represents a period of grace before the Flood. It may be, however, that the author thought of the 120 years as the maximum life-span that was only gradually implemented; cf. the slow-acting curses of Eden 3:16–19. In the post-Flood period, the recorded ages steadily decline (chap. 11), and later figures very rarely exceed 120."

Gordon J. Wenham, *Genesis 1–15*, Word Biblical Commentary 1 (Waco, TX: Word, 1987), 142

" . . . the operation of God's life-giving spirit in man crippled by sin; and in future the normal limit of his life shall not exceed 120 years."

S. R. Driver, *The Book of Genesis* (London: Methuen, 1904), 83–84

"The sense of this passage is apparently this: the earliest generations, which were the strongest on account of their nearness to the Divine source, lived almost to a thousand years, the day of the Almighty; but the span of life was diminishing from generation to generation, and in the end would be stabilized at the point where the healthiest person, if he did not suffer illness or any calamity, would be able to live only a little more than a hundred years—a hundred and twenty years according to the round figure of tradition."

U. Cassuto, A Commentary on the Book of Genesis: Part 1, From Adam to Noah, trans. Israel
Abrahams (Jerusalem: Magnes, 1961), 297–98

"The limitation of 120 years most likely refers to a reduction of the life span of humans."

John H. Walton, Victor H. Matthews, and Mark W. Chavalas, The IVP Bible Background Commentary:
Old Testament (Downers Grove, IL: InterVarsity Press, 2000), 36

"The sad reality of the narrative, however, is that such long lives do not belong to mankind as a whole but belonged to another age. . . . Henceforth man's life would be 'a hundred and twenty years' only. Such a short life, in comparison with the long lives of the previous chapter, marks man's fall and separation from his Creator."

John H. Sailhamer, The Expositor's Bible Commentary with the New International Version, ed.
Frank E. Gaebelein, vol. 2 (Grand Rapids: Zondervan, 1990), 77

"Because all the descendants of Seth followed the path of the descendants of Cain, God shortened their lives to 120 years as punishment. Though people lived about 200 years just after the Flood, their lives were to be shortened to 120 years thereafter. The words 'his days' mean that the lives of all mankind would be shortened dramatically as in the case of one man."

Suh Chul-Won, The Book of Genesis (Seoul: Grisim, 2001), 258–59

"The words '120 years' . . . it seems proper to interpret the meaning as the life span of mankind after the Flood and evidence is found in the fact that the life span of mankind gradually shortened so that it eventually did not exceed 120 years."

Wone Yong-Kuk, A Commentary of Genesis (Seoul: Se Shin Culture, 1990), 152

II. The View That the 120 Years was a Grace Period for Repentance before the Judgment

The second view argues that the 120 years was a period of grace granted to men before judgment so that they may repent and return to God.

"This does not mean that life span of man was limited to 120 years, but that there would be the judgment of the Flood after 120 years."

"They were given 120 years of opportunity to repent, but they did not obey."

Park Yune-Sun, A Commentary on Genesis, vol. 1 (Seoul: Yung Eum Sa, 1991), 132–33

"The word 'days' refers to 120 years. It, however, does not signify the period of man's life. It signifies that God reserved the judgment 120 years."

> The Oxford Bible Interpreter. Edited by Disciples Publishing House
> (Seoul: Bible Study Material Publisher, 1989), 1:391

"It means that God would judge 120 years later. . . . If people do not repent during the period of grace given by God, God's judgment will be upon them so that they perish."

> Lee Byung-Kyu, The Commentary on Genesis (Seoul: Yum Kwang, 1986), 86–87

"More likely, this phrase means that God will extend a (grace period) of 120 years before expending His wrath (in the Flood)."

> Earl D. Radmacher, gen. ed., The Nelson Study Bible: NKJV, ed. Ronald B. Allen
> (Nashville: Thomas Nelson, 1997) 16

"God has always been long-suffering, even under such awful conditions as prevailed in the days of Noah (1 Peter 3:20). Though all had rejected Him, He still granted 120 years to mankind in light of the bare possibility that at least some might 'come to repentance' (2 Peter 3:9). This was more than adequate time even for those who were infants to grow to maturity and have abundant opportunity to accept or reject God."

> Henry M. Morris, The Genesis Record: A Scientific and Devotional Commentary
> on the Book of Beginnings (Grand Rapids: Baker, 1976), 171

"Early exegesis of this verse prefers to see here a reference to the interval of time remaining before the Flood. The figure would then represent three conventional generations of forty years each."

> Nahum M. Sarna, Genesis: The Traditional Hebrew Text with New JPS Translation,
> JPS Torah Commentary (Philadelphia: Jewish Publication Society, 1989), 46

"We believe that Noah preached for 120 years, and during that time the Spirit of God was striving with men."

> J. Vernon McGee, Genesis: Chapters 1–15 (Nashville: Thomas Nelson, 1991), 119

"Nevertheless both ancient and modern Jewish expositors, e.g. Rashi and Reggio, Abenezra and Heidenheim, explain this 120 years of a respite accorded to men for the purpose of obviating by repentance the judgment of extermination."

> Franz Delitzsch, New Commentary on Genesis, vol. 2 (Minneapolis: Klock &
> Klock Christian Publishers, 1978), 230–31

"And the period of 120 years becomes one of probation, in the face of every sign that the doom cannot be averted. All of this accords with the separately established fact that the Flood story in Genesis, unlike its Mesopotamian analogues, was morally motivated."

> E. A. Speiser, Genesis, Anchor Bible 1 (Garden City, NY: Doubleday, 1979), 7

"Is this an age limit, or is it a period of grace prior to the Flood (i.e., his [remaining] days shall be 120 years)? The first alternative faces the difficulty that most of the people in the rest of Genesis lived well beyond 120 years. It is possible to interpret the longer life spans of the patriarchs as a mitigation or suspension of the divine penalty, just as an earlier announced divine penalty ('on the day you eat of it you shall surely die') was not immediately implanted.

But the (imminent) withdrawal of the divine Spirit as a means of lowering the life span of humanity does not make a great deal of sense. Rather, it seems to presage some event that is about to occur. Accordingly, we prefer to see in this phrase a reference to a period of time that prefaces the Flood's beginning. It is parallel to Jon. 4:5, 'Yet forty days, and Nineveh shall be overthrown.' God's hand of judgment is put on hold."

Victor P. Hamilton, *The Book of Genesis: Chapters 1–17* (Grand Rapids: Eerdmans, 1990), 269

"It is more likely that 'the period of 120 years becomes one of probation, in the face of every sign that the doom cannot be averted' (Speiser, p. 46)."

Clifton J. Allen, ed., *The Broadman Bible Commentary*, vol. 1, rev. ed.
(Nashville: Broadman, 1969), 142–43

"For these words, 'yet shall their days be one hundred and twenty years,' are to be taken in the sense of the traditional interpretation: one last period of grace is fixed by God for the repentance of mankind. . . . Before disposing of the guilty ones a time of grace of no less than one hundred and twenty years is allowed for their repentance."

H. G. Leupold, *Exposition of Genesis*, vol. 1 (Grand Rapids: Baker, 1942), 256

"The 120 years was taken by Luther (also Calvin and The Scofield Bible) to refer to a time of reprieve granted by God to mankind before sending the Flood ('I want to give them yet a reprieve of 120 years,' Luther Bible)."

John H. Sailhamer, *The Expositor's Bible Commentary with the New International Version*, ed.
Frank E. Gaebelein, vol. 2 (Grand Rapids: Zondervan, 1990), 77

The two differing arguments presented here on the meaning of the "one hundred and twenty years" in Genesis 6:3 are both valid arguments. It is difficult to conclude which argument is right or wrong, for each person interprets the meaning according to his or her own faith. However, one thing is clear. The "one hundred and twenty years" does not refer to the time it took to build the ark. John H. Walton also views the 120-year period as the grace period before the flood and argues that some have unnecessarily concluded that it took Noah 120 years to build the ark. Walton states, "But even if the 120 does represent the time left until the Flood, there is no hint in the text that all of this period was occupied by Noah's building activity."[52]

CHAPTER 11

The Genealogy from
Shem to Abraham

The second genealogy from Shem to Abraham continues in Genesis 11, following the genealogy from Adam to Noah in Genesis 5. This genealogy illustrates how mankind had multiplied to fill the earth and focuses attention on one figure—Abraham—who was chosen from among the multitude to lead the work of redemption. Genesis 10 introduces Noah, his three sons, and their seventy descendants. In Genesis 11, Shem was chosen among Noah's three sons. This genealogy concludes with Abraham emerging as the new starting point of redemptive history.

What is heartbreaking in the genealogy of Shem's descendants in Genesis 11 is that mankind became sinful once again after the flood and erected the tower of Babel. Shem's descendants also took part in that sin when they should have preserved their godliness. As a result, the life span of mankind was abruptly shortened from the time of Peleg, and the life span of the descendants of Shem was also progressively shortened as they continued to sin.

It was during these spiritually dark times that God chose Abraham and called him out of the land of Ur of the Chaldeans, where sin had prevailed (Gen 11:31–32). Ultimately, Abraham made the firm decision in faith to leave his elderly father and departed from Haran at the age of seventy-five to set foot on the land of Canaan (Gen 12:1–5).

11. Eleventh Generation: Shem

שֵׁם (*shem*): name, reputation, fame[53]

> Shem was born 1,558 years after Adam (before the flood, when Noah was 502 years old). He became the father of Arpachshad at the age of 100 (2 years after the flood) and lived 500 years more and had other children. He died at the age of 600 (2,158 years after Adam Gen 11:10–11). Shem lived 448 years contemporaneously with his father Noah (1 Chr 1:4). He lived 35 years more after Abraham's death, until Isaac was 110 years old and Jacob was 50 years old. Shem was 98 years old when the flood occurred and lived until the age of 600. He lived a long life and witnessed the world before and after the flood. He lived contemporaneously with fifteen generations of patriarchs, from Methuselah (8th) to Jacob (22nd).
>
> His name is recorded in the genealogy of Jesus in Luke 3:36 as Σήμ (*Sēm*).

Shem was Noah's firstborn, but the genealogy in Genesis 10 lists Noah's sons in the order of Japheth, Ham, and Shem. This was done to focus attention on Shem and his descendants who would become the center of redemptive history. Just as Noah prophesied, "Blessed be the LORD, the God of Shem" (Gen 9:26), the descendants of Shem are the central figures in the history of redemption since Jesus Christ would come through this lineage. In primeval history, all mankind were descendants of one ancestor. After the flood, Noah's direct line continued through the descendants of Shem.

Shem was born to Noah before the flood at the age of 502 (Gen 11:10), 1,558 years after Adam. Noah was 600 years old at the time of the flood, and Shem was ninety-eight years old.

> **Genesis 11:10** These are the records of the generations of Shem. Shem was one hundred years old, and became the father of Arpachshad two years after the flood.

The name *Shem* means "reputation (honor)" and "fame." The name of his brother Ham means "black" and "hot," and the name of his brother Japheth means "extend" and "enlargement."[54] Shem's name hints at Noah's desire for his son to become renowned, but not for the sake of family honor. Rather, his expectation for his son was to live a life that exalts God's name and upholds His honor throughout the earth.

(1) Shem lived to honor God's name.

The word *honor* is derived from the Latin word *honos* and means "high regard or great respect."[55] This word generally refers to the state of being highly esteemed by others and the glory that comes with it. People in this world erect monuments and set up halls of fame in order to commemorate persons who have made noteworthy contributions to the world.

A person's honor is associated with his or her name, character, and identity. Likewise, the fullness of God's glory, authority, and honor is in His holy name because it contains His grand creation (Heb 11:3; Ps 33:6), divine providence (Rom 11:36; 1 Cor 8:6), and salvation (Acts 2:21; 4:12; Rom 10:13). Above all, the Word that proceeds from His mouth will not return empty (Isa 55:11); when God speaks, His Words bear fruit. Thus, God's name has the highest authority and honor.

> **Isaiah 55:8–13** "...And it will be a memorial [שֵׁם, *shem*] to the LORD, for an everlasting sign which will not be cut off."
>
> **Psalm 135:13** "Your name [שֵׁם, *shem*], O LORD, is everlasting, Your remembrance, O LORD, throughout all generations."
>
> **Isaiah 42:8** "I am the LORD, that is My name [שֵׁם, *shem*]; I will not give My glory to another, nor My praise to graven images."
>
> **Hosea 12:5** "Even the LORD, the God of hosts, the LORD is His name [שֵׁם, *shem*]."

In this world, a person can be liable for the defamation of another person's name or character. Likewise, God holds people liable for the defamation of His great name and for using His name in vain (Exod 20:7). Using the Lord's name in vain means to mock, ridicule, or disregard His name (Gal 6:7).

Acknowledgment from the world and praise from other human beings have temporal effects. Honor received through the name of God, however, is a spring of eternal joy and blessings (Mal 4:2). Solomon's fame was great because it was "concerning the name of the LORD" (1 Kgs 10:1; 2 Chr 9:1). Therefore, those who guard the name of God with all their hearts, minds, and lives will also see their names lifted high, and will live honorable lives.

Shem also lived a faithful life, not for himself, but for the glory and honor of God's name. He lived a life that was worthy of the glorious title, the " God of Shem" (Gen 9:26).

(2) Shem received the testimony "Blessed be the LORD, the God of Shem" (Gen 9:26).

Among the children in a family, one particular child may be considered the family's "lucky charm." The parents may say, "This child brings good luck, because all the good things started happening to our family after this child was born!"

Likewise, Noah's exclamation, "Blessed be the LORD, the God of Shem" expressed Noah's vision of faith that God's blessings upon his family would continue and blossom through Shem. He sang praises with the hope that God's name would become renowned through Shem's descendants who would continue to glorify God and call upon His name. What a great honor it is for Shem to have God Almighty, the sovereign over the whole universe, declare that He would be glorified through his descendants! There can be no greater honor for any individual.

Shem's descendants continued to call on God's name in accordance to Noah's confession of faith. God identified Himself as the God of Abraham, who was a descendant of Shem. As Abraham successfully passed down his faith to his descendants, God became the God of Isaac and the God of Jacob (Exod 3:6, 15; Matt 22:32; Mark 12:26; Luke 20:37; Acts 3:13; 7:32). Abraham made an earnest effort to pass down his faith, because it was the purpose of God's calling (Gen 18:18–19).

The prophecy that Shiloh (Messiah) would come through Judah (Gen 49:10; Jacob's fourth son) whose name means "this time I will praise the LORD" (Gen 29:35) shows that praise that began with the descendants of Shem resonates through the later generations.

The coming Messiah has a name above all names (Phil 2:9) and is worthy to receive all the honor, glory, and praise (Rev 5:12). The name of the returning Lord is the "King of kings" and "Lord of lords," who will be renowned with glory and fame most high (1 Chr 16:27; 1 Tim 6:15; Rev 17:14; 19:16).

✷ Organized and presented for the first time in history

(3) Lamech died when Shem was ninety-three years old, and Methuselah died five years later when Shem was ninety-eight years old. The judgment of the flood came with Methuselah's death.

Shem lived thirty-five years longer than Abraham and was alive during the time of Isaac and Jacob. This was an amazing blessing of longevity. During the 600 years of his long life, he lived contemporaneously with

Methuselah (eighth generation from Adam) down through to Jacob (twenty-second generation from Adam)—a total of fifteen generations, including himself (Gen 5:25–32; 11:10–32; 25:7–26; 35:28; 41:46; 45:11; 47:9, 28).

These fifteen generations can be grouped as follows:

① Born before the flood (8th–11th generations): Methuselah, Lamech, Noah, Shem
② Born after the flood (12th–22nd generations): Arpachshad, Shelah, Eber, Peleg, Reu, Serug, Nahor, Terah, Abraham, Isaac, Jacob

The Genealogy of the Sons of Shem (26 people, Gen 10:21-31)

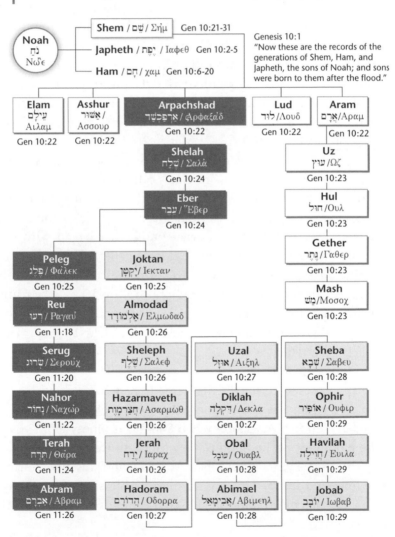

12. Twelfth Generation: Arpachshad

אַרְפַּכְשַׁד (arpakhshad): boundary[56]

> Arpachshad was born 1,658 years after Adam. He became the father of Shelah at the age of 35 and lived 403 more years and had other children. He died at the age of 438 (2,096 years after Adam, Gen 11:12–13; 1 Chr 1:24). He lived 348 years contemporaneously with Noah. He lived until Abraham was 148 years old and Isaac was 48 years old.
>
> His name is recorded in the genealogy of Jesus in Luke 3:36 as Ἀρφαξάδ (Arphaxad).

Shem had five sons after the flood: Elam, Asshur, Arpachshad, Lud, and Aram (Gen 10:1). Arpachshad was the third son (Gen 10:22). The Bible enumerates the five sons and reveals that the will of God is being fulfilled through the third son, Arpachshad, and not the first.

After Shem became the father of Elam and Asshur, he had a third son and named him *Arpachshad*, meaning "boundary" (Gen 10:22). In faith, Shem hoped that his blessings and spiritual boundaries would extend and continue to the future generations through Arpachshad.

The genealogy in Genesis 10 does not provide an answer as to why God's will was carried on through Arpachshad. However, the Bible's description of the relationship between the chosen people of Israel and the nations of Elam and Asshur at a later point in time reveals the reason as to why these two sons were set aside from God's chosen line.

Isaac Asimov states, "The first two sons of Shem are Elam and Asshur, the eponyms of the Elamites and the Assyrians, which at the time that Genesis was reduced to writing were the most powerful nations of the 'Semitic' world."[57] He writes that the word "Semitic" is in quotations because in reality the Elamites and the Assyrians were no longer considered part of the descendants of Shem.

(1) The reason Shem's first and second sons were not included in the genealogy of redemptive history.

Shem's first son was Elam.

Elam (עֵילָם) is an Assyrian word meaning "high" or "highlands." Elam is the ancestor of the Elamites, who lived in the highlands located between the Persian Gulf and the Caspian Sea on the right bank of the Tigris River (Hiddekel) in the ancient Near East. Due to geopolitical reasons, Elam had continuously engaged in battles with Sumer, Babylon, Assyria, Media, Persia, and other Mesopotamian nations in the surrounding area. The Elamite influence, which originated in the region east of Mesopotamia, had quickly expanded westward to the Jordan. When Abraham went to battle with the 318 men raised in his house to rescue Lot, he was confronted by an army of four nations led by Chedorlaomer, the king of Elam (attack by the four nations: Shinar, Ellasar, Elam, and Goiim, Gen 14:1–17).

The Elamites were skilled archers (Jer 49:35). They were a militant nation given to waging war and making conquests and the people of the world feared them (Ezek 32:24). When Assyria attacked Judah, Elam sent soldiers to assist in the destruction of Jerusalem (Isa 22:6). God declared that He would directly send plagues, pour out His anger, and send the sword to consume Elam and destroy the king and the princes who had assaulted His chosen people (Jer 49:36–38; Ezek 32:24–25).

One of the people who interfered with the reconstruction of the temple upon Israel's return from the Babylonian exile was an Elamite (Ezra 4:1–9). Thus, Elam appears as a nation that harassed the chosen people of Israel. The former region of Elam is what is now the highlands of the Khuzestan province in the southwestern part of Iran.

Shem's second son was Asshur (Assyria, Assyrians).

The name *Asshur* (אַשּׁוּר) means "a prosperous place" and is derived from the verb that means "to prosper" or "to rejoice." Assyria took advantage of every opportunity to expand and enlarge its territory; it erected the most powerful city-state of the ancient Near East. The power of the Assyrian Empire was at its peak from the ninth century BC until the seventh century BC. The capital city at the time was Assyria, but it was moved to Nineveh during the reign of King Sennacherib (705/704 BC – 681 BC).

After being conquered by Nimrod, the people of Assyria failed to inherit the faith of Shem. They became a belligerent nation like the descendants of Ham and afflicted the chosen nation of Israel. In the phrase, "From that land he went forth into Assyria" in Genesis 10:11, the pronoun "he" refers to Nimrod, Ham's grandson (Gen 10:6–8). Nimrod was the first mighty man on the earth, and it was he who invaded the land of Asshur (Gen 10:8). He was a "mighty hunter" before the Lord, a hero mighty enough to establish four great cities (Gen 10:9, 11–12). In accordance with the meaning of his name, "rebel," he turned away from faith in God, which had been passed down from Noah, and erected the tower of Babel. He stood on Satan's side, against the work of God.

The Assyrians were hostile toward the chosen nation of Israel. King Shalmaneser of Assyria destroyed Samaria, the capital of the northern kingdom of Israel during the reign of King Hoshea in 722 BC (2 Kgs 17:1–6; 18:9–12). After conquering the land of Israel, the Assyrians occupied the land and lived among the chosen people. This accelerated the corruption of the Israelites (2 Kgs 17:27–33). In addition, King Sennacherib, who had already invaded the northern kingdom of Israel, brought his army of 185,000 men down to the southern kingdom of Judah and surrounded the city of Jerusalem during King Hezekiah's reign. God, however, struck them dead (2 Kgs 18:13–19:37).

Regarding the Assyrians, God said through Isaiah, "Woe to Assyria, the rod of My anger and the staff in whose hands is My indignation" (Isa 10:5). Isaiah prophesied that judgment would eventually come upon the Assyrians, because they were proud and did not acknowledge God (Isa 10:12–16; 14:24–25).

The people of Assyria were originally of Shem's line. However, as they melded with the people of Nimrod, they drew further and further away from faith, eventually becoming enemies of God.[58] Thus, it is surely not by coincidence that the line of redemptive history continued through Shem's third son Arpachshad.

(2) Arpachshad was born to Shem at the age of 100, two years after the flood and 1,658 years after Adam (Gen 11:10).

Shem was one of the eight people who witnessed God's judgment, the consequence of sin, through the great flood. After the flood, God blessed not only Noah, but also his three sons, saying, "Be fruitful and multiply, and fill the earth."

> **Genesis 9:1** And God blessed Noah and his sons and said to them, "Be fruitful and multiply, and fill the earth."
>
> **Genesis 9:7** As for you, be fruitful and multiply; populate the earth abundantly and multiply in it.

Shem had lived through judgment and persevered through the days of suffering in the enclosed ark. Through this process, he matured spiritually to possess a *God-first* faith. This is evident in his reaction to an event that took place not long after the flood. His father, Noah, became drunk with wine and lay in his tent. When his younger brother, Ham, saw his father's nakedness, he went out and spread malicious rumors.

> **Genesis 9:22** Ham, the father of Canaan, saw the nakedness of his father, and told his two brothers outside.

The word *told* in this verse is נָגַד (*nagad*) in Hebrew, meaning "to announce," "to denounce," or "to explain" (Gen 41:24). Ham exposed his father's conduct with exaggerated detail. Shem's actions, however, were prudent and careful. He entered the room humbly, walked backwards, and covered his father's nakedness. This shows the depth of his filial respect (Gen 9:23).

After waking up, Noah pronounced severe judgment upon Ham's son, Canaan. Conversely, he blessed Shem, saying, "Blessed be the LORD, the God of Shem." He prophesied, "And let Canaan be his servant. May God enlarge Japheth, and let him dwell in the tents of Shem" (Gen 9:25–27). Consequently, Shem received the inheritance of faith from Noah.

(3) Shem hoped that the boundary of faith would be secured through Arpachshad.

Shem received God's grace and blessings in full and had a third son whom he named *Arpachshad*. The meaning of the name, "boundary," hints at Shem's fervent hope that the spiritual boundary, the foundation for the work of redemption, will be secured through his son.

Shem's expectation for Arpachshad to secure the boundaries of faith and set up a bridgehead for the gospel is reminiscent of the time when Noah sent the dove out from the ark for the second time. The tiny claws of the dove had found a small foothold to rest and brought back a freshly picked olive leaf (Gen 8:8–11). Noah, then, realized that dry ground was finally appearing and probably felt a great sense of relief and hope.

God began His work of redemption by first marking out His boundaries. He chose the small country of Israel in the land of Palestine as a foothold for His work. The chosen Israel became His own boundary and territory (John 1:11). From among all the nations that rose after the flood (Gen 10:31–32), He chose one nation for His work and made its people His own precious people (Deut 7:6; 10:15; 26:18; 32:9). Prophet Amos gives an account of the birth of the chosen nation: "You only have I chosen among all the families of the earth" (Amos 3:2). God chose Israel not because it possessed any unique qualities or merit, but rather by His absolute grace (Amos 9:7). Amos warned that they would not be able to escape God's fierce judgment if they become proud and forget the grace by which they had been chosen (Amos 3:2).

At the fullness of time (Gal 4:4), God sent Jesus to the land of Israel which He had chosen and prepared from long ago to receive the Messiah. This land was rightfully His own (John 1:11). This was the land upon which the Messiah was to lay His head (Matt 8:20; Luke 9:58). This was the boundary that He had chosen and set apart as His own since the time of Abraham.

In reality, Jesus' ministry did not extend far outside the small territory of Israel. He spent most of His time in His land. A good example is the account of His encounter with a woman from Syrophoenicia who had traveled a long distance to bring her sick daughter to Jesus (Mark 7:26). He responded coldly to her request, saying, "I was sent only to the lost sheep of the house of Israel" (Matt 15:24). When Jesus sent His disciples out to evangelize, He instructed them, "Do not go in the way of the Gentiles, and do not enter any city of the Samaritans; but rather go to the lost sheep of the house of Israel" (Matt 10:5–6).

The size of the land of Israel was inconsequential compared to the rest of the world. However, God secured His land to provide a staging ground for His work just as a bridgehead is strategically secured during a battle. Geographically, the land of Judah which God chose was situated at the center of the world, and connected to Europe, Africa, and Asia (Ezek 38:12). Like Arpachshad's name, we should also strive to become God's boundary, which He consecrates and establishes to advance His will (1 Pet 2:9).

13. Thirteenth Generation: Shelah

שֶׁלַח (*shelah*): send away or sent, sprout (shoot), outstretching (undertaking)

Shelah was born 1,693 years after Adam. He became the father of Eber at the age of 30 and lived 403 years more and had other children. He died at the age of 433 (2,126 years after Adam, Gen 11:14–15; 1 Chr 1:24–25). He lived 313 years contemporaneously with Noah. Shelah outlived Abraham by three years. He lived until Isaac was 78 years old and Jacob was 18 years old.

His name is recorded in the genealogy of Jesus in Luke 3:35 as Σαλά (*Sala*).

The name *Shelah* is derived from the Hebrew word שָׁלַח (*shalah*) and means "to throw (out)," "to send," or "to spread out."

Arpachshad named his son *Shelah* with the hope that God would send godly descendants out to all corners of the world so that the power of faith may expand its reach. Accordingly, it was during Shelah's time that the descendants of Shem spread out to the different regions. God's boundaries (central base) were secured during Arpachshad's time and enlarged during Shelah's time in order to spread the gospel to all parts of the world. This was the fulfillment of the command to "multiply" in God's command to "be fruitful and multiply, and fill the earth" (Gen 9:1, 7), which He gave immediately after the flood. Similarly, the chosen people of Israel, which began with one man, Abraham, whom God first called out from Ur of the Chaldeans, had multiplied greatly by the time the Israelites left Egypt. Exodus 1:7 testifies, "The sons of Israel were fruitful and increased greatly, and multiplied, and became exceedingly mighty, so that the land was filled with them."

(1) Israel was God's first domain, but it expanded to all nations through the Great Commission Jesus gave before His ascension (Matt 28:18–20).

Another Hebrew origin for the name *Shelah* is שֶׁלַח (*shelah*), from which comes the meaning "young branch," "shoot," or "new sprout." A sprouting branch is a new shoot that bears the hope that one day it will grow into a large tree. Jesus is the spiritual shoot who has opened the path to salvation through His death and resurrection. In the spring, shoots appear and soon sprout fresh green leaves; in time they become a great forest. Likewise, it was Arpachshad's hope that the gospel would proliferate rapidly.

With His crucifixion and resurrection as the turning point, the work of the gospel of Jesus Christ expanded from the Jews in the land of Judea to the Gentiles (Matt 28:18–20; Acts 1:8; 13:46–47). The time had come to gather the sheep from outside the pen (i.e., Gentiles) to one shepherd (John 10:16). Apostle Paul was also called for this ministry—to become a vessel to hold the Gentiles (Acts 9:15). The movement of the gospel, which had begun in Jerusalem, spread to nearby Samaria and farther out to all the ends of the earth (Acts 1:8).

(2) The progression of the work from Arpachshad to Shelah corresponds to the prospering gospel movement of the early church after Jesus' resurrection and ascension.

It is important for us to examine how the boundaries of the gospel were enlarged after the advent of the Holy Spirit upon the 120 people during Pentecost. Israel was transformed from an unbelieving land to a land of the gospel through the small group of 120 people who had gathered in Mark's upper room. Additionally, the great expansion and growth of the Word of God began when these believers were sent out to witness the gospel (Acts 2:41, 47; 4:4; 5:14, 28; 6:7; 9:31; 11:21; 12:24; 19:20). The gospel yielded abundant fruit and increased all around the world (Col 1:5–6).

The growth and expansion of the gospel movement during the era of the early church foreshadow the movement of the Word in the end time. The task of spreading the gospel has been entrusted to us today (Matt 24:14). As people entrusted with the Word of God (Rom 3:2), we must diligently teach the Word to our children, neighbors, and friends until the earth is filled with the knowledge of the Lord. Our hope and prayer is to see the day when everyone in this world, from the least to the greatest, comes to the knowledge of God (Isa 11:9; Jer 31:31–34; Hab 2:14; Heb 8:10–11; 10:16–18).

Perspective on Cainan

✳ Organized and presented for the first time in history

Noah (10th), Shem (11th), Arphaxad (12th), Cainan, Shelah (13th) (Luke 3:35–36)

Arpachshad (Arphaxad), the twelfth generation from Adam, fathered Shelah at the age of thirty-five. Arpachshad lived 403 years after fathering Shelah and had other children (Gen 11:12–13). In the biblical genealogies, there are four places that state that Arpachshad fathered Shelah (Gen 10:24; 11:12; 1 Chr 1:18, 24). In all four places, however, there is no mention of Cainan (Kenan) between Arpachshad and Shelah. This is because Cainan was not recorded in the original Hebrew text. The only place where Cainan is mentioned between Arpachshad and Shelah is in the Gospel of Luke. How should we view this?

   * Cainan in Luke 3:37 is the same person as Kenan in Genesis 5:10.

I. Cainan is Missing in the Old Testament.

1. The genealogy in Genesis 10 lists the patriarchs in the order of Noah, Shem, Arpachshad, Shelah, Eber, and Peleg (Gen 10:1–25). This indicates that Arpachshad was the father of Shelah.

> **Genesis 10:24** Arpachshad became the father of Shelah; and Shelah became the father of Eber.

2. Genesis 11:10–20 also lists Noah, Shem, Arpachshad, Shelah, Eber, Peleg, Reu, Serug, Nahor, Terah, and Abram.

> **Genesis 11:12–13** Arpachshad lived thirty-five years, and became the father of Shelah; [13]and Arpachshad lived four hundred and three years after he became the father of Shelah, and he had other sons and daughters.

II. Cainan is included in the genealogy in the Gospel of Luke.

The genealogy in Luke 3 lists the patriarchs in the order of Noah, Shem, Arphaxad, *Cainan*, Shelah, Heber, Peleg, Reu, Serug, Nahor, Terah, and Abraham (Luke 3:34–36). How do we explain this issue?

III. The Relationship between Arpachshad, Cainan, and Shelah.

The Old Testament genealogies in Genesis 10:24 and Genesis 11:12–13 omit Cainan, but Luke 3:36 includes him. Since both the Old and the New Testaments are inerrant, we may speculate as follows:

1. **After Arpachshad, the birthright must have been transferred to Cainan and then to Shelah.**

2. **Therefore, it is possible that Cainan and Shelah were twins.**

Of the two sons of Arpachshad, Cainan was the older and Shelah was the younger. Arpachshad presumably fathered both sons at the age of thirty-five.

> **Genesis 11:12** Arpachshad lived thirty-five years, and became the father of Shelah.

How can the difference between the genealogy in Genesis and the genealogy in Luke be rendered? Arpachshad's birthright was transferred from the firstborn, Cainan, to the younger son, Shelah. Although there is no mention of this in the Bible, we reckon that Cainan had committed some sin that caused him to lose his birthright. Interestingly, the book of *Jubilees* offers the following explanation regarding Cainan:

> **Jubilees 8:2–3** And Cainan grew, and his father taught him writing, and he went to seek for himself a place where he might seize for himself a city. ³And he found a writing which former (generations) had carved on the rock, and he read what was thereon, and he transcribed it and sinned owing to it; for it contained the teaching of the Watchers in accordance with which they used to observe the omens of the sun and moon and stars in all the signs of heaven.

Although we cannot accept all the pseudepigraphal writings as the truth, we can at least conclude that for some reason Cainan had forsaken God and lost his birthright. This is a plausible reason for the omission of his name from the genealogies of the patriarchs.

3. **It appears that the Gospel of Luke recorded the genealogy according to the order in which the birthright was passed on: "the son of Shelah, the son of Cainan, the son of Arphaxad."**

The genealogy in Genesis omits the transference of the birthright from Cainan to Shelah and lists Shelah directly after Arpachshad.

There are other similar instances in the Bible. For example, Esau and Jacob, twins born to Isaac and Rebekah, struggled for the birthright. The birthright from Isaac rightfully belonged to Esau the firstborn, but he despised it and sold it for a bowl of lentil stew (Gen 25:27–34). Furthermore, Jacob deceived Esau and received the blessing of the firstborn (Gen 27:25–40). Based on the transference of the birthright, the genealogy should read: Abraham, Isaac, Esau, Jacob. However, the genealogy in the Gospel of Matthew only records the names of those who inherited the birthright: Abraham, Isaac, and Jacob.

From this perspective on God's providence in the Old and New Testaments, the inclusion of Cainan in Luke 3 has no impact on the reckoning of the generations in Genesis 5 and Genesis 11.

14. Fourteenth Generation: Eber

עֵבֶר (*ever*): the one who crossed over

Eber was born 1,723 years after Adam. He became the father of Peleg at the age of 34. He lived 430 more years and had other children. He died at the age of 464 (2,187 years after Adam, Gen 11:16–17; 1 Chr 1:25). He lived 283 years contemporaneously with Noah. Eber outlived Abraham by 64 years. He lived until Isaac was 139 years old and Jacob was 79 years old.

His name is recorded in the genealogy of Jesus in Luke 3:35 as Ἔβερ (*Eber*).

The name *Eber* derives its meaning from the Hebrew word עָבַר (*avar*), which means "to pass over" or "to cross over." Thus, *Eber* means "one who crossed over" or "region across or beyond." The meaning of his name foreshadows his crossing of the Euphrates River, moving away from the land of sin and embarking on a walk of faith.

The word *Hebrew* is derived from the same root word as *Eber*, indicating that the Hebrews were descendants of Eber. Abraham, the ancestor of the Hebrew people, followed Eber's path of faith and also crossed the Euphrates to separate himself from the sinful land (Gen 14:13).

The Bible makes a peculiar statement regarding Eber: "And also to Shem, the father of all the children of Eber" (Gen 10:21). John Calvin emphasized the importance of Eber: "Moses, being about to speak of the sons of Shem, makes a brief introduction, which he had not done in reference to the others."[59]

The Bible highlights Eber's significance (fourth generation from Shem) by praising him even before enumerating the descendants in Shem's genealogy. Arpachshad and Shelah were also Shem's descendants, but they were set aside as if only the children of Eber were descendants of Shem.

The main purpose of this verse is to praise the merits of Eber's faith and call attention to Eber immediately after Shem. Furthermore, Genesis 10:21 can be interpreted as "and all the children of Eber are born of Shem," awarding value to his descendants' faith as well. God's title had changed from the "God of Shem" (Gen 9:26) to the "God of the children of Eber," focusing more specifically on the children of Eber. In this manner, Eber is highlighted as the important link to Abraham, the father of faith, in the line of Shem (Gen 11:10–27).

(1) Eber enjoyed the greatest longevity among the direct descendants of Shem, but there was a notable shortening of life span to about 200 years after the generation of his son Peleg.

The abrupt decrease in human life span by half is directly related to sin (Prov 10:27).

> **Psalm 55:23** But You, O God, will bring them down to the pit of destruction; men of bloodshed and deceit will not live out half their days. But I will trust in You.

Eber enjoyed the blessing of longevity because he had protected his faith and distanced himself from sin even when the perverse movement to build the tower of Babel was well under way. In contrast, the life span of Eber's descendants was cut in half as a curse. Instead of following their ancestors across the river, they stayed and intermingled with the descendants of Ham and participated in building the tower of Babel (Gen 10:6–10; 11:1–9).

(2) Eber crossed the Euphrates River and established the kingdom of Ebla.[60]

Many people turned away from God when the tower of Babel was being built. It was at this time that Eber crossed over the Euphrates River from Mesopotamia and erected a large city-state called Ebla in order to preserve orthodox faith in God the Creator. As a godly descendant, Eber crossed the river and waved the banner of spiritual reformation and religious purification.

According to the clay tablets discovered from this region, the kingdom of Ebla was a highly civilized city-state in the region known today as Aleppo in Syria. It is believed that Eber was its founding king and that the city-state had previously existed as a small city, but developed into a large city-state during Eber's time. Thus, Eber, the godly descendant from the line of Shem, became its first king and the kingdom was named after him. According to the clay tablets, the kingdom of Ebla flourished in the arts and academic fields and reached its peak around 2300 BC when Eber ruled. In fact, records of their tribute receipts from nations in the Euphrates region were excavated, giving credence to the theory that the kingdom of Ebla was the most powerful kingdom in the ancient Near East at that time.

According to the calculation of the years in the Bible, Eber was born 1,723 years after Adam (c. 2391 BC). He became the father of Peleg 1,757 years after Adam and lived until 2,187 years after Adam (1927 BC). Thus, the years of the kingdom of Ebla coincide with Eber's time.

This information was discovered when over 15,000 clay tablets were excavated from an abandoned region in the northwestern part of Syria and subsequently deciphered. The deciphering process was made possible with the excavation of the world's greatest Sumerian-Eblaite dictionaries containing some 1,000 words. Wone Yong-Kuk wrote in his revised edition of *The Pentateuch*, "According to the tablets, the dominion of the kingdom of Ebla expanded to the south, encompassing the entire area of Palestine, Syria from Lebanon's most modern history, and Sinai; to its west, it expanded to Cyprus; and to the east, Mesopotamia. The tablets also mention some cities of the ancient Near East, like Gaza, Megiddo, Melchizedek, Sodom and Gomorrah."[61] Based on this evidence, Eber had established a vast territory with great influence that merits the name "kingdom of Ebla."

(3) The Euphrates River that Eber and, later, Abraham crossed.

Amazingly, *Euphrates* means "storage house of heaven." During harvest time, wheat is gathered into the barn, but the chaff is thrown into the unquenchable fire. Likewise, only people like Eber who set themselves apart from the place of sin by crossing the Euphrates River will become the spiritual wheat that enters heaven's storehouse. Those who remain in the sinful world to partake in building the tower of Babel are like the chaff and cannot enter heaven.

> **Matthew 3:12** His winnowing fork is in His hand, and He will thoroughly clear His threshing floor; and He will gather His wheat into the barn, but He will burn up the chaff with unquenchable fire.

In the last days, God's judgment will also fall upon the "Euphrates." Among the plagues of the seven trumpets, the sixth plague will fall upon the "great river Euphrates" (Rev 9:13–15).

> **Revelation 9:13–14** I heard a voice . . . saying to the sixth angel who had the trumpet, "Release the four angels who are bound at the great river Euphrates."

According to Revelation 16:12, the sixth bowl will be poured out upon "the great river, the Euphrates."

> **Revelation 16:12** The sixth angel poured out his bowl on the great river, the Euphrates; and its water was dried up, so that the way would be prepared for the kings from the east.

According to Jeremiah 51:61–64, the book that declared Babylon's destruction was thrown into the Euphrates. Thus, the great tribulation of the end time will be poured out upon the Euphrates and those who cross the river to escape tribulation will survive.

(4) The "God of Eber" later became the "God of Abraham."

Like Eber, Abraham crossed the Euphrates to enter the land of Canaan when he left Ur of the Chaldeans. In doing so, Abraham completely departed from his ancestors Peleg, Reu, Serug, Nahor, and Terah who had intermingled with the sinful world and plunged into darkness after the time of Eber (Gen 11:31–12:4; Josh 24:2–3; Acts 7:2–4).

Abraham's contemporaries identified Abraham as a "Hebrew" (Gen 14:13), meaning "one who crossed the river," acknowledging that he was a descendant of Eber. Both words, *Eber* (עֵבֶר) and *Hebrew* (עִבְרִי), are derived from the verb *avar* (עָבַר) and have the same meaning. Abraham, who was Eber's seventh generation, reconnected the channel of orthodox faith that had been severed after Eber. Therefore, the "God of Shem" became the "God of Eber," and continued as the "God of Abraham."

15. Fifteenth Generation: Peleg

פֶּלֶג (*peleg*): division, separate, split

Peleg was born 1,757 years after Adam. He became the father of Reu at the age of 30. He lived 209 years more and had other children. He died at the age of 239 (1,996 years after Adam, Gen 11:18–19; 1 Chr 1:25). His life span was shortened to about half of the average lifespan during Eber's time. Thus, Peleg was the first one to die among the 10 generations after the flood. He lived 239 years contemporaneously with Noah.

His name is recorded in the genealogy of Jesus in Luke 3:35 as Φάλεκ (*Phalek*).

The name *Peleg* originates from the Hebrew word פָּלַג (*palag*), which means "to split" or "to divide." His name thus means "division," "separation," and "split." Genesis 10:25 confirms that the world was divided during his time in accordance with the meaning of his name. The godly man Eber probably named his son Peleg with the hope that he would live a holy life, separated and consecrated from the sinful world. Peleg's life, unfortunately, fell short of his father's expectations.

(1) During Peleg's time, languages were confused and mankind was scattered as a result of the construction of the tower of Babel (Gen 11:1–9).

The phrase "for in his days the earth was divided" in Genesis 10:25 speaks of the time when God had confused the people's language during the construction of the tower of Babel and thwarted their plans. Since it was impossible to build such a complex structure without being able to communicate clearly, the people were eventually scattered abroad (Gen 11:9). This is how the city in which the tower was being built earned its name.

> **Genesis 11:9** Therefore its name was called Babel, because there the LORD confused the language of the whole earth; and from there the LORD scattered them abroad over the face of the whole earth.

Men forgot how fierce God's judgment could be, even after they experienced the catastrophic flood that swept the whole world as a result of their sins. Once again, they stirred up His wrath with the construction of the tower of Babel.

(2) The most peculiar characteristic of Peleg's time was that human life span was shortened by half compared to that of his father Eber's time. Peleg was the first to die among the ten generations of patriarchs after Noah.

✴ The reason for the shortened life span during the time of Peleg closely examined and presented for the first time in history

Eber lived 464 years, but Peleg lived only 239 years. Reu lived 239 years, and Serug lived 230 years. They lived just over 200 years and did not enjoy the longevity of their ancestors. In fact, they lived only about half the life span of their ancestors. After the flood, Peleg died suddenly, while all the other godly patriarchs in the line of Shem were still alive and healthy. The shortening of life span during Peleg's time indicates that Peleg and his contemporaries sinned before God and did not fear Him (Ps 55:23; Prov 10:27).

> **Ecclesiastes 8:13** But it will not be well for the evil man and he will not lengthen his days like a shadow, because he does not fear God.

Judging from Genesis 10:25, "for in his days the earth was divided," the construction of the tower was the great sin of challenging God. Vivid memories of the dreadful judgment of the flood that destroyed mankind should have spurred them to sever themselves from sin and draw closer to God. Instead, they garnered all human wisdom to build the tower in an attempt to elude God's judgment in case there was another (Gen 11:3–4). The underlying reason for this challenge against God was that they believed His judgment by the flood was unjust. Even Peleg, the offspring of godly Eber, had fallen into the temptation of making concessions for worldly gain and power. Ultimately, he also participated in the construction of the tower and committed a grave sin against God.

In his writings about ancient biblical times, Kim Sung-Il notes that Nimrod had lifted his name high among his followers and wanted to construct the tower in order to prevent them from rebelling against him. He asserts that it would have been impossible to do so without the sophisticated construction skills of Shem's descendants so they, too, must have taken part in this work.[62]

After the flood, the tides of sin and corruption swept away even the godly descendants of Shem. It was reminiscent of Noah's time, when sin had so filled the world that the sons of God saw the beauty of the daughters of men and intermarried with them (Gen 6:2). The fall of the descendants of Seth brought such sorrow and pain to God's heart that He was sorry that He had created them. This was the deciding factor for the judgment of the flood (Gen 6:5–7). Likewise, Peleg stood in the path of sin although he was supposed to carry on the faith in the line of Shem. If it were not for God's covenant of the rainbow given after the flood, this charge was great enough to warrant yet another catastrophe similar in magnitude to that of the great flood. Therefore, the sudden decrease in the average life span during Peleg's time can be interpreted as a form of God's judgment upon man. Even Noah (Adam's tenth generation) outlived Peleg (Adam's fifteenth generation) by ten years. Peleg's life was shortened because he participated in sinning against God.

(3) Peleg lived contemporaneously with Abraham (his sixth generation) for forty-eight years.

According to the chart of the chronology of the patriarchs, ten generations of ancestors in the line of Shem (from Noah to Terah) were all alive during Abraham's lifetime. It is conceivable that Noah, Shem, Arpachshad, Shelah, and Eber had already migrated toward Haran by Abraham's time.[63] Hence, Abraham most likely lived with Peleg, Reu, Serug, Nahor, and Terah, ancestors who did not preserve their faith, until he left Ur of the Chaldeans.

At the age of forty-eight, Abraham witnessed the unprecedented premature death of his ancestor Peleg at the age of 239. The following year, when he was forty-nine years old, he again witnessed the premature death of his grandfather Nahor at the age of 148. God had forsaken them because they had strayed too far away from their faith. Through their deaths, Abraham must have felt and realized many things. God called Abraham out and consecrated him while he was living among these ancestors (Gen 12:1).

16. Sixteenth Generation: Reu

רְעוּ (*reu*): friend, neighbor[64]

> Reu was born 1,787 years after Adam. He became the father of Serug at the age of 32. He lived 207 more years and had other children. He died at the age of 239 (2,026 years after Adam, Gen 11:20–21; 1 Chr 1:25–26). He lived 219 years contemporaneously with Noah.
>
> His name is recorded in the genealogy of Jesus in Luke 3:35 as Ῥαγαύ (*Rhagau*).

The name *Reu* is derived from the noun רְעִי (*rei*), meaning "pasture" or "pasturage," and the verb רָעָה (*raah*), meaning "to pasture," "to tend," "to associate with," and "to be a friend of."

Unstable times followed after the departure of Eber because there was no spiritual leader to provide guidance. Realizing this, Peleg named his son *Reu*, hoping that he would develop good relationships in this world and find success. Instead of teaching his son to become a friend of God, he foolishly desired for his son to develop good social relationships with the people of the sinful world.

(1) Reu probably lived a nomadic life.

The origin of the name *Reu* means "to pasture," "to tend," or "to graze." This shows that he must have lived a nomadic life. Raising livestock and farming were two primary forms of livelihood in ancient agrarian societies.

As nomads, people moved from one place to another in search of water and grazing fields. They generally engaged in vast migrations in the spring or summer season and even moved around within pastures. A great migration likely occurred after the foiled construction of the tower of Babel, and it was probably at this time that they became nomads. Reu's dedication to this way of life is evident in his name. He migrated from place to place in search of green pastures for his livestock and to secure a place to settle.

The lives of saints on this earth also involve continuous migration. The Bible describes such people as "strangers" (1 Pet 2:11) and "sojourners" (1 Chr 29:15). The word *sojourn* refers to a "temporary stay."

Saints are on this earth temporarily; eventually they will move on to their eternal home in heaven (Heb 11:13–16).

(2) Reu was faithful in his friendships with other people.

The name *Reu* also has a derived meaning "to associate with" or "to be a friend of." Before the attempt to build the tower of Babel, everyone lived in one community and spoke one language.

Genesis 11:1 Now the whole earth used the same language and the same words.

However, God squelched their foolish rebellion by confusing their language and scattered them across the earth. Relationships are essential for human existence and they are established mainly through communication using a common language. The confusion of languages was detrimental because it not only affected daily conversation, but also led to differences in ways of thinking, eventually resulting in chaos beyond what we can imagine.

God nullified the people's plans to challenge Him by heightening the degree of differences, misunderstandings, and hostility among them. This led to the formation of new communities as people began to relocate from one place to another in search of people who spoke similar languages. Within these new communities, new relationships may have developed between people who shared similar interests. Generally, establishing new ties and relationships are the first priority in these new-found communities. Thus, Reu's name was an accurate reflection of a time in which there was a desperate need for friends who shared common interests and the same spirit.

However, it is essential to note that friendships outside of God are Satan's snares that bind the feet of the saints to this sinful world (Jas 4:4). If Reu had turned his focus to hold hands with God and reconcile his relationship with Him, he would not have been so anxious about his earthly relationships. Like Abraham, Reu could have left the land of his dwelling in order to begin a new life as a sojourner to recover true faith.

What became of mankind after being scattered across the earth? As people settled down and built communities, they began once again to erect invisible cities of sin. People who were accustomed to sinning bonded together and grew in strength for the purpose of opposing and sinning against God. The seeds of darkness and the powers of evil always assemble quickly to build communities of sin.

(3) A true believer must be worthy to be called a "friend of God."
Eber and other godly ancestors from the line of Shem crossed the river and established a holy community of faith (kingdom of Ebla) during Reu's lifetime. Peleg and his descendants perhaps were confident that they could continue their lives of faith without crossing the river to the other side. However, they could not maintain the purity of faith in a humanistic society full of idolatry. Around Abraham's time, not too long after the attempt to build the tower of Babel, the tides of evil ensnared the godly descendants of Shem into total corruption and idolatry (Josh 24:2, 14).

These were the circumstances under which God called Abraham. Just as God had called Noah to build the ark at a time when sin had filled the earth, He also called Abraham in times of great apostasy in order to establish His kingdom.

In response to God's calling, Abraham forfeited all that was life to him and severed his family ties and friendships without hesitation (Gen 12:1; Acts 7:3). He did not know where he was headed (Heb 11:8), but he obeyed God's calling (Gen 12:4) and began his new life as a sojourner. Peleg, Reu, Serug, and Nahor had not been able to do this, but Abraham was resolute. He gave up his friendship with this world because he longed after a close friendship with God (Jas 4:4). As a reward, he gained the title "friend of God" (Ps 25:14) and became the only person in the Bible to earn such a noble title (2 Chr 20:7; Isa 41:8; Jas 2:23). Today, we must ask ourselves whether we are friends with this world or with God.

17. Seventeenth Generation: Serug

שְׂרוּג (*serug*): vine-shoot,[65] firm strength,[66] bow[67]

Serug was born 1,819 years after Adam. He became the father of Nahor at the age of 30. He lived 200 more years and had other children. He died at the age of 230 (2,049 years after Adam, Gen 11:22–23; 1 Chr 1:26). He lived 187 years contemporaneously with Noah.

His name is recorded in the genealogy of Jesus in Luke 3:35 as Σερούχ (*Serouch*).

The name *Serug* (שְׂרוּג) originates from the word שָׂרַג (*sarag*), which means "to mesh together," "to be intertwined," and "to intertwine themselves."[68] The purpose of meshing together and intertwining is to build strength. The firmly attached tendrils growing on walls are strong and sturdy because of the numerous well-intertwined branches growing out to the sides. An archer's arrow drawn on the bow also symbolizes strength. Thus, Reu probably named his son Serug with the hope that his community would be strengthened, which was critical for survival in the chaotic world after the confusion of languages.

The strength of this community, however, was neither strength from faith nor strength from above. It spawned from materialism and humanism as people lived intertwined with the world.

(1) Serug relied totally on his own power and strength.

This is evident from the derived meaning of his name—"arrow."

① In the Bible, arrows were used as offensive weapons during battles. The Bible speaks of bows and arrows in relation to wars and battles: "bow of war" (Zech 9:10), "bow of battle" (Zech 10:4), "bow of Elam, the finest of their might" (Jer 49:35), "he who sat on it had a bow . . . and he went out conquering and to conquer" (Rev 6:2), and "[men] who . . . shot with bow, and were skillful in battle" (1 Chr 5:18).

② It was common for those who had fallen away from the line of faith to become archers or belligerent people. Shem's first son, Elam, was one of the finest archers (Jer 49:35). Ishmael, the son of Abraham's maid-servant, was an archer (Gen 21:20), and Isaac's son, Esau, also hunted with bow and arrow (Gen 27:3). They sought after warfare and conquests and became violent nations that attacked and afflicted the chosen people of God later in time.

It appears that Serug possessed nothing that could aid him in settling in the land immediately after the foiled construction of the tower of Babel. Because threats from foreign nations were commonplace, it is likely that Serug raised up military power in preparation for war and used bows and arrows as weapons. Instead of arming himself with faith in God, he acted as the gentile nations did and sought to protect himself by building a unified military force armed with bows and arrows.

Isaiah prophesied about those who do not seek the Lord but instead rely on strong nations, taking comfort in the large numbers of horsemen and chariots. He proclaimed that they will be cursed and destroyed (Isa 31:1–3) because they, too, are neither spirit nor God, but mere flesh.

(2) A true believer must rely on God's strength.

A soldier may prepare for battle with swords and spears, but all these instruments of war mean nothing without God because victory belongs to Him (Prov 21:30–31). The battle is the Lord's (1 Sam 17:47), and His salvation is not based on external factors (1 Sam 14:6). At times, the Lord Himself fights battles for His people (Exod 15:3; 14:13–14).

Well aware of this, the psalmist confessed, "For I will not trust in my bow" (Ps 44:6). There are so many things that are impossible by our own human strength and ability. At the outset, things may seem ostensibly achievable, but they do not work out as easily as expected. Human strength eventually succumbs to forces that are stronger. A believer must trust in the power and might that come from the Word of God and sincerely seek His grace (Acts 19:20; Heb 4:12). The joy of the Lord is the strength of His people (Neh 8:10). He fills those who believe and trust in His Word with amazing new strength so that they can overcome any crisis (Ps 146:3-5; Isa 40:31; Zech 4:6).

> **Psalm 119:133** Establish my footsteps in Your word, and do not let any iniquity have dominion over me.

18. Eighteenth Generation: Nahor

נָחוֹר (*nahor*): to blow out[69]

> Nahor was born 1,849 years after Adam. He became the father of Terah at the age of 29. He lived 119 more years and had other children. He died at the age of 148 (1,997 years after Adam, Gen 11:24–25; 1 Chr 1:26). He lived the shortest life among all twenty generations of patriarchs. He lived 148 years contemporaneously with Noah.
>
> His name is recorded in the genealogy of Jesus in Luke 3:34 as Ναχώρ (*Nachor*).

The name *Nahor* (נָחוֹר) means "to be out of breath," "to pant," and "to blow out." The root of this word is נַחַר (*nahar*) and means "snorting." Judging from the fact that Peleg lived 239 years, Reu 239 years, Serug 230 years, and Terah 205 years, we can conclude that Nahor, who died at the age of 148, did not fully live out his years. It was probably a sudden death from a disease or an accident under God's curse. His unexpected death must have been a shock to his family and the patriarchs in the line of Shem.

(1) Nahor's life appears to have been shortened due to sin.

Peleg was the first to die among the ten generations after the flood, but Nahor lived the shortest life. He died suddenly at the age of 148, only a year after Peleg. In the Bible, sudden deaths are associated with sin (Ps 55:23; Prov 10:27; Eccl 7:17; 8:13; Job 22:15–16). The Bible presents two cases in which people suddenly perish.

First, the proud will perish.

Proverbs 29:1 A man who hardens his neck after much reproof will suddenly be broken beyond remedy.

Second, liars will perish.

Proverbs 6:12–15 A worthless person, a wicked man, is the one who walks with a perverse mouth, [13]who winks with his eyes, who signals with his feet, who points with his fingers; [14]who with perversity in his heart continually devises evil, who spreads strife. [15]Therefore his calamity will come suddenly; instantly he will be broken and there will be no healing.

Nahor was at the prime of his life when he was struck with a devastating plague that ruined him. The meaning of his name indicates that he had dedicated his whole life to being preoccupied or obsessed with something. Whether it was wealth or honor, he probably dreamed of being great and stopped at nothing to achieve his goals. He poured out all—his wealth, his time, and the vitality of his youth—into the world. In today's terms, he had made it big, both in fame and money. He found satisfaction in his own calculations and was deceived by his own wit. He was so absorbed with his secular life (pursuit of wealth, honor, and fame) that he progressively lost himself until he became completely oblivious of the importance of his soul and life.

(2) Nahor was probably a man of greed deeply immersed in secularism. In accordance with Proverbs 28:16, Nahor would have enjoyed longevity if he had scorned greed. However, his life came to an abrupt end, because he could not overcome his greed.

> **Proverbs 28:16** A leader who is a great oppressor lacks understanding, but he who hates unjust gain will prolong his days.

In Luke 12:15, Jesus said, "Be on your guard against every form of greed." In Ephesians 5:3, Paul said, "But immorality or any impurity or greed must not even be named among you." Greed leads people to marshal all sorts of lies. It makes people forsake God or even use Him to achieve their selfish desires. At times, it manipulates a devoted heart of faith for evil purposes, filling it with the greed of the flesh, which is idolatry (Col 3:5). Nahor possessed this kind of greed.

Nahor probably expended all his energy chasing his goals and busied himself traveling far and wide. However, the result was futile because God suddenly took his soul back. Nahor boasted as if he possessed the whole world, but he was a fool who lost himself in the end (Matt 16:26; Luke 9:25). In Luke 12:20, Jesus deplored such fools: "You fool! This very night your soul is required of you; and now who will own what you have prepared?"

God would have been greatly pleased if Nahor had expended all his energy to guard his faith, to consecrate himself holy in this world, and to battle against the sinful world. God is pleased when we live by the principle that we came from the womb naked and naked we will return (Job 1:21; Eccl 5:15; 1 Tim 6:7–9). Nahor, nonetheless, found satisfaction only when he draped himself with honor, wealth, and riches. He found security and joy in them; they made life worth living. He spent his whole life chasing after these things, panting and gasping to satisfy his desires.

The meaning of Nahor's name bears no trace of godliness as a believer. It only shows that he had lived his life totally separated and alienated from God. In Genesis 6:3, God said that the end of such a person is just flesh, because the spirit of God will depart. Although Nahor confessed that he believed, he indulged in sensual pleasures and materialism from all of which God is absent.

Apostle Paul said that the wrath of God is revealed from heaven against all those who are ungodly, unrighteous, and more detestable than the unbelievers (Rom 1:18). His indictment of heathens found in Romans 1:21–32 is as follows:

> Even though they knew God, they did not give thanks (1:21).
>
> Even though they knew God, they became futile in their speculations (1:21).
>
> Even though they knew God, they became fools without wisdom (1:22).
>
> Even though they knew God, they exchanged His glory for idols (1:23).
>
> Even though they knew God, they exchanged the truth for a lie (1:25).
>
> Even though they knew God, they were filled with degrading and indecent thoughts (1:26–27).
>
> Even though they knew God, they did not see fit to acknowledge God any longer (1:28).
>
> Even though they knew God, they planned only evil and were ungrateful (1:29–31).
>
> Even though they knew that such practices are worthy of death, they not only continued to do the same without feeling any shame, but also gave hearty approval to those who practiced them (1:32).

This is what happened to Nahor. Regardless of how much you possess, if God takes away the breath of life that He breathed into Adam, like Nahor, you will "pant" until life comes to an end (Gen 2:7; Job 33:4).

The corruption of the descendants in the godly line of Shem accelerated with the passage of time. Reu prioritized human relationships over his relationship with God. Serug trusted in his own strength. Nahor lived as a man of greed absorbed in secularism.

These people were not completely ignorant about God. However, with time, they completely forsook their faith and fell tragically into worshiping detestable idols (Josh 24:2, 15). Their faith regressed and became fully distorted to one based on the flesh.

The desires of the flesh set people against the Holy Spirit and cause them to turn away from the Word of truth (Gal 5:17). This is similar to the act of sowing two types of seeds in a vineyard (Deut 22:9), making the ox and the donkey plow together (Deut 22:10), and mixing wool and linen together (Deut 22:11). It represents detestable faith that strives to bind believers with nonbelievers, Christ with Belial, and the temple of God with idols (2 Cor 6:14–16).

We must do away with greed which is idolatry (Col 3:5) and boldly reject carnal faith that results from entwining with the world. We must become God's own people who pant from working zealously to fulfill His will.

19. Nineteenth Generation: Terah

תֶּרַח (*terah*): to stay, to delay

Terah was born 1,878 years after Adam. He became the father of Abram at the age of 70 and died at the age of 205 (2,083 years after Adam, Gen 11:26–32; 1 Chr 1:26–27). He lived 128 years contemporaneously with Noah.

His name is recorded in the genealogy of Jesus in Luke 3:34 as Θάρα (*Thara*).

The name *Terah* (תֶּרַח) means "to stay" or "to delay." He left Ur of the Chaldeans with Abraham and moved to Haran en route to the land of Canaan, but he tarried in Haran (Gen 11:31–32). He died forty years before Abraham in the land of Haran at the age of 205. He was the nineteenth generation from Adam, and he lived 128 years contemporaneously with Noah, the tenth generation. This, however, does not mean that he lived with Noah in the same location during those 128 years.

(1) Terah was an idol worshiper (Josh 24:2–5, 14–15).

Terah was a descendant of Noah, Shem, and Eber. This lineage of orthodox believers passed down faith as an inheritance. However, Terah could only boast of the faith of his ancestors since he had already sold off his inheritance of faith. He was so consumed with idolatry that his faith shook from its roots. Joshua 24:2 specifically states, "From ancient times your fathers lived beyond the River, namely, Terah, the father of Abraham and the father of Nahor, and they served other gods."

(2) Terah left Ur of the Chaldeans, the city of idols, but he settled in Haran.

> **Genesis 11:31** Terah took Abram his son, and Lot the son of Haran, his grandson, and Sarai his daughter-in-law, his son Abram's wife; and they went out together from Ur of the Chaldeans in order to enter the land of Canaan; and they went as far as Haran, and settled there.

The main event noted in Terah's genealogy in Genesis 11:27–32 is Abraham's departure from Ur of the Chaldeans for the great journey to the land of Canaan. This was the dramatic scene where God totally separated Abraham from the core of evil where the tower of Babel was being built in order to use him.

God appeared to Abraham in Ur of the Chaldeans as the God of glory and commanded him, "Leave your country and your relatives, and come into the land that I will show you" (Acts 7:2–3). When Terah heard about this encounter from Abraham, he got caught up in the grandeur and enthusiasm of the calling. Terah took an even greater initiative to obey the calling by *taking* Abraham and leaving with him from Ur of the Chaldeans (Gen 11:31). Unfortunately, Terah did not complete the journey into the land of Canaan. He remained in Haran and died there at the age of 205 (Gen 11:32). Terah's life was true to the meaning of his name "to delay." While Terah and Abraham were tarrying in the land of Haran, God appeared to Abraham once again and commanded, "Go forth from your country, and from your relatives and from your father's house, to the land which I will show you" (Gen 12:1). This time, Abraham fully obeyed and departed from Haran for the land of Canaan (Gen 12:5). From this point, Abraham became the focal point of God's new work of salvation.

(3) After Terah, Abraham came to the forefront of the history of redemption.

The genealogy of Shem in Genesis 11 lists the names of fathers and sons and the age the fathers had sons (Gen 11:10–26). However, unlike the genealogy in Genesis 5, it does not list how many years each ancestor had lived before he died. In Terah's case, however, this information is provided in order to draw attention to his death.

> **Genesis 11:32** The days of Terah were two hundred and five years; and Terah died in Haran.

Genesis 11 concludes with Terah's death. The commotion of the tower of Babel being built—the echos of betrayal and opposition against God—was now silenced. The odor from the carnal acts of the supposed descendants of faith (Peleg, Reu, Serug, and Nahor) dissipated. Everything faded away and came to an end with Terah's death, leaving one man standing at the front line of the history of redemption—Abraham.

Even the descendants of Shem from the line of orthodox faith were defiled by idolatry, and God urgently called Abraham out of this darkness. After the tower of Babel, mankind fell into a mire of sin so great that God's work of salvation was almost cut off. With the death of Terah, however, darkness that had loomed over the line of Shem was lifted, and a new work of salvation began through Abraham.

The "God of Shem" (Gen 9:26) became the "God of Eber" (Gen 10:21), and now, He is the "God of Abraham." Ham's sin after the flood had cast a pall of dark clouds over the line of faith, but the words of hope, "Blessed be the LORD, the God of Shem" (Gen 9:26), were fulfilled when Abraham was singled out from the line of Shem. Now, the path of salvation for all mankind is opened wide.

20. Twentieth Generation: Abraham

אַבְרָהָם (*avraham*): father of the multitude,
father of nations

Abraham was born 1,948 years after Adam. He became the father of
Isaac, the covenantal son, at the age of 100. He died at the age of 175
(2,123 years after Adam, 1 Chr 1:27–28; Gen 21:5; 25:7; 17:1–22). He
lived 58 years contemporaneously with Noah. Within the 10 generations after Noah, the patriarchs who had died before Abraham were
Arpachshad, Peleg, Reu, Serug, Nahor, and Terah. The patriarchs who
died after Abraham were Shem (died 35 years after Abraham), Shelah
(died 3 years after Abraham), and Eber (died 64 years after Abraham).

His name is recorded in the genealogy of Jesus in Luke 3:34 as Ἀβραάμ
(*Abraam*).

The name *Abram* (אַבְרָם, *avram*) means "exalted father" or "honorable
father," but the name *Abraham* (אַבְרָהָם), which God gave to him at the
age of ninety-nine, means "father of the multitude" and "father of nations" (Gen 17:5). The name underscores the crucial role that Abraham
would play in fulfilling God's administration of redemption.

Adam was the first father of mankind, Noah became the father of the
new world after the flood, and Abraham was the father of the chosen
people of Israel. In Christ, he also became the father of faith for all
spiritual people from all nations.

The history of redemption that had begun with Seth, and continued through Noah during the age of the flood, now reached Abraham.
Failure, corruption, and betrayal had seeped into the line of Shem after
the tower of Babel, but God chose Abraham from the house of Terah.
When Abraham was born, it had only been 292 years since the flood,
and only 100 years since the building of the tower of Babel, but sin was
brimming over like boiling water. However, a new administration of
redemption began with the calling of Abraham.

(1) Abraham received God's calling in Ur of the Chaldeans (Gen 11:31; Acts 7:2–4).

✳ God's two callings of Abraham organized and presented for the first time in history

Abraham was first called by the God of glory in Ur of the Chaldeans. *Ur* (אוּר) originally means "light" or "fire." Scholars suggest that this name reflects the reverence and worship of fire in that period, which is further evidence that Abraham had lived in a markedly idolatrous age. In Joshua 24:2, Joshua said to the people, "From ancient times your fathers lived beyond the River, namely, Terah, the father of Abraham and the father of Nahor, and they served other gods." One day, the God of glory appeared to Abraham and commanded him to leave Ur of the Chaldeans (Acts 7:2–3). Hence, Abraham followed his father Terah out of Ur of the Chaldeans and settled in Haran (Gen 11:31).

(2) Abraham fully obeyed God's second calling in Haran and became a blessing (Gen 12:1–3; Heb 11:8).

Haran was one of the magnificent cities of Paddan-aram located in the northern region of Mesopotamia. It is presumed that many people from the line of Shem lived around this area (Gen 10:22; 24:4; 25:20; 28:5).

Abraham left Ur of the Chaldeans and settled in Haran. Haran was a temporary stop on the way to Canaan, but Abraham's filial piety for his father kept him from leaving. Terah was born among the sins of his fathers; he was raised eating and drinking in the midst of sin. He had become so accustomed to sinning that he could not sever ties with sin during the stopover in Haran. He settled there in fulfillment of the meaning of his name "to delay" and "to stay."

Abraham had lived a long time in Haran with Terah when God called him yet a second time, at the age of seventy-five, to finally leave Haran for Canaan (Gen 12:5). God commanded Abraham, "Go forth from your country, and from your relatives and from your father's house, to the land which I will show you" (Gen 12:1).

Abraham obeyed this command and let go of his hold on Terah. It took great spiritual resolve to completely break his attachment with his father in order to wholly follow the Word and head toward Canaan (Gen 12:4). Acknowledging Abraham's faith, the author of Hebrews testifies, "By faith Abraham, when he was called, obeyed by going out to a place which he was to receive for an inheritance; and he went out, not knowing where he was going" (Heb 11:8). Abraham was seventy-five years old when he departed from Haran. He lived 100 more years and became the father of Isaac and the grandfather of Jacob before dying at the age of 175.

(3) Abraham lived with Isaac for seventy-five years and with Jacob for about fifteen years.

Hebrews 11:9 states, "By faith he lived as an alien in the land of promise, as in a foreign land, dwelling in tents with Isaac and Jacob, fellow heirs of the same promise." What was Abraham's primary activity as he dwelt in his tent? Abraham occupied himself with the work of passing down his faith to his descendants. According to Genesis 18:18–19, God called Abraham for this precise reason. To Abraham's credit, he fully completed this task and yielded the fruit of faith through his son Isaac. This was evident in Isaac's obedience when God commanded Abraham to offer Isaac, his only son of the covenant whom he had begotten at the age of 100, as a burnt offering (Gen 22:1–2, 9).

During the fifteen years that he lived with Jacob, Abraham undoubtedly passed down his faith by recounting stories. He told of God's calling in Ur of the Chaldeans, his delay in Haran, his departure from Haran, all of God's amazing works during the 100 years after he left Haran, and the fulfillment of God's covenant regarding the land and the descendants. Abraham's exemplary life of faith undeniably had a greater impact than his words.

Three generations—Abraham, Isaac, and Jacob—had become one in faith. God was now called the God of Abraham, the God of Isaac, and the God of Jacob, and His amazing work of redemption began to unfold through them (Exod 3:6, 15–16; Matt 22:32; Mark 12:26; Luke 20:37; Acts 3:13; 7:32).

(4) Abraham lived fifty-eight years contemporaneously with Noah.

✳ Organized and presented for the first time in history

Abraham became the father of Isaac at the age of 100, and he died at the age of 175. According to the biblical genealogies, all ten generations after Noah were alive at Abraham's birth. Abraham was born 290 years after Arpachshad and all these ancestors were still alive.[70] According to the chronology of the patriarchs, Noah was 892 years old and still alive when Abraham was born. Noah lived 350 years more after the flood

(Gen 9:28). Abraham was born 292 years after the flood. Although the Bible does not directly state these facts, these numbers can be deduced from Shem's genealogy. Shem gave birth to Arpachshad two years after the flood (Gen 11:10). Adding two years to the sum of all the ages in which the patriarchs in this genealogy fathered their sons will result in the year of Abraham's birth after the flood. Arpachshad had Shelah at the age of thirty-five, Shelah had Eber at the age of thirty, Eber had Peleg at the age of thirty-four, Peleg had Reu at the age of thirty, Reu had Serug at the age of thirty-two, Serug had Nahor at the age of thirty, Nahor had Terah at the age of twenty-nine, and Terah had Abraham at the age of seventy (Gen 11:12–26). Thus, Abraham was born 292 years after the flood (2 + 35 + 30 + 34 + 30 + 32 + 30 + 29 + 70).

Since Abraham was born 292 years after the flood and Noah lived 350 more years after the flood, Noah and Abraham lived contemporaneously for fifty-eight years (350 − 292). Abraham had lived with Noah until Noah died at the age of 950. This is an amazing fact. Although there were 390 years between the generations of Shem and Abraham, God's covenant that began with Shem after the flood had been passed down until it reached Abraham. Noah's faith surely had a positive influence on Abraham.

God's work of salvation, which had begun with Adam and was passed down through Noah (Adam's tenth generation), finally reached Abraham (Noah's tenth generation) to usher in a new start. Then, it unfolded with a new people of God (descendants of Abraham) and the new land of God (Canaan).

PART FIVE

A New Work of Salvation

The Bible contains God's administration for the redemption of fallen mankind. The genealogies in the book of Genesis clearly illustrate this divine administration through the two distinct spiritual lines: the line of Seth and the line of Cain. The incredible contrast between these two lines clearly shows how the saints who will fulfill God's plan for redemption will lead lives set apart from the world. The genealogies in Genesis 5 and Genesis 11 conclude the generations of the line of Seth with Abraham and at the same time usher in a new era in the history of redemption through him. The flow of the lineage from Seth until Abraham can be summed up as the process of being *set apart* from the world by adhering to the Word of God. The Bible teaches us that those who consecrate themselves from this world will become key figures who fulfill God's administration of redemption.

Now, we will examine the differences between the line of Seth and the line of Cain and the redemptive significance of this process through which Abraham emerges separated from the world.

CHAPTER 12

The Differences Between the Line of Cain and the Line of Seth

Adam and Eve had two sons, Cain and Abel, after they were expelled from the garden of Eden. When Cain committed the evil act of killing Abel, God appointed another seed, Seth, in Abel's place (Gen 4:25). Adam's two sons were now Cain and Seth. Although they were from the same parents, these two sons became the ancestors of two very distinct lines. Seth became the ancestor of the genealogy of the chosen people who obeyed God's Word and advanced the fulfillment of His plan for salvation. Cain became the ancestor of the genealogy of people who challenged God's will, persecuted His chosen people, and hindered the work of salvation. These two spiritual lines flow distinctly through the Old and New Testaments.

According to our studies of the lines of Seth and Cain, Seth's descendants had their roots in God and were active participants in His work of redemption. As a reward, they enjoyed longevity on this earth. In contrast, the descendants of Cain flourished in the secular world, but they were cut off from God. They stood on the side of the wicked and afflicted the chosen people, hindering the flow of redemptive history. What are the specific differences between the two lines?

1. The Genealogies of Cain and Seth Have Different Beginnings.

The beginning of all things is important; a bad start can have a negative impact on what follows. The two genealogies had very different beginnings.

First, the genealogy of the line of Cain began with Cain's departure from the presence of God.

Genesis 4:16 states, "Then Cain went out from the presence of the LORD, and settled in the land of Nod, east of Eden." Cain fathered his son Enoch after his departure from God, setting the tone for the rest of his line—a genealogy with no ties to God. Those who leave God will perish regardless of their notable worldly achievements (Ps 73:27). Jeremiah 17:5 states, "Thus says the LORD, 'Cursed is the man who trusts in mankind and makes flesh his strength, and whose heart turns away from the LORD.'"

Second, the genealogy of the line of Seth began with God.

Genesis 5:1–3, which introduces the genealogy of Adam's descendants, states that God had created Adam and Adam had a son at the age of 130 whom he named *Seth*. Thus, the genealogy of Seth traces back to Adam and ultimately to God.

The genealogy of Jesus in Luke 3 also traces its roots back to God, "the son of Seth, the son of Adam, the son of God," testifying that God's plan for salvation is fulfilled through the line of Seth. Another affirmation of this fact is that the descendants of Seth who were alive during Noah's time were given the honorable title "the sons of God" (Gen 6:2).

There are also many verses in the Bible that clearly state that we are sons of God and that He is our Father.

> References: Exod 4:22; Deut 1:31; 14:1; 32:5–6; 2 Sam 7:14; 1 Chr 22:10; Isa 1:2; 9:6; 63:16; 64:8; Jer 3:4, 19; 31:9; Hos 11:1; Mal 2:10; Ps 2:7; 68:5; 89:26–27; Matt 5:45; 6:4; 7:11; 10:20, 29, 32; 11:25; 23:9; Mark 11:25; Luke 2:49; 6:36; 10:21–22; 11:2; 12:30; John 1:12; 4:21; 8:41, 54; 20:17; Gal 4:6; Eph 1:17; 1 Pet 1:17

Applying this truth to the lives of believers today, we can conclude that those who do not pray have departed from God, while those who pray to God have their beginnings with Him (Deut 4:7). Those who distance themselves from the Word of God have forsaken Him, while those who draw near to His Word have their beginnings with Him (Ps 1:1–3).

2. The Genealogies of Cain and Seth Show Different Ways of Life.

We must focus on the differences in the way the descendants of Cain and Seth lived their lives. Generally, there are two ways in which human beings live their lives on this earth. Some people live self-centered lives focused on their own success and happiness. Others live God-centered lives focused solely on glorifying Him.

First, the descendants in the line of Cain lived self-centered lives.

These men introduced in Genesis 4 were founders of new cultures, civilizations, and professions. They were considered successful from the world's perspective. After Cain departed from God's presence, he built the first city and named it *Enoch* after his son (Gen 4:17). He secured himself in the city he built and exalted his own name. This way of life reached its climax with Lamech, the seventh generation. Lamech was an extremely self-centered man who killed a young boy for inflicting a small wound on him.

Lamech's sons achieved fame as originators of various civilizations. Genesis 4:20–22 describes Jabal as the father of those who dwell in tents and have livestock. His brother Jubal was the father of all those who play the lyre and pipe and Tubal-cain was a forger of sharp implements made of bronze and iron. However, their lives did not exalt God's name; their lives were completely self-serving and had absolutely nothing to do with God. The tower of Babel was a clear manifestation of their ways. Their main purpose for building cities and towers was to make a name for themselves (Gen 11:4).

Second, the descendants in the line of Seth lived God-centered lives.

For these men who appear in Genesis 5, there is no mention of earthly achievements, new discoveries, or anything else through which they could make a name for themselves. Their lives were focused on glorifying God. Enosh called upon the name of the Lord and worshiped Him. Mahalalel sang His praises. Enoch walked with God for 300 years. As his name indicates, Methuselah lived his life with his eyes fixed firmly upon God's judgment that would bring the world to an end. Lamech hoped that God's rest would be established through his son Noah. Noah built the ark and lived a life of obedience to the Word of God. They all lived God-centered lives that manifested His glory.

From the beginning of the history of mankind until today, all lives took one of these two paths—the path according to the line of Cain or Seth. The path according to the line of Cain may have attained earthly achievements that endowed them with fleeting wealth, honor, power, and fame. However, no matter how lavish their lives may have been, the Bible warns that woe will be upon those who go the way of Cain. Those who follow the path of Cain are like trees twice dead and uprooted, like wild waves of the sea casting up their own shame like foam, and like wandering stars for which the gloom of utter darkness has been reserved forever (Jude 1:11–13). They are like oak trees whose leaves have dried up, like a garden with no water (Isa 1:30), and like broken cisterns that cannot hold water (Jer 2:13). No matter how much water they drink, they will become increasingly thirsty. Furthermore, they are like a bush in the desert that does not see when prosperity comes (Jer 17:5–6). Worries, concerns, sadness, and pain will not cease to engulf them. All this will happen to them because they have forsaken God, the fountain of living waters.

On the contrary, the descendants of the line of Seth will continue to thrive like a healthy tree, full of sap and green and yielding fruit even in their old age because they have glorified God's name (Ps 92:14). Why? It is because the God of their faith is the fountain of living waters (Jer 2:13; 17:13). He watches over their lives from beginning to end, exalts their name above every name, and ensures that their names are never erased (Phil 2:9).

3. The Genealogies of Cain and Seth Have Different Records of Birth and Death.

The genealogy of the line of Seth in Genesis 5 was recorded in a specific format: "He became the father of X, then he lived Y years, and all his days were Z." This genealogy accurately records the year of birth, death, and life span. The genealogy of the line of Cain, however, has no record of birth, death, or life span. What does this mean?

First, the difference in the genealogical records signifies that there are lives that God acknowledges and lives that He does not. There is no mention of when these people were born, how long they lived, or when they died. This indicates that God did not esteem the lives they led. The world may acknowledge lavish and successful lives, but the years of those whom God does not acknowledge will not be recorded.

On the other hand, there are exact records of the births, lives, and deaths of the descendants of Seth because their years were esteemed by God. God carried out His plans through this line that He acknowledged. Psalm 1:6 states, "For the LORD knows the way of the righteous, but the way of the wicked will perish."

Second, the difference in the genealogical records indicates that there was a contrast in the succession and continuation of faith.

Faith in God and the spiritual inheritance were not passed down through the generations of the line of Cain. Their lives were extremely individualistic and self-centered. They built and lived in personal strongholds of self-absorption and obstinacy until their lives came to a futile end.

The stream of faith, however, continued to flow down through the generations of Seth's line without ceasing. The descendants of Seth diligently passed down to their children the Word of God and the works of faith which they had also inherited from their fathers (Joel 1:3; Ps 78:3–8; Isa 38:19).

For this reason, the record of Cain's line came to an abrupt end after only seven generations, while the record of Seth's line continued from Adam to Abraham, the twentieth generation. Although there were slight digressions along the way, there were no breaks in the lineage of the godly descendants or in the works of faith until the coming of the Messiah. It continued from Adam to the Messiah and to us today. This enduring genealogy shows that although individuals died, God's work of life committed to overcoming the curse of death continues without rest through the godly descendants.

Third, it distinguishes the lives of people who are like "beasts" from the lives of true "men."

The lives of the men in Cain's line were like those of beasts. For beasts, the cycle of birth and death has no meaning. The children in the line of Cain never once gave thought to the redemptive significance of the times in which they lived. They did not live their lives by grace; they lived for themselves and their own satisfaction. The Bible says that those who lack understanding are no different from beasts (Ps 49:12, 20; Eccl 3:18–19).

However, the children in the line of Seth were awarded the status of men, not of beasts. Genesis 5:2 says, "[He] named them Man." Genesis 5:3 also says that Adam gave birth to Seth. These verses underscore the fact that the line of Seth was passing down the form of the true "man" whom God had created in His own likeness.

4. The Genealogies of Cain and Seth Have Differing Records of Longevity.

There are no records of the years of birth or death for the descendants of Cain. Hence, there is no way to know how long they had lived on this earth. On the contrary, records show that the descendants of Seth enjoyed longevity on earth. The blessing of longevity was God's special privilege awarded to Seth's descendants but not to Cain's descendants. The phrase, "So all the days that X lived were Y years," which appears at the end of each patriarch's record, is an illustration of this blessing (Gen 5:5, 8, 11, 14, 17, 20, 27, 31). "So all the days that X lived were Y years" did not only mean that they lived long lives, but also that the blessing was marked by both spiritual and physical well-being. Longevity did not mean long life in a frail or diseased body; it was accompanied by good health and blessings. The word *live* (חָיָה, *hayah*) in this verse means "to live prosperously" and "to revive from sickness, discouragement, or death."

Being able to live out all the years that God had determined for them is a testimony of His grace and protection. The descendants of Seth had children even when they were well advanced in years. This is another indication that they had enjoyed good health through God's blessings (Prov 4:20–23). What was the secret behind their longevity?

First, they feared God.

The Bible explains that the secret to longevity is the fear of God (Deut 4:40; 5:16; 6:2–3; 11:9; 22:7; Exod 20:12; 1 Kgs 3:14; Job 22:15–16; Ps 21:4; 55:23; 91:16; Prov 3:1–2, 7–8, 16; 4:20–23; 9:11; 10:27; 16:31; Eccl 7:17; 8:12–13; Eph 6:1–3).

Proverbs 10:27 states, "The fear of the LORD prolongs life, but the years of the wicked will be shortened." To fear God means to wholeheartedly revere and serve Him, acknowledging that He is the One to be awed. The author of Ecclesiastes draws this conclusion when he writes, "The conclusion, when all has been heard, is: fear God and keep His commandments, because this applies to every person" (Eccl 12:13). The command "to fear God" appears in many places throughout the Bible (e.g. Lev 19:14, 32; Deut 5:29; 6:2; 10:12, 20; Prov 3:7; 23:17). The fear of the Lord is the beginning of all wisdom (Job 28:28; Ps 111:10; Prov 1:7; 9:10). Those who fear God keep away from evil and turn away from its path (Prov 3:7; 8:13; 16:6, 17; Job 28:28). The fear of God is the path to blessings without want (Isa 33:6; Ps 34:7–9; 128:1; Prov 14:26–27; 22:4). In 2 Corinthians 7:1, the end time is described as a world covered with filthy sins. The only way for us to preserve our spirits and keep our bodies blameless and unblemished is to have the fear of God. The fear of God perfects holiness and allows us to see God (Heb 12:14).

Second, they distanced themselves from sin.

If we want to enjoy longevity, first, we must immediately do away with sins that are close to us in our lives. Sin shortens our lives and prevents the blessings of heaven from reaching us (Jer 5:23–25). The descendants of Seth enjoyed longevity because they repented and distanced themselves from sin. In the Bible, Methuselah enjoyed the greatest longevity (969 years; eighth generation from Adam), followed by Jared (962 years; sixth generation from Adam), and then Noah (950 years; tenth generation from Adam). Their longevity calls for a reflection upon the truth that mankind was originally created to live eternally (1 John 2:25).

Man was originally created for eternal life, but death came by way of sin (Rom 5:12; 6:23). Man, however, did not immediately die, but lived a long life because God delayed the punishment of sin. Nevertheless, man's life span grew shorter and shorter as people continued to sin despite God's love. Human life spans were shortened drastically after the flood. Later, when man attempted to exalt his own name and challenged God by constructing the tower of Babel, God responded by shortening man's life span again by half. In the beginning, the descendants of Adam enjoyed astonishingly long lives that approached 1,000 years. After the flood, man's life span ranged between 400 to 600 years. It was reduced again to about 200 years after the attempt to build the tower of Babel. After Abraham, no one lived over 200 years. Moses said that his eyes did not grow dim until he was 120 years old, but in Psalm 90 he sang, "As for the days of our life, they contain seventy years, or if due to strength, eighty years" (Ps 90:10).

Shortened life spans are a sure indication that sin had seeped deeply into the lives of mankind (Ps 55:23). Furthermore, sin had a staggering impact not only on man's life span, but also on the environment—elements in nature that man breathes, eats, and drinks (Hos 4:2–3; Amos 4:6–10). According to God's principle of creation, the earth rotates on its own axis while simultaneously revolving around the sun, maintaining 24-hour days and four beautiful seasons of the year (Gen 1:14). The countless number of stars also keep their place and maintain order in the universe. This strict yet wondrous display of order manifests God's great love and His marvelous works (Ps 139:14).

The universe was originally created to benefit mankind. However, the wickedness of man was great on the earth and the earth was filled with violence (Gen 6:5–7, 11–12). God was sorry that He had made man, and He judged the world with the flood. The harmony of nature, climate, and temperature, which had once been perfectly suitable for life, were altered after the flood (Gen 8:22). Climate change meant that nature no longer provided the perfect conditions for life. After the flood, abnormal changes in the climate and seasons (severe cold or extreme heat) sped up the aging process and caused diseases leading to significantly shortened life spans. Genesis 8:21–22 explains that such changes took place because "the intent of man's heart is evil from his youth." From this point on, nature did not only bestow benefits, but also brought harm to mankind (Jer 5:23–25). This was clearly the result of sin. Regarding this, God said to Adam, "Because you have listened to the voice of your wife, and have eaten from the tree about which I commanded you, saying, 'You shall not eat from it'; cursed is the ground because of you; in toil you shall eat of it all the days of your life" (Gen 3:17).

Third, they honored their parents.

The Bible states that those who honor their parents will enjoy longevity (Eph 6:1–3; Deut 5:16). The fifth commandment also states, "Honor your father and your mother, that your days may be prolonged in the land which the LORD your God gives you" (Exod 20:12). Accordingly, the descendants of Seth who had enjoyed longevity must have also honored their parents. Why is it so important to honor our parents? It is a way of confessing that we remember the origin of our existence. Furthermore, honoring our parents is equivalent to honoring God our Creator. In the Ten Commandments, the fifth through the tenth commandments pertain to relationships between people. Among these, the fifth is the only commandment that includes the phrase, "the LORD your God," because honoring our parents leads to honoring God. By honoring our parents, we are led to remember our God—the life-giver and the origin of our existence.

We have learned that those who obey the Word of God and keep from sinning will receive the blessing of longevity (Prov 3:1–2). We must distance ourselves from sin for miserable and fearful are its consequences. We must also fear God and fulfill our God-given duties. Then, good opportunities will come along, good things will happen, spiritual works of life will occur, and our lives will prosper and advance. As we have confirmed through Seth's descendants, the eternal Word of God must continue to be passed down not only to the current generation, but also to all future generations until the second coming of the Lord.

Despite the inevitability of death for all mankind after Adam, why did God show His love and mercy to the godly descendants by blessing them with longevity? There was a greater purpose than the biological multiplication and increase in the number of mankind.

First, it was for the fulfillment of God's blessing to be fruitful, to multiply, and to fill the earth (Gen 1:28; 9:1, 7). In accordance with this blessing, there were no generational breaks in the line of Seth. Thus, they grew in number and formed the nation of Israel through the descendants of Abraham. Furthermore, a countless number of spiritual descendants of Abraham are born through Jesus Christ who came as a descendant of Abraham (Gal 3:7–9, 29).

Second, it was for the preservation of the holy seed so that God's plan for redemption could be passed down through the generations of godly descendants. The godly patriarchs spent the long years of their lives imparting God's Word to their descendants (Gen 18:18–19). The descendants, in turn, received proper indoctrination of the Word. Through their longevity, God achieved His plan for the transmission of His Word.

In Genesis 5 the phrase, "became the father of" (or "begot"), appears twenty-eight times in the Hebrew Hiphil stem, indicating that God was actively and providentially intervening in the births of the children.[71] The continuity of the godly line of Seth is proof that God's absolute sovereign work had sustained it.

Ultimately, God preserved His holy seed by granting longevity to the godly descendants who, like a ray of light, shined through the dark generations. The longevity of the godly seed was the channel through which God passed down His Word. It was His providential plan to deepen and strengthen His holy and intimate fellowship with His people and to assure the succession of His covenants for their complete fulfillment.

The day will come when the issue of sin is finally resolved and creation is restored to its original state, so that there may be eternal life without death (Rev 21:1–4). Isaiah prophesied that the day will come when nature will not harm mankind (Isa 11:6–9; 65:17–25; cf. Ps 121:6). The day will come when the earth is filled with the knowledge of the glory of the Lord (Hab 2:14). This will be the day when all creation will be made anew through the second coming of Jesus Christ (Rev 21:5). This is the day for which all creation has been anxiously longing (Rom 8:19–23). A new world will be created in which there will no longer be tears, death, mourning, or crying (Rev 21:3–4).

God chose and called Abraham from the line of Seth to prepare for the coming of this glorious day. In truth, until Abraham appeared at the forefront of the history of redemption, God's work focused mainly on calling His chosen people out from the sinful world in order to set them apart.

CHAPTER 13

The Work of Separation

Genesis 12:1 Now the LORD said to Abram, "Go forth from your country, and from your relatives and from your father's house, to the land which I will show you."

The history of Israel began with God's command to Abraham for consecration—to go forth. God focused on separating His people until He was able to establish the nation of Israel in order to send the Messiah to this earth.

What did God separate His people from? It was separation from the pervasively wicked world in which the patriarchs lived. The primary purpose of the genealogies of Seth (Gen 5:1–32) and Shem (Gen 11:10–32) was to demonstrate how God had set apart and protected the lineage of His chosen people from Adam to Abraham.

The ultimate purpose for separation was to carry forward the work of salvation, which began with Adam and continued through Abraham, the first direct ancestor of the chosen nation of Israel, until the coming of the Savior. God wanted to prevent the lineage of godly faith from being cut off before the final hour of the work of redemption (Mal 2:15; Hos 11:4). This was precisely why He diligently segregated His people from the powers of darkness, either through His love and protection or with a stick or whip.

The work of separation, nevertheless, is always accompanied by pain. It cannot be carried out or even understood without painful tears. Abraham, the father of faith, was the fruit of God's tears and sweat, the steadfast offspring dedicated to the work of salvation.

1. The Work of Separation among the Patriarchs after Noah

The names of the patriarchs in the line of Seth, especially from

Arpachshad to Abraham, progressively reveal the process of separation essential for the establishment of faith. God opened up a new era after the flood and wanted the godly patriarchs to be completely victorious in the battle against idolatry. He also wanted them to set out on a pilgrim's journey in order to preserve the tradition of faith. They had to continue on this journey forgoing the time to settle down and enjoy the comforts of life. It was only after this that the "God of Shem" became the God of his descendants (Gen 9:26). The names of Shem's descendants reveal the unavoidable pain of separation. Unfortunately, Shem's descendants who came after Peleg did not live according to the positive meanings of their names. Instead of setting themselves apart from the world, they intermingled with the world.

From this point, we will examine God's methods of separation suggested in the meaning of their names and how they apply to us today.

(1) Arpachshad

Arpachshad was Shem's son and his name means "boundary." He and his people separated themselves from the land of their origin and set up new boundaries. Israel was originally a small nation, but God chose the Israelites as His holy people and set the boundaries to distinguish them as His own (Exod 19:6; Deut 7:6–7). When Jesus left the glory of His throne in heaven and came to this earth, He came to His land within His own boundaries (John 1:11). We are also God's own people within His boundaries. How must God's own people, the people of His inheritance, live?

First, we must obey God's Word.

Just as citizens of a country are expected to abide by its laws, we must also abide by the law of His Word if we are truly part of His domain. God said to His people in Exodus 19:5, "Now then, if you will indeed obey My voice and keep My covenant, then you shall be My own possession among all the peoples, for all the earth is Mine."

Second, we must become His holy domain.

Exodus 19:6 calls those who have become part of God's domain a "holy people," and 1 Peter 2:9 calls them a "holy nation." God, our master, is holy, and thus we, who are His territory, must also be holy (Lev 11:45). We must sanctify ourselves so that the hands of sin and darkness may not touch us (1 John 5:18) until the coming of our Lord (1 Thess 5:23).

When we set ourselves apart from the world, we are no longer under Satan's rule. We are under God's boundless care and endless counsel. For this reason, we are called "Thy people, Thine inheritance" (Deut 9:26, 29), "His people" (Deut 32:43), "a treasured possession" (Deut 26:18), and "a consecrated people to the LORD" (Deut 26:19). God promised that He would set His nation high above all nations (Deut 4:6–8; 26:19; 28:1). Thus, we, who are under His sovereign rule, are the most blessed on this earth (Deut 33:29).

(2) Shelah

Shelah was Arpachshad's son and his name means "to throw out" or "to send away." This refers to separation caused by being thrown toward a determined location or by being sent out with a specific purpose. If it is the will of God, we must make the resolute decision to leave our current dwelling place and head toward the newly designated place no matter how lowly, how unfamiliar, or inconvenient the place may be. Whether "valley of Achor" (Isa 65:10; Hos 2:15) or desolate waste, if that is where God's will lies, then we must take the gospel and run to the place where we are dispatched.

As Jesus was ascending into heaven after His resurrection, He commissioned His disciples not to leave Jerusalem (Acts 1:4); Jerusalem was His marked territory. After they received the Holy Spirit, however, He commanded them to leave Jerusalem, saying, "But you will receive power when the Holy Spirit has come upon you; and you shall be My witnesses both in Jerusalem, and in all Judea and Samaria, and even to the remotest part of the earth" (Acts 1:8). God wanted the members of the early church to be *sent out* throughout Judea, to Samaria, and to the ends of the earth with the gospel in hand. For this purpose, after the advent of the Holy Spirit at Pentecost, fierce persecution in Jerusalem scattered the believers throughout Judea, Samaria, and the ends of the earth (Acts 8:1). This was God's holy throw.

Being sent away from one's current dwelling place to a different one marks the beginning of a lonely journey. In reality, it is hard to accept and obey the command to depart to a designated place. However, if we are sent for the sake of the gospel, we will receive the blessing of the expansion of our boundaries and the enlargement of our borders, much like the blessing of Jabez (1 Chr 4:10).

Today, we need to be sent out with the gospel in hand to places of unbelief where the gospel has not yet been preached. We must conquer lands governed by Satan in order to expand God's boundaries. God delights in the feet of those who preach the gospel (Isa 52:7; Rom 10:15; Eph 6:15). Instead of taking comfort in "our boundaries," we must take the gospel of life and salvation and bravely throw it to the world (Matt 4:18–22; 28:18–20). Through this work, God's boundaries will extend to the remotest parts of the earth.

(3) Eber

The name *Eber* means "to cross the river and continue advancing toward a certain place." This evokes the image of people who have been dispatched with a mission. They face fierce obstacles and trials, but persevere without looking back until they reach their destination.

Likewise, our journey of faith is a long-distance race with many hurdles along the way. These hurdles can be ourselves (Prov 16:32), the members of our family, relatives, friends, the threat of death, or the riches of this world. However, we must set ourselves apart from the obstacles without complaining about them or avoiding them all together. We must hold on to the Word of God for the power to prevail and continue to advance forward. In order to do this, we must continuously overcome ourselves, battling against our own thoughts and bearing the pain of cutting off certain human ties if necessary (Luke 9:61–62).

There were innumerable rivers and barriers standing in Apostle Paul's way (2 Cor 11:23–30) when he broke out of the boundaries of the Law and was thrown out as a vessel for the Gentiles (Acts 9:15). However, Paul leaped over these obstacles by relying only upon God. He confessed in 1 Corinthians 15:10, "I labored even more than all of them, yet not I, but the grace of God with me."

King David encountered many obstacles in each of the battles that he fought, but he was victorious because he trusted in God. Regarding his feats, King David declared in Psalm 18:29, "For by You I can run upon a troop; and by my God I can leap over a wall." Today, we hope to become spiritual Ebers by crossing over rivers of sin and setting ourselves apart so that the boundaries of the gospel may greatly expand.

(4) Peleg

The name *Peleg* means "separate" or "divide." First, this is a reference to the division of nations resulting from the attempt to build the tower of Babel (Gen 11:9). However, it is also a reflection of God's desire for separation. At a time when faith was defiled and commingled, God called for the separation between faith and disbelief, good and evil, light and darkness, and the spirit and the flesh (2 Cor 6:14–16). Although Peleg was a descendant of the godly line of Shem, he participated in the construction of the tower of Babel. Those who built the tower possessed arrogant desires to exalt their own names rather than God's. They also wanted to safeguard themselves by building their own city. Satan coaxed the people to build towers of arrogance and complacency in order to prevent the will of God from advancing. Peleg had commingled with such people.

God's work of separation began when men united to build their own city and tower. God intervened by confusing their language (Gen 11:7). Through His intervention and separation, God prevented the people from committing even greater sins and prepared for the birth of Abraham through the lineage of Peleg many years later.

The patriarchs from Peleg until Abraham (Peleg, Reu, Serug, Nahor, and Terah) could not completely separate themselves from sin. They were not able to fulfill God's hope of separation bound in the meaning of their names. Consequently, their names serve as a guide to understanding the redemptive significance of the process and method through which God set Abraham apart.

Experiencing pain from various forms of separation is mandatory for those who seek to enter the kingdom of heaven, the spiritual Canaan. We must separate ourselves and come out from the Babylon of all unbelief (Rev 18:2–4). This means separation from a double-sided faith that seeks the counsel of the wicked. It is separation from the path of sinners who compromise with evil; it is separation from the seat of scoffers (Ps 1:1).

At the end of the painful struggle for separation, we will find God standing and waiting for us. God will take care of us and wipe away all our tears. He will untangle all of our problems in one sweep (Luke 18:8). Hallelujah!

(5) Reu

The name *Reu* means "friend" or "special relationship." This suggests that we need to have faith great enough to be called a "friend of God" in order to separate ourselves from this world (Gen 18:17; John 15:14–15). God is the Creator, but He is a personal God who wants to build an intimate relationship with His chosen people (Job 29:4; Ps 25:14; Amos 3:7). Abraham was considered a "friend of God" after he left his father's house through faith (2 Chr 20:7; Isa 41:8; Jas 2:23). There are no secrets between friends; Abraham knew in advance about the judgment that would fall upon Sodom and Gomorrah (Gen 18:17). John 15:14–15 teaches us how we can also be called a "friend of God."

> **John 15:14–15** You are My friends if you do what I command you. [15]No longer do I call you slaves, for the slave does not know what his master is doing; but I have called you friends, for all things that I have heard from My Father I have made known to you.

What must we do to become a friend of God? We need to obey completely and do exactly as Jesus commands. John 15:14 states, "You are My friends if you do what I command you." Faith without works is dead (Jas 2:26). A true friend is one who can be by our side at any time or hour. Let us draw closer to God—our eternal friend (Ps 73:28; Jas 4:8). God draws near to us when we pray (Deut 4:7). If the president of a country were to become our good friend, our status in society would surely change overnight. How much more so if we become a friend of God? We must also separate ourselves from this world, obey and follow the Word, and become a true person of prayer so that we may also be called a "friend of God."

(6) Serug

The name *Serug* means "intertwined tendril" or "firm strength." Intertwining with God is a great way to free ourselves from this world and restore our relationship with Him. Like tendrils that cling steadfast to the wall, separation from the world is possible when the souls of the believers are intertwined and bound in God's Will and His Word so that they do not fall into the world (John 15:7). Christians cannot consecrate themselves from the world by their own will or strength; they can be made holy only through the Word of God and prayer (1 Tim 4:5). Separation is possible only when God's sovereign love is poured out upon His people through grace. God's sovereign love is the "firm strength" that holds His believers.

In 2 Corinthians 5:14 Apostle Paul tells us, "For the love of Christ controls us." The word *control* in this verse is also translated as "attract." The New International Version translates this verse as "For Christ's love compels us." To control is συνέχω (*synechō*) in Greek, meaning "to hold fast," and is used in connection with the act of herding cattle from all sides. The love of Jesus Christ holds us firmly by the hand and guides us forward just as a shepherd guides his sheep. This is the irresistible force of His grace that seeks to save His people (Rom 8:30). No one in this world can overcome God's stubborn love.

The love of Christ also had a strong hold on Apostle Paul. Christ's love constrained him so that he did not live for himself; it enabled him to walk the path of a difficult calling. Paul remained focused on God until God was fully satisfied. God's love was so great that Paul could not help but go out and evangelize; he could not help but offer his whole being in faithfulness. God's love was so great that Paul forfeited all his possessions, his honor, and his knowledge. For Paul, everything was rubbish before the love of Christ (Phil 3:8). Christ's love was so great that Paul did not hesitate to give up his life with joy in Rome.

Yes, true separation is possible only when we are enthralled by the love of Christ. Once we truly experience His love, we will have no regard for the great personal loss or the immeasurable pain and suffering that come with separation. When we are led by the love of Christ, we will be able to walk the path of separation with joy, even if it may be the path to martyrdom.

(7) Nahor

The name *Nahor* means "to be short of breath" or "to pant." On the positive side, the name depicts a person who, with every ounce of strength, confronts and battles the evil of this world until he is victorious. It describes a heart that seeks to protect and keep the Word of God from Satan. It describes the immense effort to resist being tainted by the sins of the world and to separate from the old habits and ways of life. Apostle Paul called this battle "the good fight" (2 Tim 4:7). This conflict is not with an external enemy; it is an internal struggle against the evil within (Rom 7:16–25). It is the act of "buffet[ing] my body and mak[ing] it my slave" (1 Cor 9:27). Paul advises us to "compete" aggressively for the final victory (1 Cor 9:25).

As we carry out the Lord's work, there are many times when our zeal gets the best of us and we work to satisfy ourselves and our own greed (Matt 16:22–23). At times, our zeal is motivated by the awareness of other people's gaze; sometimes, it comes from our own competitiveness. Human zeal gone astray displeases God. It may please other human beings for a moment, but God looks into our hearts, and He does not acknowledge this kind of zeal (1 Sam 16:7). It is all in vain. When this kind of zeal becomes the motivation for work, it will only lead to exhaustion without yielding fruit. As Paul stated, our zeal has to be a godly zeal and godly jealousy (2 Cor 11:2). When we receive the zeal of God's Spirit, God will do the work. He will provide us with all the strength, ability, wisdom, and wealth that we need (Phil 2:13).

Jesus always worked with godly zeal (John 5:17). This was especially evident in the Garden of Gethsemane when He prayed earnestly to resolve the issue of sin for each and every one of us (Luke 22:44). He shed so many tears for us; He vindicated us countless number of times (Heb 5:7). He fought intensely against Satan to the point of bloodshed on our behalf.

Paul also worked with this godly zeal and made seven exclamations in 2 Corinthians 7:11, six of which begin with the word "what." This word *what* is ἀλλά (*alla*) in Greek and means "more on the other hand" or "more besides." We must exhaust our efforts to become more faithful to the work entrusted to us, to pray more, to serve more, to evangelize more, to labor more, and always persevere to perform God's work (1 Cor 15:58; 1 Thess 4:1; 2 Tim 4:2). Laboring harder is the way to repay God for the grace that we have received and the holy way to separate ourselves from the path of sinners (1 Cor 15:10).

(8) Terah

The name *Terah* means "to stay" or "to delay." Terah lived a wretched life worshiping idols in Ur of the Chaldeans, the seedbed of sin (Josh 24:2). However, he was enthralled by the fear of the God of glory who appeared to his son Abraham (Acts 7:2–3). Momentarily, he repented and abandoned his old way of life; he left Ur of the Chaldeans with Abraham and separated himself from the city of idols (Gen 11:31).

However, Terah was unable to completely cut ties with his old sinful ways and he settled in Haran where he eventually died (Gen 11:32). Nonetheless, even moving out of Ur of the Chaldeans and crossing the river to Haran was a great feat for Terah, who had lived a life totally immersed in idol worship.

Terah's life teaches us that we need to live a pilgrim's life if we want to become a blessing (בְּרָכָה, *berakhah*), possess spiritual and material wealth, and bear many descendants of faith as Abraham had (Gen 12:2). If Terah had moved from Haran to Canaan with Abraham, he would have become the father of faith along with Abraham. Like Abraham, he would have possessed a great name and the respect of his descendants. Yet, Terah lived out the meaning of his name "to delay" or "to stay." Satan often uses the abundance of wealth like that of Haran to keep us from moving toward the spiritual Canaan and to delay the fulfillment of God's will.

Haran was an important center of commerce because of its location midway between Canaan and Mesopotamia. Since considerable commercial activity took place there, it was a city of plenty. Like Terah, people's hearts are often held down by the treasures and riches of this world (Matt 6:21; Luke 12:34). If we dedicate our lives to following the path of wealth, bowing before money, and using money as the gauge of success, then our hearts have already forsaken God. We cannot serve both God and money (Matt 6:24). God tells us not to fix our hopes on the uncertainty of riches (1 Tim 6:17). The love of money is the root of all sorts of evil (1 Tim 6:10). Judas loved money and fell into temptation (John 12:4–6). It led him to betray Jesus and hand Him over for money—an eternal fatal mistake that cannot be wiped away. In the end, he hanged himself and died a tragic death (Matt 27:5; Acts 1:16–18).

The verb *separate* means "to disconnect," "to sever," "to set apart," or "to make a distinction between." Doing this is not as easy as it sounds. We must first feel great indignation for the sins that we have committed and then pound our hearts in earnest repentance (Ps 32:3; 34:18; Prov 28:13). We cannot draw near to God when we remain connected to the world by sin. Sin only separates us from God and accuses us before Him. The sins that we commit will follow us like a shadow throughout our lives; they will look for us and testify against us (Num 32:23; Isa 59:12). Revelation 17:16 explains that sin will make us desolate, strip us naked, and will burn us up with fire. So persistent and vicious is sin that Jesus, though He was without sin, fell on His knees and rubbed His forehead against the ground in fervent prayer in order to free us from our sins (Luke 22:44). Like Jesus, we must feel great scorn for sin, and we must repent thoroughly of our sins so that sin cannot adhere to us in any way. We must become totally separated from sin.

It is only then that we can fully obey the command to "Leave!" If there is anything that keeps us from walking the path of a pilgrim, we must sever ourselves from it through faith. True faith is answering God's command with "Yes" and "Amen" and following through with action even though His plan may not be immediately comprehensible (2 Cor 1:20). We must not become complacent and relish in the fact that God has chosen us. We cannot advance even one step without self-sacrifice, without faithfulness, and without focusing our eyes on the final goal each and every day.

As biblical history shows, God will see the end of what He has determined—His plan for the salvation of mankind. Until this is fulfilled, we must not seek the comforts of this world. If we do not waver or retreat, then we can advance forward one step at a time to enter God's kingdom as holy saints set apart from this world.

2. The Work of Separation in Abraham's Life

There were four crucial levels of separation in Abraham's life. These four levels represent different levels of Christian faith.

The First Separation: separation from his homeland and relatives and separation from Terah (Gen 12:1; Acts 7:2–4)

Abraham's ancestors lived and worshiped idols in Ur of the Chaldeans (Josh 24:2, 15). His departure from this land represents the first step in faith for Christians: separation from the world.

Ur of the Chaldeans was a fertile land located southeast of Baghdad and was the center of the ancient civilization as well as the center of idolatry. Idol worship was at its peak during Abraham's time, and Terah was more absorbed in worshiping idols than in worshiping the true God. This was when God commanded Abraham, "Leave your country and your relatives" (Acts 7:3). He obeyed and departed from Ur of the Chaldeans with his father Terah and arrived in Haran. Terah, however, was ensnared by the ease of life in Haran; he settled there although it was a rest stop on the way to Canaan.

At last, when Abraham was seventy-five years old, God called him a second time. This time He commanded Abraham to leave not only his country and his relatives, but also his father's house (Gen 12:1). This was a direct and intensified command spurred on by Abraham's failure to fully obey God's command when he was called out of Ur the first time. Genesis 12:4–5 clarifies that it was only after Abraham had fully obeyed God's command to separate from his father's house that he was able to enter Canaan.

> **Genesis 12:4–5** So Abram went forth as the LORD had spoken to him; and Lot went with him. Now Abram was seventy-five years old when he departed from Haran. ⁵Abram took Sarai his wife and Lot his nephew, and all their possessions which they had accumulated, and the persons which they had acquired in Haran, and they set out for the land of Canaan; thus they came to the land of Canaan.

✳ The two contradictory records regarding Terah's death (Gen 11:31–32; Acts 7:2–4) closely examined and presented for the first time in history.

Because Abraham was living in a patriarchal society, it was difficult for him to reject his father's wishes and leave him behind. He was seventy-five years old, and his father Terah was 145 years old and alive when he left Haran (Gen 12:4; 11:26). It must have been heartbreaking for the firstborn in charge of the household to leave his father in his old age. The verse in Acts 7:4, "From there, after his father died, God had him move to this country in which you are now living," shows how determined Abraham had been to follow the Word of God. The word for *death* in Acts 7:4 is ἀποθνήσκω (*apothnēskō*) in Greek and is used to represent symbolic death (1 Cor 15:31). This meant that Abraham was able to completely sever Terah from his heart; not even a trace of Abraham's filial devotion for his father could be found (Luke 14:26). Terah died sixty years later in Haran at the age of 205 (Gen 11:32). Abraham overcame the pain of this separation and followed the Word with faith (Gen 12:4).

The Second Separation: separation from Lot (Gen 13)

Genesis 13:10–11 shows that Lot was greedy. God separated Abraham from such a person. This represents total separation from lingering worldly desires and indecisiveness even after the initial separation from the world.

> **Genesis 13:11–12** So Lot chose for himself all the valley of the Jordan, and Lot journeyed eastward. Thus they separated from each other. ¹²Abram settled in the land of Canaan, while Lot settled in the cities of the valley, and moved his tents as far as Sodom.

When Lot parted ways with Abraham, he selected all the valley of the Jordan because it was well watered everywhere all the way to the land of Zoar, like the garden of the Lord. His choice shows that Lot was worldly and greedy for wealth.

> **Genesis 13:10** Lot lifted up his eyes and saw all the valley of the Jordan, that it was well watered everywhere—this was before the LORD destroyed Sodom and Gomorrah—like the garden of the LORD, like the land of Egypt as you go to Zoar.

Lot had accompanied Abraham throughout his journey out of Ur of the Chaldeans into Canaan, the foreign land of the Gentiles. Separating from Lot was heartbreaking since he was the only relative who had been with him through the toughest times until they finally settled in Canaan.

Only those who can overcome the pain of separation can become true disciples of Jesus. In Luke 14:26, Jesus says, "If anyone comes to Me, and does not hate his own father and mother and wife and children and brothers and sisters, yes, and even his own life, he cannot be My disciple." He continues in Luke 14:33, "So then, none of you can be My disciple who does not give up all his own possessions." Today, we can also become true disciples when we cut our ties to the secular and materialistic things of this world.

The Third Separation: separation from Ishmael (Gen 21)

After Isaac the covenantal son was born, Abraham drove out Ishmael, his first son whom he had fathered through human thoughts and schemes (Gen 21:10–14). This represents the level of faith in which we deny ourselves by surrendering our own plans and powers to submit before the great will of God.

Galatians 4:30 But what does the Scripture say? "Cast out the bondwoman and her son, for the son of the bondwoman shall not be an heir with the son of the free woman."

In Genesis 17:18 Abraham confessed, "Oh that Ishmael might live before You!" Genesis 21:11 tells us, "The matter distressed Abraham greatly because of his son." This tells of Abraham's love for his seventeen-year-old son nurtured during the years they lived together. Abraham's deep attachment for his first son, however, did not stop him from resolutely obeying God's command to send his son and his mother Hagar away. Separation from Ishmael must have caused Abraham great anguish—the pain of having his flesh torn away.

We must also drive out the "Ishmaels" in our lives today. We must deny ourselves of the things that we love dearly—things that we cannot let go of even though we know that they have nothing to do with the will of God. In doing so, we can be truly qualified to possess the inheritance of God like Isaac (Gal 4:28–31).

The Fourth Separation: separation from Isaac (Gen 22)

After Abraham drove Ishmael out, God commanded Abraham to offer up Isaac, his only son whom he loved, as a burnt offering. In faith, Abraham obeyed (Gen 22:1–12). Of course, God ultimately saved Isaac from Abraham's hands, but this near-sacrifice required Abraham to offer his most beloved and cherished son. He had truly intended to offer up to God that which held the greatest value to him (Gen 22:16–17). For Abraham, this separation was equivalent to death; it shook the very foundation of his existence. Abraham was required to sever his bond not only with the son born to him according to the flesh, but also with Isaac, the covenantal son, the last object of his affection.

Abraham overcame this incomprehensible test through his total trust in God. This is mature faith—the ability to return to God what belongs to Him. In essence, he was confessing that even the blessings that had originally come from God ultimately belong to Him. The twenty-four elders make a similar confession in Revelation 4:10–11; they glorify God by casting down before His throne the crowns that they had received from Him (Rev 4:4), confessing in song that all things created belong to God.

Revelation 4:10–11 The twenty-four elders will fall down before Him who sits on the throne, and will worship Him who lives forever and ever, and will cast their crowns before the throne, saying, [11]"Worthy are You, our LORD and our God, to receive glory and honor and power; for You created all things, and because of Your will they existed, and were created."

The Christian journey of faith is similar to these steps of separation. Faith matures through separation (Isa 52:11). We cannot advance forward to the new place to which we are called unless we forsake our sinful past, old habits, and old ways. If we cannot completely abandon them as God commands, then those very things will return to us in the future as thorns and snares (Josh 23:13; Judg 2:3).

God first commanded Abraham to leave Ur of the Chaldeans, his beloved hometown (Gen 12:1). He, again, commanded Abraham to leave Haran where he had moved with his father and briefly enjoyed a life of abundance. Both times, he submitted and departed on a pilgrim's journey not knowing his final destination (Heb 11:8). From a societal viewpoint, this path meant forfeiting his rights, losing his resting place, and living a lonely sojourner's life. It was an impossible journey to undertake if he had not endured the separations with tremendous determination and courage.

By faith and the fear of God, Abraham endured and overcame the pain of separation from his father Terah, his nephew Lot, his son Ishmael, and his covenantal son Isaac and ultimately reached the apex of faith.

> **Genesis 22:12** He [the angel of the LORD] said, "Do not stretch out your hand against the lad, and do nothing to him; for now I know that you fear God, since you have not withheld your son, your only son, from Me."

God acknowledges those who obey the command for separation as people who fear Him and He fulfills the work of redemption through them. Believers today must follow in Abraham's footsteps of faith in order to become true spiritual Hebrews and cross over the spiritual Euphrates River. In the eyes of some, this path may appear imprudent, like the journey of a wretched wanderer without a final destination. However, this path taken in obedience to the Word of God is a holy and honorable path.

(1) What must we do to achieve holy separation?

First, we must come out from the world, the spiritual Babylon, and refrain from participating in its sins (Rev 18:4). Next, we must live lives consecrated from this world. In 2 Corinthians 6:14–7:1, we learn about the principles of holy consecration. Although Christians physically live in this world, our lives must be thoroughly set apart from the world. We must not compromise with the world, but instead we must maintain holiness befitting the children of God (Lev 11:44–45; 1 Pet 1:15–16). In addition, we must reject worldly philosophies and liberal theologies that are outside the Word of God. The influence of these teachings will ultimately cause us to steer away from the pure gospel.

(2) What kind of blessing awaits those who walk the holy path of separation?

God gave a great blessing to Abraham who walked the holy path of separation (Gen 22:17). This great blessing, according to the Living Bible translation, is an "incredible blessing"—an immense blessing unimaginable to the human mind. This blessing goes over and beyond human comprehension. This "great blessing" was fulfilled when Jesus came as the descendant of Abraham (Matt 1:1). God Almighty, the Lord over all the universe and creation, came upon this earth as a descendant of Abraham. What greater blessing could there be? Even today, anyone who follows the Word and overcomes the pain of separation as Abraham had done will receive the same "great blessing" that Abraham had received (Gal 3:6–9). Hallelujah!

> **Genesis 22:15–18** Then the angel of the LORD called to Abraham a second time from heaven, [16]and said, "By Myself I have sworn, declares the LORD, because you have done this thing and have not withheld your son, your only son, [17]indeed I will greatly bless you, and I will greatly multiply your seed as the stars of the heavens and as the sand which is on the seashore; and your seed shall possess the gate of their enemies. [18]In your seed all the nations of the earth shall be blessed, because you have obeyed My voice."

CHAPTER 14

Abraham from the Redemptive Historical Perspective

The Bible was written by God and contains no meaningless narratives. The primary purpose of the genealogies recorded until this point was to reveal the root of Abraham; it was a deliberate effort to introduce Abraham. At the same time, it was a record of God's tears and diligence in choosing Abraham and preparing him to become the passageway for the Messiah who will come to save mankind.

Most of the genealogies recorded in the Bible list the most important figure at the end so that a new era begins with that person. The genealogy in Genesis 11 was recorded with Abraham in mind and reveals the crucial role that he would play in the future. This is similar to the genealogy in Matthew 1:1–17, which was recorded with the works of Jesus Christ in mind (Gal 3:16; Gen 17:19; 22:12–18).

Abraham, Adam's twentieth generation, was an important figure because he opened the first gateway through which the Messiah would come. This is why Jesus' genealogy begins with Abraham. Matthew 1:1 introduces Jesus as the "son of David, the son of Abraham," not as the son of Adam. Without hesitation, the Jews called Abraham their father (John 8:39). When Lazarus died, he went to heaven and was in Abraham's bosom, while the rich man went to hell. Even from hell the rich man brazenly cried out, "Father Abraham" (Luke 16:24, 30). All nations of faith throughout the world began with Abraham. His importance carries on through the New Testament as the Bible tells us that those who are of faith are blessed with Abraham (Gal 3:6-9).

1. The Work of Sin Proliferated until the Birth of Abraham

God's work, which began with creation, was carried out in parallel to the major sinful events in the world until Abraham's time. Starting with Adam's bite into the forbidden fruit (Gen 3), Cain's murder (Gen 4), Lamech's song (Gen 4), the marriage of the sons of God and the daughters of men (Gen 6), the judgment of the flood (Gen 7–9), and the construction of the tower of Babel (Gen 11), sin amplified and man grew farther and farther away from God. Sin, which began with one individual, increased to a group level and expanded further to a national level.

After the flood, sin resurfaced for the first time through Ham, and its powers grew to infect all mankind, eventually leading to the construction of the tower of Babel. Sin truly holds enormous power. Before the judgment of the flood, it had successfully placed the sons of God under its grip. Then, just before the judgment of the tower of Babel, it assembled a powerful community to rebel against God. This was an attempt to encroach upon heaven, His sacred dwelling place, through the construction of a high-reaching tower and city. The people of this humanistic community relied on their own wit and cut themselves off from the line of salvation that God had given to mankind. Historically, the attempt to build the tower of Babel took place about one hundred years after the judgment of the flood. In such a short period of time, sin spread, infected, and covered the world like a poisonous mushroom.

Calculation:

The sum of the patriarchs' ages at the birth of their first sons from the time Arpachshad was born to Shem (two years after the flood) until Peleg was born to Eber (Gen 11:10, 12, 14, 16).

2 (years after the flood) + 35 + 30 + 34 = 101

Noah and Shem had been saved from the dreadful flood and were alive when the tower of Babel was being built. Noah had witnessed how the world had been judged because of its overflowing sins. His righteous heart was torn once again as he watched men's evil intentions at work in building the tower. Noah probably spent the 350 years of his life after the flood the same way he had previously lived—expending all his energy in preaching to the successive generations about the divine preservation of this earth through God's administration of redemption.

2. God Preserved Faith throughout the History of Sin and Wickedness.

God preserved the framework of faith, the last remaining holy stump, so that the history of redemption would not be cut short, even with the ever-expanding work of sin, from the fall of Adam until the chaos of the tower of Babel in Genesis 11 (Isa 6:13; 2 Pet 2:5).

God clothed Adam and Eve with garments of skin before He banished them from Eden (Gen 3:21). For Cain, God put a mark on him as a sign of His protection to prevent him from being killed after he was cursed to wander the earth (Gen 4:15). For Noah, God preserved his family and proclaimed a message of blessings and prosperity once again through the covenant of the rainbow (Gen 8:17; 9:1, 7).

God revealed the bright future of redemptive history amidst His continuous judgments, reaffirming His intention to save mankind. The light of God's grace and love shined brilliantly through His judgments and punishments. His grace abounded even more where sin increased (Rom 5:20). This framework of faith can only be preserved by God's grace.

3. The Beginning of a New Work of Salvation through Abraham

The history of redemption that began to unfold in Genesis 12 after judgment upon the tower of Babel encountered a revolutionary turning point. Until then, God had worked universally with all mankind. Now, He was beginning a new history of redemption by electing one ordinary man, Abraham, the son of an idol maker from Ur of the Chaldeans. Consequently, it appears that the prospect of redemptive work had narrowed significantly in Genesis 12. However, the election of Abraham was a critical event in the history of redemption because it opened the first gateway for the coming of the seed of the woman as promised in Genesis 3:15.

From this point, God's administration for the redemption of all nations on the face of this earth was to be fulfilled through Abraham, the main focus of the genealogy of Shem. Just as God promised when He first called Abraham, although he began as one person, he ultimately became the starting point for the salvation of all nations.

Genesis 12:3 [The LORD said to Abram,] "And I will bless those who bless you, and the one who curses you I will curse. And in you all the families of the earth will be blessed."

Ezekiel 33:24 "Son of man, they who live in these waste places in the land of Israel are saying, 'Abraham was only one, yet he possessed the land; so to us who are many the land has been given as a possession.'"

Hebrews 11:12 Therefore there was born even of one man, and him as good as dead at that, as many descendants as the stars of heaven in number, and innumerable as the sand which is by the seashore.

When Abraham was ninety-nine years old, God renewed His covenant and gave him and his wife Sarai new names. Abram received the name *Abraham*, meaning "father of a multitude of nations" (Gen 17:4–5; Rom 4:17), and Sarai received the name *Sarah*, meaning "mother of nations" (Gen 17:15–16). After the coming of Jesus Christ, Abraham's fatherhood expanded to include all those who believe in Jesus Christ (Rom 4:11–12, 16, 23–24; Gal 3:7, 29).

The God whom the Israelites had encountered through their own history is not just the God of the Jews. As evident in Genesis 1 to Genesis 11, He is the God of the universe. He created the universe; His providence is over all mankind; He sustains the world. Furthermore, after God's covenant with Abraham, the history of Abraham's descendants was not theirs alone. Their history was an extension of the history of redemption, which contains God's plans to fulfill His covenant with Abraham and ultimately achieve salvation for all mankind.

The work recorded in Genesis 1 through Genesis 11 was only a prelude, a mere introduction, to Abraham's calling. The actual redemptive work began with Abraham in Genesis 12. The genealogy of Shem recorded in Genesis 11 was the dawning of the history of redemption that announced "the appearance of Abraham for the salvation of the whole world."

Now, God had cut the ribbon for His plan to save all mankind through Abraham (Gen 18:18; 22:18). This was a glimpse of hope and the first streak of daylight shining upon times of despair after the attempt to build the tower of Babel. Abraham stood at the center of this hope and light. God's redemptive work that had begun to progress with the election of Abraham was completed through the coming of the Messiah from among the descendants of Abraham. God's covenant with Abraham, "In your seed all the nations of the earth shall be blessed" (Gen 22:18), did not pertain to Abraham; it was a covenant to be fulfilled when the Messiah comes as a descendant of Abraham.

The genealogy in Genesis 11 is testimony to the trustworthiness and faithfulness of God, who remembered and fulfilled His promise of salvation through the seed of the woman despite man's endless disbelief and disobedience (Rom 3:3; 2 Cor 1:18; 1 Thess 5:24; 2 Tim 2:13; Heb 10:23).

The genealogy of the godly descendants will endure until the second coming of our Lord. We must strive to become godly descendants that God desires by properly understanding the divine administration of redemption which He seeks to fulfill in the end time.

Now, there is only One whose coming we must anticipate: Jesus Christ who died on the cross and resurrected for us. On the day He returns in all His glory, the work of redemption which began with the calling of Abraham will see its final consummation. At that time, the devil which stood against God and interfered with His work of salvation will be thrown into the lake of fire and brimstone (Rev 20:10). I pray today that we summon all of our strength to race toward the kingdom of heaven, focusing our hope on that day of final victory.

כל בר דעת דרך המסעות ארבעים שנה במדבר 'והרוחב והאורך של אה׳ץ הקדושה מנהר מי

מדבר צין הוא קדש

ים המלח

עתר

מקרה

עיר כרמל

שבט

באר שבע

שמעון

שבט

ארץ פלשתים

מדבר שור

מדבר פארן

מדבר סיני

לוח המסעות במדבר
אשר על פי הסעו ועל פי יחנו

א׳ רעמסס	טו׳ רתמה	כט׳ הרהגדגד
ב׳ סכת	טז׳ רמן פרץ	ל׳ יטבתה
ג׳ אתם	יז׳ לבנה	לא׳ עברנה
ד׳ פיהחירת	יח׳ רסה	לב׳ עציןגבר
ה׳ מרה	יט׳ קהלתה	לג׳ מדברצין
ו׳ אילם	ד׳ הרספר	לד׳ הרההר
ז׳ ים סוף	דא׳ חרדה	לה׳ צלמנה
ח׳ מדברסין	דב׳ מקהלת	לו׳ פונן
ט׳ רפקה	דג׳ תחת	לז׳ אבת
יו׳ אלוש	דד׳ תרח	לח׳ דיבןגר
יא׳ רפידם	דה׳ מתקה	לט׳ עלמן דבלה
יב׳ מדברסיני	דו׳ חשמנה	מ׳ הרי עברים
יג׳ קברתהתאו	דד׳ מסרות	מא׳ ערבתמואב
יד׳ חצרות	דה׳ בני יעקן	

ארקב גשן

פתם

שרה

צען

אלכסנדרי

Conclusion

The history of God's work of redemption is not separate from the history of this world. The two are intertwined. The history of redemption has been developing and unfolding since before the beginning of time in accordance with God's pleasing will and by His absolute sovereignty. Secular history is significant because it is the channel through which God fulfills His purpose in the work of redemption. Through the passage of time, the tides of the world changed continuously and history underwent countless transformations. Yet, God's work of redemption continued to flow dauntlessly and will not cease until the consummation of salvation at the return of Jesus Christ. In this light, we must discover the stream of redemptive revelations that flows ceaselessly through the genealogies in Genesis. Then, we will be able to unearth the treasures of God's amazing providence of salvation hidden within the years of the generations.

Furthermore, God's administration of redemption is also hidden in all the corners and crevices of the Bible (John 5:39, 45–47; Luke 24:25–27, 44). God's history of redemption will surely be fulfilled according to His Word written in the Bible (Matt 5:18; 24:35; Luke 21:33; Isa 55:10–11). The Word is the beginning, the plan, the blueprint, and the powerful force that propels God's history of redemption to its fulfillment (Rev 1:17; 22:13). God created the entire universe through this Word (Ps 33:6, 9; John 1:3, 10), and the Word upholds it and guides it (Rom 11:36; Heb 1:3). It is also the Word that judges the fallen world in the end (2 Pet 3:7). As the end approaches, God's Word will fill all the earth (Isa 11:9; Hab 2:14), and this wonderful vision is prophesied in numerous places in the Bible.

Ezekiel 47 compares the evangelical movement of salvation manifested through Jesus Christ to the living waters flowing out of the temple. The temple was a reservoir, and the water in it was not still, but flowing. This is symbolic of the ever-flowing living waters. This water increased, and as it increased, it trickled out little by little from the temple. In no time, it turned into a great body of water. It reached the great sea, giving life to the dying and causing the trees on the banks of the river to bear new fruit and no leaves withered. Everywhere this water reached, even the waters of the sea became fresh (healing), and there were many fish. Wherever this water went, everything flourished and came to life (Ezek 47:8–9). Fishermen would come and go, for there were many fish according to their kinds, like the fish of the Great Sea (Ezek 47:10). By the river on its bank, on both sides, there were all kinds of trees bearing fruit for food every month; they grew leaves for healing (Ezek 47:12). This was all "because their water flows from the sanctuary" (Ezek 47:12).

This is the prophecy that the living waters of God's Word will flow out from the church, the body of Jesus Christ, and give life to all the world and the nations in it (John 4:13–14; 6:63; Rev 22:1–2).

Even now, the spiritual water of life flowing from Golgotha, where Jesus Christ's cross stood, springs up endlessly and flows continuously to every corner of the universe to give life. Today, every church throughout the world that proclaims the gospel of the blood shed on the cross (gospel of life) is a spiritual Golgotha. From there, the living waters break through the grounds of deep sin and spring up. Then, it flows continuously, increases, and grows. Life-giving work is occurring through the living waters in the churches that have the living Word of the cross (1 Cor 1:18), the Word of the precious blood shed on Golgotha for the atonement of all mankind. The soul of one who drinks from the living waters is like a "watered garden," because God continuously directs the stream of water from the depths of the earth toward the garden (Jer 31:12; Isa 58:11). Thus, the watered garden is a place where the living waters never cease to flow; the green pastures are endless. No one will languish (Jer 31:12); there will be vitality. Our souls are satisfied and our bones strengthened (Isa 58:11); our physical health is ensured. Only peace and joy overflow bountifully (Isa 66:12).

Prophet Zechariah received a revelation of the living waters flowing out of Jerusalem toward the eastern sea and the western sea (Zech 14:8; cf. Isa 2:2–4; Mic 4:1–2). Prophet Joel also saw that a spring would go out from the house of the Lord to water the valley of Shittim (Joel 3:18). The valley of Shittim was arid and barren and life could not survive. However, this barren land will become abundant with grapes, greenery, and flocks of sheep giving milk through the overflowing waters (Joel 3:18). At one time, the priests mourned because there was nothing in the temple to give as an offering to the Lord (Joel 1:9,13). Now, it will become a fountain of living waters that satiates thirst and saves mankind.

A true church needs to become the altar from which the Word of the living waters springs forth so that souls may never thirst again. Jesus Christ is the source of the water of life (Rev 21:6). The Israelites drank the living waters from a rock in the wilderness (Ps 105:41; 78:16). Water poured out when Moses struck the rock. The New Living Translation translates it as ". . . and water gushed out. So the entire community and their livestock drank their fill" (Num 20:11). When the water came out of the rock, it gushed out as from a waterfall and formed a river for millions of people to drink in the wilderness (Ps 105:41). This rock foreshadows Jesus Christ. First Corinthians 10:4 confirms "And all drank the same spiritual drink, for they were drinking from a spiritual rock which followed them; and the rock was Christ." Yes, only Jesus Christ is the source of the living waters.

> **John 7:37–38** Now on the last day, the great day of the feast, Jesus stood and cried out, saying, "If anyone is thirsty, let him come to Me and drink. [38]He who believes in Me, as the Scripture said, 'From his innermost being will flow rivers of living water.'"

Here, the work of the living waters signifies the work of God's Word and the Holy Spirit. Both the Word and the Holy Spirit come from Jesus. When Ezekiel prophesied according to God's command, the dry bones came together and breath went into them. They came to life, stood on their feet, and became an exceedingly great army (Ezek 37:7, 10). Likewise, the breath of life (Holy Spirit) works through the Word, and where the living Word is proclaimed, the Holy Spirit works powerfully and works of life occur (Acts 10:44). Therefore, the church of the living waters is a church where Jesus is alive and His Word works powerfully. This is the kind of church that we strive to become—a church where the Holy Spirit dwells fervently, powerfully, and abundantly.

Amos 8:11–13 states,

> "Behold, days are coming," declares the Lord GOD, "When I will send a famine on the land, not a famine for bread or a thirst for water, but rather for hearing the words of the LORD. People will stagger from sea to sea and from the north even to the east; they will go to and fro to seek the word of the LORD, but they will not find it. In that day the beautiful virgins and the young men will faint from thirst."

Likewise, the world is experiencing a "famine of the Word," and it is becoming harder and harder to find the Word of the living waters. We need to initiate a fundamental movement within the church so that the Word of the living waters may overflow.

Only Jesus Christ is the true Shepherd who leads us beside quiet waters and to the spring of the living waters (Ps 23:1; John 10:11, 14). He makes us lie down in green pastures, allowing us to eat in abundance without want. Revelation 7:17 states, "For the Lamb in the center of the throne will be their shepherd, and will guide them to springs of the water of life; and God will wipe every tear from their eyes." When we follow our true Shepherd, we will be able to live a life that overflows with blessings for eternity.

Now, we greatly anticipate the One who died for us on the cross and resurrected—the one who leads us to the spring of the living waters, our true Shepherd, Jesus Christ. On the day our Lord gloriously returns, the history of redemption, which began and progressed through the genealogies of Genesis and was manifested through the calling of Abraham, will finally come to its complete fulfillment and fruition. On that day, the devil, who challenges God and interferes with His work of salvation until the very end, will be thrown into the lake of fire and brimstone (Rev 20:10).

Let us run our race toward the kingdom of God with our hope firmly focused on that final day of victory. Moses' sincere cry to "remember the days of old, consider the years of all generations" (Deut 32:7) in preparation for entry into Canaan is now resounding in our ears as we prepare for our entry into the kingdom of God. This is God's firm command and the voice of His call for us to remember and deeply understand the history of God's work of redemption through the years of all generations in the Bible.

The moment we understand God's administration of redemption hidden in the Bible, He will acknowledge us as godly people of faith and as the burning lamp in a world cloaked in dark clouds of sin and wickedness. God uses the spirit of His godly people as His lamp even in this present day (Prov 20:27). I pray with all my heart that the line of the godly offspring may continue until the prophecy of our Lord's return is fulfilled on this earth. Amen.

Commentaries

Dr. Min Kyung-Bae

Distinguished Professor at Baekseok University
Honorary Professor at Yonsei University

I am grateful for this opportunity to share my thoughts regarding the work of our most honorable and respected pastor, Rev. Abraham Park.

Rev. Park is not an author of many books. Yet, this remarkable book displays his gift for writing. In reading this book I realized that his calling to publish books like this one is as great as his calling for ministry at a large church like the Pyung Kang Che-il Presbyterian Church.

After reading the first few pages, I reacted to the book's profound message with tearful prayers and thanksgiving. As I continued to read each page, I was assured, time and time again, that this book, its style and writing, manifests a careful study of the Scriptures and was penned by someone who possesses a profound understanding of the Bible. I have conviction that this kind of writing was possible only through an immeasurable amount of tears, meditation, research, prayer, and thanksgiving. The writing is an outburst of the wonders of truth and love. Rev. Park is a minister who has spent many years on his knees in prayer, reading the Holy Scriptures hundreds of times, studying the Hebrew language, and researching a wide range of theological texts. He completed all these works with the enlightenment of the Holy Spirit. His writing, page after page, is typified by his complete reliance on the Holy Scriptures. His writing is candid and to the point, without unnecessary citations of other works or illustrations. It confirms that the gospel and the message of salvation given to the church cannot be explained by anything other than the canon of the Holy Scriptures. This work is a masterpiece of clarity and truth—a rare find in our time. This is why I boldly assure the reader that this book will remain a timeless work that warrants a place on the bookshelves of every believer, every church, and every university.

Rev. Park's expansive knowledge and understanding of the Bible are incomparably profound. All the verses of the Bible seem to be chronologically indexed in his mind—like a vein in the Holy Scripture's inexhaustible gold mine that he has fully mapped. Rev. Park has the uncanny ability and insight to select the most appropriate text as links to connect the most significant and complex passages that explain God's truth.

Another facet of this book that caught my attention is that it is well organized, written in a form that it is easy to follow, and filled with the fruit of his studies from as early as 1968. He has also shared this message and this method of study since 1983 through his preaching and ministry both at home and abroad. This book is the result of fifty wonderful years during which his ministry developed and has been supported by over forty years of prayer and extensive meditation. Thus, this book is a solemn notice to our academic world.

My description of this book's core value begins here. At one time, I thought it was impertinent for a "historical theologian" to write a review on a book that deals extensively with "biblical theology" based on Genesis and the Old Testament. To my own amazement, as I read the book, I saw that it is truly a work that ought to be deemed the "Magna Carta" of historical theology. The historical interpretations in this book spotlight the beauty of depth and insight usually found in the pages of biblical commentaries. I do not say this merely because I am a historical theologian. I found that the very premise and method of study for historical theology, its actual history, acute discernment of historical writing, and its descriptions are clearly evident in this book. This is a new revelation into the study of biblical history. Surely, this book sets a new precedent for all future studies of such history. I found this explicitly typified in the first three chapters.

What is even more astounding to me is that I have always regarded Deuteronomy 32:7–8 as the premise of all of my studies of history and Rev. Park also places this verse on the cover of his book. "Remember the days of old; consider the years of all generations. Ask your father, and he will inform you, your elders, and they will tell you."

Rev. Park uses this verse as the compass and the grand premise for this book as well as his writings on history and theology. I have never read any of Rev. Park's writings prior to this book, and I am sure that he has never read any of mine. Even if he has, I doubt that he could easily find the pages where I make mention of this verse, since it was only a minute part of my work. I was struck with admiration and wonder when I saw this verse used as the pillar of his work.

It is clear why I read this book through and through without being able to put it down. Upon reflection, I realize that I would have been greatly disappointed if I were not asked to write a review of such a great piece of work. What a shame it would be if I had missed the opportunity to share this important message about this book. Although it may not have been the original intention of the author, this book introduces an innovative method and system of study that qualify as models for any study of biblical history in modern times. It is truly a Christian representation of historical philosophy.

The full title of this book is *The Genesis Genealogies: God's Administration in the History of Redemption*. The author affirms that the book of Genesis is not only an introduction to the entire Bible, but also a blueprint of the history of the redemption of mankind and the world. In this illuminating view of the Genesis account, Rev. Park sees a compact and picturesque version of the Bible—a "micro-Bible." It is like a biblical parallel to the principle of modern biogenetic theory claiming that the development of a microscopic stem cell taken from flesh or bone can become the seed for recreating an entire body. He also purports that thorough understanding of the Book of Genesis by itself will uncover the mysteries of the redemptive history of mankind which is also found throughout the Holy Scriptures. Hence, this book can also be appropriately called "God's Work of Salvation as Viewed through the Genesis Genealogies." It truly is a work that deals with more than just the origin of creation, or Genesis, for it logically organizes insights into God's work of redemptive history through the Scriptures.

Rev. Park states that faith comes from the past. He argues that the "days of old" refers to a history of God's love and tears and includes the entire process of His redemptive work. These words of wisdom pierce the soul and the core of the Scriptures. The entire Bible is God's "history book" for Christians who believe that the relationship between faith and history is the central theme of the Scriptures. However, many people do not think about this vital point. Perhaps, some choose to avoid this point in theological discussions due to its relativity and presumed earthliness. The fallacy of pietistic theology, if there is any, is the belief that salvation comes from isolation or alienation from the world. It is clearly revealed and explained in this book that salvation and God's providence are fulfilled in our day-to-day lives. In other words, this book does not treat faith as a mere religious ritual, but makes it widely applicable to everyday life. This is the fulfillment of the long-cherished desire of Lee Kwang Soo, who in 1917 desperately hoped that the Korean church would adopt such thought and reflection. Thus, I say that this book is truly an achievement and work worthy of praise.

Rev. Park discovers the great foundation of historical salvation and redemption from the genealogies of the patriarchs. From his studies, he is able to distinguish God's redemptive plan from the years of the patriarchs. Furthermore, the manner in which he precisely interprets the names of the patriarchs from the source language is most fascinating. He reveals how the names and their meanings are directly related to the historical circumstances of each patriarch's era. I marveled at his ability to perceptively apply this new and fresh method of analogy. This perspective allows his readers to view the stories of the patriarchs as a type, not just in light of the stories of their lives, but how they are connected to our current generation. The intimacy between the Biblical message and our reality cannot be explained any more vividly than this. Turning the Bible into a book that is "my story" is the outstanding achievement of this book.

The author unravels the mystery of God's work of redemptive history by connecting the lives of each patriarch one by one. This brings one to the conclusion that salvation is not accomplished by chance or through an unintended event. This kind of historical interpretation confirms that biblical history is a continually developing story in which salvation is fulfilled through a gradual process, not by sudden change. Rev. Park construes this gradual process in the revelation that Ezekiel received by the river Chebar, in which living water trickles from the temple of God, gradually becoming a stream of water, then a river, then a much greater river, and finally a sea. This interpretation allows us to view eschatology as a completion of redemptive history fulfilled at the glorious return of our Lord rather than through a fearful judgment that comes abruptly at the "end time." Blessed with this understanding, one can look forward with thanksgiving and praise to the eschatological grace and blessings that are to come. This message reaffirms a gospel that marks Christianity as the religion of thanksgiving, joy, and bright hope. At the same time, it is an indirect exclamation that history upon this earth is God's history of life and blessings.

Through devout faith and theology, the author has truly accomplished the great work of overlapping redemptive history with the history of the secular world. This surmounts the early Augustinian dichotomy of redemptive history and secular history that separated Christianity and the secular world. It is a monumental achievement in orthodox theology that warns against schismatic and mystical seclusion.

It is amazing that this concept could be sieved from the study of Genesis. If history progresses in a linear path and comes to its completion at the second coming of the Lord, then this is similar to the general structure for sacramental and incarnational theology, which are the mainstream theologies today. Rev. Park accurately highlighted and exalted this belief in his book as the very foundation of Christian faith. This accomplishment befits the meaning of Rev. Park's epithet "Hui Sun" (Hui means "light" or "to shine" and Sun means "to spread," "to provide," or "to declare"). It is essential for the Korean church to embrace, enhance, and adopt this kind of theology.

This book is a guide that takes us into the marvelous depths of the Holy Scripture. It will become a time-honored achievement and deserves attention from all churches today for its great accomplishment in the theological and biblical study of the genealogies of Genesis.

Dr. Andrew J. Tesia
President of the Research Institute of Reformed Theology

Everyone who has received salvation, including laypeople, pastors with a special calling, and theologians, must continue to study the inspired revelation, the Word of God, throughout their lives and apply what they have learned. Just as food is essential for the sustenance of life, this effort is essential for our spiritual survival. Among the various approaches available for correct understanding and application of the Word, total trust and faith in the Word as well as persistent effort and research are imperative. This is an absolute calling that all Christians must respond to in gratitude for the Lord's grace and love. Therefore, all Christians (including pastors and theologians), as debtors to God's grace, must always walk with the Word as the deer pants for the water brooks (Ps 42:1). It is not an easy task to discover a coherent theme and gain penetrating insight on the revealed Word. This is because of the long duration of time, historical circumstances, and the varied experiences and educational backgrounds of the authors during the recording of the inspired Word. It is impossible to comprehend God's profound will with our limited capacity, even through persistent readings and studies of the Word. At the second coming of the Lord, in the last days, "when the perfect comes, the partial will be done away" (1 Cor 13:10). I sincerely long for the day of the Lord's coming. Maranatha!

Recently, Rev. Abraham Park attempted something that no one has attempted before through his two books: *The Genesis Genealogies* and *The Covenant of the Torch*. They are sure to astonish the world.

I first met Rev. Park about ten years ago at a world missions conference that I attended through the invitation of my friend Rev. Andrew Phipps. I was greatly blessed as I listened to Rev. Park preach vividly about Jesus Christ's suffering and crucifixion through the powerful work of the Holy Spirit. Over the past ten years, I have heard his sermons about four times. I was greatly inspired and truly received grace each time I heard his messages. My soul, which had dried up from conventional faith, felt revived, like a fish thrown back into the water. Then one day, Rev. Phipps gave me two manuscripts that Rev. Park authored. I read them right away. I could not put them down until I finished reading them. They are simply marvelous.

Rev. Park uses covenantal links to dynamically unfold the enormous biblical discourse from the perspective of God's redemptive plan. No one else has come close to such an endeavor. He logically and perfectly depicts this theme as the central theme of Christian theology as well as the theme of his own faith and theological belief. This is for certain the result of his lifelong devotion to prayer and his study of the Word with gratitude for the Lord's grace. He has read the Bible hundreds of times since his calling, and his books are compilations of the Word of God and the spiritual mysteries of the Bible that he was awoken to through the process. Through the two books, we pastors and theologians will have to examine ourselves to see if we have lived our lives fulfilling the tasks we were given. At times, we must lend our ears to his discussions and confront the challenges.

First, by clearly organizing the Bible from the salvation and covenant perspective, Rev. Park has attempted something that has not been attempted during the two thousand years of the church's history. There are countless biblical commentaries and interpretations available. Furthermore, many pastors are studying and preaching the Bible based on various existing theological frameworks, typically those based on Calvinism and orthodox theology founded upon conservative faith. Nevertheless, one cannot help but be amazed at Rev. Park's work, which approaches the Bible, the original text of Christianity, as a great discourse and unfolds it coherently from the covenantal perspective. His two books truly reveal the essence of his immense theological beliefs and the perfect and logical development of his competence. More than anything, it is shocking to see a man of little scholarship (as he confesses to be) explain the profound Word in such a clear and easy way. It is amazing to see how both *The Genesis Genealogies* and *The Covenant of the Torch* are so perfectly arranged and harmonized. The mathematical calculations of the chronological years in history since the time of Adam cause readers to marvel at his immense effort and achievement. His achievement is truly a stern admonition to pastors and theologians who profess to be what they call "conservative" but have spent and are spending their time in denominational power struggles rather than working to fulfill their God-given tasks! A tearful, contrite heart is required.

Second, Rev. Park is now in his early eighties, but in both *The Genesis Genealogies* and *The Covenant of the Torch*, he pours out the spiritual mysteries of the Bible to which he was enlightened in a clear, detailed, and powerful literary style. As if overtaken by a magical spell, readers will become breathless and transfixed by the continuous tension and anticipation that he builds. Above all, his literary style has powerful spiritual charisma that captivates the reader. I believe that this is because Rev. Park himself has lived his whole life captured by the Word. Hence, his sermons call to mind the great "Prince of Preachers" who shook up not only England but also all the rest of the world in the mid-nineteenth century, Charles Haddon Spurgeon. Spurgeon faced challenges during a period in time when society was rapidly inclining toward the liberal left. Solitarily, he poured the Word of God into the minds of people through his sermons from the pulpit and his written works. The thousands who congregated at the London Central Baptist Church were captivated by his sermons as they listened breathlessly, with the exception of occasional bursts of acclamation and shouts of joy. He proclaimed the Word of grace that he received with great strength and zeal; it was like a spiritual lion's roar. Unfortunately, he spent long, heartbreaking years facing much dissension, misunderstandings, disputes, and refutations. Nevertheless, with conviction in the Word of God, he pushed on with his pastoral ministry, standing firmly upon the orthodox belief of Calvinism.

Language represents one's beliefs. In that respect, Rev. Park may actually be the master of language that the Lord has sent to us during these turbid times where the Word of God has become scarce, and good and evil hard to distinguish. Despite his advanced age, his skill and ability to freely narrate the Word of God in his own words stand unrivaled. He is undeniably a faithful servant of God, completely captured by the Word and inspired by salvation.

Third, the foundation of Rev. Park's faith and theology was established through unspeakable suffering and affliction. Through times of trial and isolation he looked only upon God and trusted only in Him. He concentrated solely on faithfully raising his sheep—the congregation entrusted to him. He was captivated by a strong sense of calling and was unable to escape God's hands even for one moment. He fully dedicated himself to the Lord and is a guardian of Calvinism, which holds biblical inspiration in one hand and God's sovereign authority in the other. As is well known, St. Augustine spent his youth in dissipation and pagan philosophy. He was even dedicated to Manichaeism at one time. However, after he met the Lord, he put an end to his old way of life and completely dedicated himself to the Lord. He gave thanks for the grace and love of the Lord of creation and found peace through repentance. Who among us today can criticize him, ostracize him, and condemn him as a libertine or a heretic? The grace and blessings that the church has received through him over the past fifteen hundred years of church history are immeasurable. How his *Confessions* have consoled many Christians, especially those who were struggling! He is considered one of the few preeminent figures of church history. There is no such thing as a perfect person in this world. I find Rev. Park's two books to be as moving as St. Augustine's *Confessions*, and readers will discover a yearning for God burning like an active volcano.

Fourth, the core of Christian theology is the progression from prophecy to fulfillment toward completion through the interpretation of the Bible using the Bible. At the center of this development is the variety of types that appear in the Old Testament, Christ's suffering and crucifixion, and completion through the second coming in the end. Through his great suffering and trials Rev. Park has developed a strong yearning for the return of the Lord and His glory. This is illustrated in his description of the patriarchs from Abraham to Isaac, Jacob, and Joseph, and to Moses and Joshua after the Exodus. It will be depicted in greater detail in books to follow. Therefore, his understanding of the biblical history of redemption, which is the covenantal belief, is based completely on the Bible. This is possible because he was educated and trained in a conservative theological seminary and denomination. That is why, even in his advanced age, he has embarked on this great project that no one else has dared to attempt. Truthfully, who among us, whether pastor or theologian, can coherently unravel this great discourse?

Rev. Park's well-versed knowledge of God's Word, the Bible, throws a great challenge to theologians whose knowledge is limited to one area of theology, for the Bible needs to be understood thoroughly and in its entirety. Theologians are generally very proficient in the areas of their study and research, but Rev. Park shows his spiritual power and knowledge in all areas of theology, which enables him to freely and appropriately use different parts of the Bible.

This is a lifelong project that Rev. Park has solely endeavored as part of his unyielding vow with God in response to the grace and love that he has received. His head and heart are filled with the Bible and the fervent zeal to think and live with the Word. In this sojourner's world we have discovered an old servant struggling to pour himself out as a drink offering on the Lord's altar, just like Apostle Paul.

Fifth, the well-organized logic and real challenges and applications of Rev. Park's work are distinguished yet natural. The details and motivating power come from his many years of experience and lifelong pastoral ministry.

His applications are concise and entirely based on the Bible. Although he uses very concise and plain language, his sentences contain a concentrated form of theological depth that no other pastor or theologian can mimic. He addresses highly debated issues that even theologians cannot easily address, such as the relationship between Abraham and Jacob, the relationship between Judah and Joseph, and the various themes that develop through Moses' life. His discoveries that the duration of the construction of Noah's ark was less than the well-accepted 120 years and of the forty-two camp sites during the Israelites' wilderness journey are the first of their kind since the time of Noah and Moses. This is a marvelous and celebrated achievement unimaginable even for a scholar who has dedicated his entire life to the study of the Bible and theology.

Unfolding the great discourse using a concise sermon format and storytelling style stands out in the world of theology, which places importance on logic and proof based on scholarship. Rev. Park unravels this discourse smoothly and with the sincerity of a grandfather narrating a story to his grandchild. His thorough Biblical insight gives him the agility to maneuver through the Bible and the ability to visually illustrate the Old and New Testaments as with a computer. His analysis of heretofore unresolved theological issues can easily be considered a masterpiece.

Finally, what is most urgently needed in all the churches today? Proper understanding of the Bible and its application in life are necessary to overcome the long period of stagnation. This is the goal that the church needs to pursue in the rapidly changing twenty-first century in order to recover the lost glory of old. For this purpose, we must first learn to live out the Word of God, develop our theological awareness, and revitalize the redemptive movement. Frankly, an understanding of the inspired Word of revelation, the Bible, and effective application in life are the universal hope of all pastors. Learning to effectively deliver the Word from the pulpit is a lifelong assignment for pastors. To be able to do this, they must first gain thorough knowledge of the Bible. This knowledge refers not merely to literal interpretation, but also to the ability to see the entire flow and to accurately reveal the meaning of each part. Another crucial task is to shed light on how the revelations of the Bible are fulfilled in history. Paradoxically, we are living in an age where the Word of God is overflowing and scarce at the same time. Thus, we must fathom the depth of God's will using the redemptive and covenantal approach. I joyfully recommend Rev. Park's *The Genesis Genealogies* and *The Covenant of the Torch* to all the churches of the world, for they not only satisfy the spiritual aspirations of thirsting Christians, but are also an absolute necessity for those who desire a more mature life of faith. I pray that you read these books once and receive a double portion of blessings.

Andrew J. Tesia

Andrew J. Tesia

DR. CHA YOUNG-BAE
Former President at Chongshin University

The Bible is the Word of the living God. If the Bible did not exist, all mankind would remain in darkness without any hope. The book of Genesis is not only the introduction to the Bible, but also the basis of the principle of salvation recorded throughout the Bible. Without knowing Genesis, we cannot understand the core of the Bible. Genesis is composed of ten genealogies (*toledoth*). Thus, by studying these genealogies, we can fathom God's will for salvation, which permeates the whole Bible.

This book examines the Genesis genealogies from the perspective of salvation. What a welcoming shock it was to read this book for the first time! I could not contain my astonishment because Rev. Abraham Park is over eighty years old, but the depth of his book exceeds all imagination.

There have been many books, both local and international, written about the genealogies in Genesis. However, I regard *The Genesis Genealogies* as unrivaled in the subject of its study. Rev. Park's book chronologically organizes the lives of all the people who appear in the genealogies from Adam to Abraham. This would have been a difficult task even for the expert theologians in this field of study. It is even more remarkable for an aged pastor to organize such a complex genealogy and draft an accurate timeline. Furthermore, because the book is Bible-centered and written from the perspective of salvation, Jesus Christ is distinctly revealed in every corner of the book. The author's ability to organize such an extensive and sophisticated subject is evidence that he has dedicated much time to comprehensive research.

A book reveals an author's ideology. This book clearly manifests the author's Bible-based and Gospel-based faith. From my reading of *The Genesis Genealogies*, I believe that Rev. Abraham Park is a man of the gospel, and that his faith is sound because it seeks to reveal "only Jesus."

It is fortunate for the churches in Korea that a book containing such precious information is receiving the spotlight during increasingly dark times. It is a great blessing from God. I highly recommend this book with the sincere hope that it will be widely read by pastors and laypersons alike, and that it will play a critical role in the movement of the Churches' return to the Word of God. I pray for the overflowing blessing from the triune God for all those who read this book.

Cha Young-Bae

Dr. Cho Youngyup
Professor at Kyeyak Graduate School of Theology

I offer my sincere congratulations to Rev. Abraham Park for introducing his precious work *The Genesis Genealogies: God's Administration in the History of Redemption* to the Churches in the fiftieth-year anniversary of his ministry.

I got a glimpse of the author's character, faith, and scholastic attitude as I read his introduction. He says that although this book "may be inadequate as fruit presented before God" and "is certainly not a theological or scholarly treatise," he asks readers to "read this book with a Christlike heart of understanding, forgive any awkward sentences, and generously tolerate any unintended mistakes." He continues, "When Peter asked, 'Lord, how often shall my brother sin against me and I forgive him?' Jesus answered, 'I do not say to you, up to seven times, but up to seventy times seven' (Matt 18:21–22). I ask that you overlook my shortcomings with the love and mercy of Christ. If anything has been accomplished through this inadequate servant, I confess that it was not the work of this eighty-year-old sinner, but completely the work of the Lord."

I started to read this book with skepticism, wanting to find out and understand who Rev. Park really is. Scrutinizing this book from the first page to the last, I was able to see that he has critically and accurately studied the Genesis genealogies from the perspective of redemptive history. Moreover, the whole book is weaved together using the Scriptures. I believe that this is just one example that shows Rev. Park's proficient and thorough understanding of the Bible.

I joyfully recommend this book and pray that whoever reads it, whether professor, minister, theological student, or layperson, will be inspired and give thanks for the grace of God's work of redemption and return unto Him all the glory.

Cho Youngyup

Rev. Lim Tae-Deuk

Senior Pastor at Dae-Myung Church in Daegu
Former Moderator of the Hap-dong General Assembly of the
Presbyterian Church in Korea

I wholeheartedly congratulate Rev. Abraham Park, senior pastor of Pyung Kang Che-il Church, for completing and publishing *The Genesis Genealogies* to commemorate the Jubilee year (50 years) of his ministry. Knowing that leaving behind a book of written words is a far more challenging and difficult task than spoken words, I believe that this work is the fruit of a pastor who has read the Holy Scriptures hundreds of times.

The Genesis Genealogies chronologically sequences the various people who appear in Genesis, examines the succession of faith, and the succession of disbelief. It profoundly probes into the environments and backgrounds of each and every period using the foundation of the Holy Scriptures. It also imparts a clear understanding of the difference between Cain's genealogy in the succession of disbelief and Seth's genealogy in the succession of faith. In addition, looking through the lens of God's redemptive history, the book unravels the legendary course of Abraham's separation from the world and insightfully explains it based on the Scriptures. Rev. Park has the dexterity that allows him to present profound content in a book that is interesting and easy for anyone to read and understand. This is truly a product of great toil.

The book addresses questions on genealogies held by Biblical scholars. For example, there are differing views on the meaning of the 120 years (Gen 6:3). Some argue that man's life span was shortened to 120 years after the flood, while others argue that it took 120 years for Noah to build the ark. Without bias, Rev. Park explains these misperceptions by analyzing the Scriptures in a way that any layperson can easily understand. For those in doubt, the profound research of the Holy Scriptures found in this book will impart a powerful conviction.

Those who have met Rev. Park or have directly witnessed his ministry often fall in love with the soundness and purity of his faith. They are awed by the power of the Word as he preaches only of Jesus Christ. He is a man of humility who always speaks of how thankful he is that "such an unworthy man" like himself can serve by preaching the glorious gospel of Jesus Christ beyond his eighty years of age. This book, *The Genesis Genealogies*, reveals Rev. Park's true character.

I encourage all who desire to live a life of faith centered on the Scriptures and those who wish to become a part of the godly lineage to read this book many times. Recognizing that the descendants of unbelief will gradually drift away from the realm of God's blessing, I sincerely hope that those who read this book will carry on the genealogy of the godly descendants. I recommend this book with the utmost joy.

Lim Tae-Deuk

Dr. Horiuchi Akira

Representative Pastor of Grace Missions Evangelical Free Church of Japan
Chairman of the Food for the Hungry International (F. H. I.)
Chief Director of King's Garden in Mie (Social Welfare Organization)

After reading this book, I was touched by the realization that the essence of the Biblical message is founded on historical facts. I was able to gain insight and understanding that was not possible from other books. I felt the joy of studying the Bible, the Word of God, and became filled with vitality. Faith that was stagnant knowledge is now applied to daily life and actions. This faith will show through deeds and works in everyday life and it will no longer be about spoken words.

I shared fellowship with the author for about 40 years and had the opportunity to observe his life and the formation and growth of his church. I have seen and heard him from near and far, and learned much from his attitude of faith. The author truly loves God and his neighbors, and consistently testifies that the Bible is God's Word. One of the characteristics that stand out in this book is the author's interpretation of the Bible based on deep spirituality and abundant Biblical knowledge like the works of F. B. Meyer.

During my long-term relationship with Rev. Park, he and his church have inspired the congregation of my church to read the Bible carefully and diligently, trust in God's promises, pray, and serve the Lord faithfully. He has encouraged us to expend our efforts for evangelism and to lead people to Christ for salvation. Consequently, our church pushed forward to become a church that loves Jesus and our neighbors, which resulted in the births of eight local churches.

As I recommend this book, I pray that every reader of this book will discover the great work and truth of our God the Creator who works in the midst of those who believe and receive God's abundant blessings.

Bibliography

Allen, Clifton J., ed. *The Broadman Bible Commentary*. Vol. 1. Rev. ed. Nashville: Broadman, 1969.

Alter, Robert. *The Five Books of Moses: A Translation with Commentary*. New York: W. W. Norton, 2004.

Asimov, Isaac. *Asimov's Guide to the Bible*. 2 vols. in 1. New York: Avenel Books, 1981.
Boice, James Montgomery. Genesis: An Expositional Commentary. Vol. 1. Grand Rapids: Zondervan, 1982.

Brown, Francis. *The New Brown, Driver, Briggs, Gesenius Hebrew and English Lexicon: With an Appendix Containing the Biblical Aramaic*. Peabody, MA: Hendrickson, 1979.

Calvin, John. *Commentaries on the First Book of Moses Called Genesis*. Vol. 1. Translated by John King. Grand Rapids: Baker, 1989.

———. *Commentaries on the Gospel According to John {1–11}*. Translated by William Pringle. Grand Rapids: Baker, 1989.

Cassuto, U. *A Commentary on the Book of Genesis: Part 1, From Adam to Noah*. Translated by Israel Abrahams. Jerusalem: Magnes, 1961.

Cho, David Yonggi. *Commentary on the Genesis I*. Seoul: Seoul Logos, 1996.

Delitzsch, Franz. *New Commentary on Genesis*. Vol. 2. Minneapolis: Klock & Klock Christian Publishers, 1978.

Disciples Publishing House, ed. *The Grand Bible Commentary: With Comprehensive and Synthetic Exegetical Study Methods*. 16 vols. Seoul: Bible Academy, 1991–1993.

———. *The Oxford Bible Interpreter*. 130 vols. Seoul: Bible Study Material Publisher, 2002.

Driver, S. R. *The Book of Genesis*. London: Methuen, 1904.

Fausset, A. R. *Fausset's Bible Dictionary*. Grand Rapids: Zondervan, 1979.

Freeman, Travis R. "A New Look at the Genesis 5 and 11 Fluidity Problem." *Andrews University Seminary Studies* 42, no. 2 (2004): 259–86.

Hamilton, Victor P. *The Book of Genesis: Chapters 1–17*. Grand Rapids: Eerdmans, 1990.

Henry, Matthew. *Matthew Henry's Commentary*. 6 vols. Peabody, MA: Hendrickson, 1991.

Holladay, William L. *A Concise Hebrew and Aramaic Lexicon of the Old Testament: Based upon the Lexical Work of Ludwig Koehler and Walter Baumgartner*. Grand Rapids: Eerdmans, 1988.

Kang, C. H. and Ethel R. Nelson. *Discovery of Genesis: How the Truths of Genesis Were Found Hidden in the Chinese Language*. St. Louis: Concordia, 1998.

Kim, Eui-Won. *Heaven, Earth, and the Toledoth of the Patriarchs*. Seoul: Presbyterian General Assembly Education Department, 2004.

Kim, Hee-Bo. Patriarchal Fathers in the Old Testament. Seoul: Presbyterian Theological Seminary Press, 1979.

Kim, Suh-Taek. *The Great Flood and the Covenant of the Rainbow*. Seoul: Hong Sung Sa, 1997.

Kim, Sung-Il. *Exploring Origin of the Korean Nation: Discovering the Route of the Shemites*. Seoul: Research Institute for Creation History, 1997.

Klein, Ernest. *A Comprehensive Etymological Dictionary of the Hebrew Language for Readers of English*. New York: Macmillan, 1987.

Koehler, Ludwig, and Walter Baumgartner. *The Hebrew and Aramaic Lexicon of the Old Testament: Study Edition*. Vol. 2. Translated and edited by M. E. J. Richardson. Boston: Brill, 2001.

Külling, Samuel R. *Are the Genealogies in Genesis 5 and 11 Historical and Complete, That Is, Without Gaps?* Riehen: Immanuel-Verlag, 1996.

Lange, John Peter. *A Commentary on the Holy Scriptures: Genesis*. Translated and edited by Philip Schaff. Grand Rapids: Zondervan, 1893.

Lee, Byuung-Kyu. *The Commentary on Genesis*. Seoul: Yum Kwang, 1986.

Lee, Sang-Kun. *The Lee's Commentary on the Gospel of Matthew*. Seoul: Presbyterian General Assembly Education Department, 1966.

"A Letter to the Readers: [Discoveries at Ebla]." *The Biblical Archaeologist* 40, no. 1 (March 1977): 2–4.

Leupold, H. G. *Exposition of Genesis*. Vol. 1. Grand Rapids: Baker, 1942.

McGee, J. Vernon. *Genesis: Chapters 1–15*. Nashville: Thomas Nelson, 1991.

Morris, Henry M. *The Genesis Record: A Scientific and Devotional Commentary on the Book of Beginnings*. Grand Rapids: Baker, 1976.

Neufeldt, Victoria, ed. *Webster's New World College Dictionary*. 3rd ed. New York: Macmillan, 1996.

Park, Yune-Sun. *A Commentary on Genesis*. Vol. 1. Seoul: Yung Eum Sa, 1991.

———. *A Commentary on John*. Seoul: Yung Eum Sa, 1966.

Radmacher, Earl D., gen. ed. *The Nelson Study Bible: NKJV*. Edited by Ronald B. Allen. Nashville: Thomas Nelson, 1997.

Sailhamer, John H. *The Expositor's Bible Commentary with the New International Version*. Frank E. Gaebelein. Vol. 2. Grand Rapids: Zondervan, 1990.

Sarna, Nahum M. *Genesis: The Traditional Hebrew Text with New JPS Translation*. JPS Commentary. Philadelphia: Jewish Publication Society, 1989.

Speiser, E. A. *Genesis*. Anchor Bible 1. Garden City: Doubleday, 1979.

Spence, H. D. M., and Joseph Exell, eds. *The Pulpit Commentary*. Vol. 1, *Genesis*, Exobody, MA: Hendrickson, 2004.

Suh, Chul-Won. *The Book of Genesis*. Seoul: Grisim, 2001.

Suk, Won-Tae. *A Commentary on Genesis*. Seoul: Gyung Hyang, 2002.

———. *Complete Sermon Collection*. Vol. 2. Seoul: Gyung Hyang, 1985.

Walton, John H. Genesis. NIV Application Commentary. Grand Rapids: Zondervan.

———. Victor H. Matthews, and Mark W. Chavalas. *The IVP Bible Background Old Testament*. Downers Grove, IL: InterVarsity Press, 2000.

Weingreen, J. *A Practical Grammar for Classical Hebrew*. 2nd ed. Oxford: Clarendon.

Wenham, Gordon J. *Genesis 1–15*. Word Biblical Commentary 1. Waco.
Wone, Yong-Kuk. *A Commentary of Genesis*. Seoul: Se Shin Culture,
Kuk. *The Pentateuch*. Rev. ed. Seoul: Lifebook, 2004.

———. *A Dictionary of Biblical Archaeology*. Seoul: Lifebook, 1984.

Notes

1. A poetic name for Israel meaning "upright one."

2. Henry M. Morris, *The Genesis Record: A Scientific and Devotional Commentary on the Book of Beginnings* (Grand Rapids: Baker, 1976), 154.

3. Travis R. Freeman, "A New Look at the Genesis 5 and 11 Fluidity Problem," *Andrews University Seminary Studies 42*, no. 2 (2004): 266.

4. Samuel R. Külling, *Are the Genealogies in Genesis 5 and 11 Historical and Complete, That Is, Without Gaps?* (Riehen: Immanuel-Verlag, 1996), 30–31.

5. Kim Eui-Won, *Heaven, Earth, and the Toledoth of the Patriarchs* (Seoul: Presbyterian General Assembly Education Department, 2004), 233–34.

6. Matthew Henry, *Matthew Henry's Commentary* (Peabody, MA: Hendrickson, 1991), 5:20, 141, 275, 806; 6:868–69.

7. "*You brood of vipers:* This is similar to the Lord's rebuke toward the Pharisees (Matt 23:23). . . . Although they were confident that they were Abraham's children, Jesus was telling them that they are actually children of the serpent, the messenger of Satan who tempted Adam in Eden" (Lee Sang-Kun, *Lee's Commentary on the Gospel of Matthew* [Seoul: Presbyterian General Assembly Education Department, 1966], 33.).

   "*I speak the things which I have seen with My Father; therefore you also do the things which you heard from your father:* The Jews did what they heard from their father (i.e., the devil)" (Park Yune-Sun, *A Commentary on John* [Seoul: Yung Eum Sa, 1966], 63.).

   "*You are of your father the devil:* What he had twice said more obscurely, he now expresses more fully, that they are *the devil's children.* . . . He calls them *children of the devil*, not only because they imitate him, but because they are led by his instigation to fight against Christ" (John Calvin, *Commentaries on the Gospel according to John {1–11}*, trans. William Pringle [Grand Rapids: Baker, 1989], 44.).

8. Gordon J. Wenham, *Genesis 1–15*, Word Biblical Commentary 1 (Waco, TX: Word, 1987), 111; Suh Chul-Won, *The Book of Genesis* (Seoul: Grisim, 2001), 238.

9. H. D. M. Spence and Joseph Exell, eds., *The Pulpit Commentary*, vol. 1, *Genesis, Exodus* (Peabody, MA: Hendrickson, 2004), 87; *The Oxford Bible Interpreter*. Edited by Disciples Publishing House (Seoul: Bible Study Material Publisher, 1989), 1:337.

10. *The Oxford Bible Interpreter*, 1:371.

11. Spence and Exell, *Genesis*, 88.

12. Disciples Publishing House, *Oxford Bible Interpreter*, 1:339.

13. Wenham, *Genesis 1–15*, 112; Spence and Exell, *Genesis*, 88.

14. Wenham, *Genesis 1–15*, 112; Spence and Exell, *Genesis*, 88.

15. Wenham, *Genesis 1–15*, 112; Spence and Exell, *Genesis*, 88.

16. Henry M. Morris, *The Genesis Record: A Scientific and Devotional Commentary on the Book of Beginnings* (Grand Rapids: Baker, 1976), 155.

17. John P. Lange, *Commentary on the Holy Scriptures: Critical, Doctrinal and Homiletical—Genesis*, trans. and ed. Philip Schaff (Grand Rapids: Zondervan, 1893), 261.

18. Spence and Exell, *Genesis*, 88.

19. Wenham, *Genesis 1–15*, 112; Spence and Exell, *Genesis*, 88.

20. Spence and Exell, *Genesis*, 88.

21. Henry M. Morris, *The Genesis Record: A Scientific and Devotional Commentary on the Book of Beginnings* (Grand Rapids: Baker, 1976), 252.

22. Kim Eui-Won, *Heaven, Earth, and the Toledoth of the Patriarchs* (Seoul: Presbyterian General Assembly Education Department, 2004), 157.

23. Park Yune-Sun, *A Commentary on Genesis*, vol. 1 (Seoul: Yung Eum Sa, 1991), 123.

24. Wenham, *Genesis 1–15*, 115; *The Grand Bible Commentary: With Comprehensive and Synthetic Exegetical Study Methods*. Edited by Disciples Publishing House. 16 vols (Seoul: Bible Study Material Publisher, 1991), 385.

25. Robert Alter, *The Five Books of Moses: A Translation with Commentary* (New York: W. W. Norton, 2004), 33; Kim, *Heaven, Earth, and the Toledoth of the Patriarchs*, 153.

26. Morris, *The Genesis Record*, 155; Park Yune-Sun, *Commentary on Genesis*, 119.

27. William L. Holladay, *A Concise Hebrew and Aramaic Lexicon of the Old Testament: Based upon the Lexical Work of Ludwig Koehler and Walter Baumgartner* (Grand Rapids: Eerdmans, 1988), 385.

28. Morris, *The Genesis Record*, 155; Park, *Commentary on Genesis*, 119.

29. Wenham, *Genesis 1–15*, 115.

30. Spence and Exell, eds., *Genesis*, 95, Suh Chul-Won, *The Book of Genesis* (Seoul: Grisim, 2001), 232.

31. Spence and Exell, *Genesis*, 95; *The Oxford Bible Interpreter* (Seoul: Bible Study Material Publisher, 2002), 1:368.

32. Spence and Exell, *Genesis*, 95.

33. Augustine, *Expositions on the Psalms*.

34. Spence and Exell, *Genesis*, 95; Suh, *Book of Genesis*, 235.

35. Wenham, *Genesis 1–15*, 127; Spence and Exell, *Genesis*, 95.

36. Suh, *Book of Genesis*, 237.

37. Spence and Exell, *Genesis*, 95.

38. Ibid.

39. Matthew Henry, *Matthew Henry's Commentary*, 1:40.

40. Ibid., 1:41.

41. Morris, *The Genesis Record*, 155.

42. James Montgomery Boice, *Genesis: An Expositional Commentary*, vol. 1 (Grand Rapids: Zondervan, 1982), 292.

43. Ibid.

44. Spence and Exell, *Genesis*, 96; Suh, *Book of Genesis*, 242.

45. Kim Hee-Bo, *Patriarchal Fathers in the Old Testament* (Seoul: Presbyterian Theological Seminary Press, 1979), 31.

46. Spence and Exell, *Genesis*, 96.

47. Boice, *Genesis*, 255–56.

48. Morris, *The Genesis Record*, 161.

49. Suh, *Book of Genesis*, 245; Boice, *Genesis*, 256.

50. Park, *Commentary on Genesis*, 124.

51. Boice, *Genesis*, 256.

52. John H. Walton, *The NIV Application Commentary: Genesis* (Grand Rapids: Zondervan, 2001), 296.

53. J. Wenham, *Genesis 1–15*, 129; Ernest Klein, *A Comprehensive Etymological Dictionary of the Hebrew Language for Readers of English* (New York: Macmillan, 1987), 664.

54. A. R. Fausset, *Fausset's Bible Dictionary* (Grand Rapids: Zondervan, 1949).

55. Victoria Neufeldt, ed., *Webster's New World College Dictionary*, 3rd ed. (New York: Macmillan, 1996), 648.

56. Francis Brown, *The New Brown, Driver, Briggs, Gesenius Hebrew and English Lexicon: With an Appendix Containing the Biblical Aramaic* (Peabody, MA: Hendrickson, 1979), 75; *The Oxford Bible Interpreter* (Seoul: Bible Study Material Publisher, 2007), 1:594.

57. Isaac Asimov, *Asimov's Guide to the Bible*, 2 vols. in 1 (New York: Avenel Books, 1981), 53.

58. Boice, *Genesis: An Expositional Commentary*, 335.

59. John Calvin, *Commentaries on the First Book of Moses Called Genesis*, vol. 1, trans. John King (Grand Rapids: Baker, 1989), 320.

60. Kim Sung-Il, *Exploring Origin of the Korean Nation: Discovering the Route of the Shemites* (Seoul: Research Institute for Creation History, 1997), 88–93.

61. "A Letter to the Readers: [Discoveries at Ebla]," *The Biblical Archaeologist* 40, no. 1 (March 1977): 2–4. Wone Yong-Kuk, *The Pentateuch*. Rev. ed. (Seoul: Lifebook, 2004), 93.

62. Kim, *Exploring Origin*, 120.

63. Wone Yong-Kuk, *A Dictionary of Biblical Archaeology* (Seoul: Lifebook, 1984), 701–5.

64. Ludwig Koehler and Walter Baumgartner, *The Hebrew and Aramaic Lexicon of the Old Testament: Study Edition*, vol. 2, trans. and ed. M. E. J. Richardson (Boston: Brill, 2001), 1264; *Oxford Bible Interpreter*, 1:637.

65. Spence and Exell, eds., *Genesis*, 171.

66. Ibid.

67. Disciples Publishing House, *The Grand Bible Commentary: With Comprehensive and Synthetic Exegetical Study Methods*, vol. 1 (Seoul: Bible Study Material Publisher, 1991), 457.

68. Wenham, *Genesis 1–15*, 251–52.

69. Ibid., 252.

70. Ibid., 251.

71. Causative verbal form. For example, "He is great" is derived in the Hiphil stem as "He caused to be great" (J. Weingreen, *A Practical Grammar for Classical Hebrew*, 2nd ed. [Oxford: Clarendon Press, 1959], 112.).

Index

Page numbers relating to the Excursus 2 table are in Italics.

"Ask your father" command (Moses), 16–17, 24–26; "asking" interpretations in, 25; "fathers" defined in, 24–25; "telling" interpretations in, 26
Asshur/Assyrians, 147–49

Babel (city), 80–81, 84, 90, 163. See also tower of Babel
Babylon, 23, 50, 69, 84; destruction of, 85, 159
Basemath, 84
Berodach-baladan, King (of Babylon), 69
Bible, accuracy of, 53
Boaz, 40

Cain, 18, 42; birth/death records in line of, 186–88; city built by, 66–68, 79; curse, by God, on, 66–68, 210; Enoch's genealogy in line of, 66–68, 184–85; Esau's sins in relation to, 84; genealogy of, 40, 46, 49, 58–85, 103, 130, 183–92; image and likeness of, 100; Irad's genealogy in line of, 68–69; Ishmael's sins related to, 83, 84–85; Lamech's genealogy in line of, 72–77, 82, 85, 93, 122–25, 185, 209; lifestyle representations in line of, 185–86; longevity records in line of, 93–94, 188–92; Mehujael's genealogy in line of, 70–71; Methushael's genealogy in line of, 71–72; murder by, 40, 60–62, 93, 99–100, 183; name's meaning, 59; Nimrod's sins related to, 79–83, 84–85; Nod settlement by, 65–66; Satan's influ-

ence on, 61–65; Seth's line in comparison to line of, 182–92; Seth's line influenced by, 78–85, 129–30, 139; sin's spread via line of, 58–85, 130, 209; worship's evolution and, 103
Cainan, 52; perspectives on genealogy of, 154–55
Calvin, John, 156
Canaan (region), 219; Abraham's call, by God, to, 142, 156, 159, 165, 172–74, 175–78, 182, 193, 200–02, 202–07; commands, by Moses, regarding, 16–17, 26; invasion of, 148. See also Israel
Canaan (son of Ham), 83–85, 150
Chedorlaomer, King (of Elam), 148
Christ. See Jesus Christ
Christ's second coming and, 219; point in time related to, 22; research/study implications in, 23
1 Chronicles 1:1–4, 24–27, 52
2 Chronicles 3:1–2, 54
commands, by Moses (in Deuteronomy): "Ask your father," 16–17, 24–26; "Consider the years of all generations," 9, 16–17, 22–23, 49, 219; "Remember the days of old" command, 9, 16–17, 18–21, 49, 219;
1 Corinthians: 10:4, 218; 15:10, 196; 15:51–54, 118
2 Corinthians: 1:5, 124; 5:14, 199; 7:11, 200; 11:4, 64; 7:1, 189
Covenant of the (rain)bow, 80, 133, 162, 210

creation: groaning of, 34; of heaven and earth, 42–43; of man, 42; as theme of redemptive history, 30, 38
Cush, 79, 83

David, King (of Israel), 13, 25, 54, 69; genealogy of, 38–40, 50; as "man of God," 72, 196
Deuteronomy: 9:14, 71; 26:5, 177; 30:16, 114; 32:7, 9, 26; "Ask your father" command in, 16–17, 24–26; "Consider the years of all generations" in, 9, 16–17, 22–23, 49, 219; "Remember the days of old" command in, 9, 16–17, 18–21, 49, 219
the devil. See Satan
divine administration: meaning of, 32; predestination of, 33, 35–36. See also administration, redemptive

earth, creation/genealogy of, 42–43
Eber: Euphrates crossing by, 156–59, 157, 196; genealogy of, 48–49, 52, 91, 146, 152, 156–59; life span of, 135, 154, 157, 162, 163; name's meaning, 156, 196; patriarchs living contemporaneously with, 91–92, 146, 162, 178; redemptive significance of, 156–59, 248
Ebla, 157–58, 165
Ecclesiastes 12:13, 189
Eden. See garden of Eden
Edomites, 83
Egypt, slavery of Israelites in, 18–20, 23, 53–54, 152
Elam/Elamites, 147–48

84–85, *92*, 145–46, 155, 167, 176, 178, 204–06; of Ishmael, 40, 44, 83–85, 167; of Jacob, 38, 43–44, 49, 52, 55, 85, *90–91*, 145–46, 155, 178; judgments by God represented in, 42, 44, 59, 65, 65–68, 81–84, 93, 98, 114–18, 120–22, 125–26, 128–34, 134, 150, 157–58, 160–62, 185, 189–90, 197, 198, 210, 136–137, 139–41; language confusion represented in, 81–82, 160–61, 164–65, 197; lifestyle representations in, 185–86; longevity records in, 47, 93–94, 111, 121–22, 157, 169, 188–92, 138–39; mankind's origin in, 42, 95–97; mankind's scattering in, 81–83, 160–61, 164–65; material selected for, 46; Messiah's first coming revealed in, 10, 30, 34–36, 48–49, 53, 88, 96, 106, 129, 207, 211–12; Messiah's second coming revealed in, 30, 35–37, 88, 118–20, 129, 191–92, 212, 216, 219; names' significance in, 47, 67–68; of Noah, 38, 39–40, 41, 42, 46–47, 49–52, 82, 88, *90–91*, 115, 121–24, 125–31, 134, 142–44, 138–40; opposing path representations in, 71–72; redemptive significance of, 11, 22–23, 36–37, 42–43; relationships between generations and, 46; separation from God themes in, 65, 76–83, 157, 160–61, 163–65,

170–72, 184, 186, 187; separation from sin themes, 142, 156–59, 165, 173–78, 182, 192–207; of Shem, 38, 40, 43, 46–49, 52, *90*, 127, 132–33, 136–38, 142–51, 156–57, 167, 177, 211; from Shem to Abraham, 142–79; sin's descendants in, 79–85; strength concepts in, 73, 78, 123–24, 166–68, 198–99; structure of, 39–40; study, method of, for, 46–49; of Terah, 44, 49, 52, *91–92*, 132, 146, 159, 169, 173–77, 200–02; timeline, calculation of, in, 49, 52, 53–55, 97, 101, 115, 117, 129–30, 209, 155; transfigurations represented in, 93, 97–98, 99, 101, 102, 105, 107, 110, 112–19, 122–23, 130; worship's evolution in lines of, 103–09, 185. See also Cain; patriarchs of Genesis; Seth; specific genealogies

Gethsemane, Garden of, 36, 200
Gibeon 25
God: "blotting out" by, 71–72; covenant of the (rain)bow by, 80, 134, 162, 210; fear of, 76, 133, 188–89, 206; friends of, 163–65, 198; honoring of parents and, 150, 190; Israelites' betrayal of, 16, 62; language, confusion of, by, 82, 160–61, 164–66, 197; name of, 144–45; omnipotence of, 68–69; providence of, 42, 82–83, 144; scattering of humans by, 80–82,

160; seed of, 35, 61–65, 192; unity of man apart from, 65, 75–76, 81–82, 157, 160–61, 164–66, 185, 186; walking with, 72–73, 89, 93, 98, 114–17, 120–21, 123, 184; Word of, 12, 62–63, 81–82, 93, 115–18, 124, 136, 153, 182, 184–87, 191–92, 194–96, 198–99, 203, 216–19. See also judgment(s), God's; Word of God

Golgotha, 217
Gomorrah, 158, 198, 204
the great flood: ark's passengers during124–25, 133; covenant of the (rain)bow after, 80, 134, 162, 210; date of, *90*, 121; as God's judgment on man, 42, 44, 80, 116–17, 119–21, 124–25, 127–34, 136–37, 139–40, 142, 150, 161–62, 185; repentance period prior to, 122, 135–36, 139–41; revelation of, *92*, 116–17, 119–20, 130, 136–37, 185; sin's rebound after, 142, 209; warnings of, 121, 124–25, 128
greed, 169–71
groaning, 34, 102

Hagar, 83, 205
Ham: genealogy of, 40, 43, 52, 79, 83–85, 126, 130, 136–37, 138, 143, 150, 157, 209; name's meaning, 143; Noah's judgment on, 150
Haman, 84
Hammedatha the Agagite, 84
Hannah, 82, 111
Haran (city), 43, 162,

significance to genealogies of, 47

Nebuchadnezzar, King (of Babylon), 69

Nimrod: Assyria invasion by, 148; genealogy of, 78–80, 84–85; name's meaning, 78; tower of Babel construction by, 78, 79–82, 85, 149, 161

Noah, 18; ark built by, 90, 121, 124–25, 130–31, 132–33, 135–37, 186; genealogy of, 38, 40–41, 42, 43, 48–49, 50–52, 83, 88, 90, 93, 117, 123–26, 127–33, 135–37, 143–45; great flood and, 44, 90, 122, 124–25, 127–28, 133–34, 186, 209–210; Ham's judgment by, 150; life span of, 90, 94, 129, 162, 189; name's meaning, 126; patriarchs living contemporaneously with, 48, 90–92, 102, 105, 107, 109, 115–16, 119, 122–23, 124, 129–30, 132, 143, 146, 152, 154, 160, 162–63, 166, 168, 172, 176, 177–78; redemptive significance of, 44, 92, 124–25, 126–29, 130, 131–34, 142, 175, 177, 185; Shem's blessing by, 150; siblings of, 124–25; spread of gospel and, 81, 136, 140, 209

Nod, 65–66, 184

Oholibamah, 84

"120 years" (of Genesis 6:3): ark construction theories related to, 135–37, 141; longevity theories related to, 138–39; repentance period theories related to, 139–41

Park, Yune-Sun, 94, 126

Passover, Feast of, 20

patriarchs of Genesis:
Abraham (Abram), 16, 23, 26, 39–40, 42–44, 48–53, 54, 90–92, 111, 128, 133, 142, 145, 146, 152, 154, 156, 158, 159, 162, 165, 172–74, 175–78, 182, 191–92, 193, 197, 202–12; Adam, 10; 18, 30, 34–35, 37, 38–39, 42–43, 45–49, 51–52, 55, 59–60, 64, 65, 88, 89–92, 93–101, 102, 103, 105, 107, 109, 112, 115–17, 119, 122–23, 129–30, 156, 183–84, 189, 190, 210; Arpachshad, 52, 90–92, 131, 143, 146–47, 147–52, 147, 150–51, 52, 154–55, 156, 162, 175, 177, 194–95; "Ask your father" command in relation to, 24–25; Eber, 48–49, 52, 91–92, 135, 146, 152, 154, 156–59, 162, 163, 178, 196, 248; Enoch, 48–49, 52, 66–68, 89, 93, 98–99, 101, 102, 105, 107, 109, 111, 112–18, 119–20, 121–22, 128, 184; Enosh, 52, 89, 94, 99, 102–104, 115, 185; Jared, 52, 89, 93–94, 107, 109, 110, 111, 112, 115, 129 189; Kenan, 52, 89, 93–94, 102, 105–09, 108, 115, 129; Lamech, 49, 52, 90, 92, 94, 95, 116, 121, 122–26, 130, 146, 185–86; Mahalalel, 52, 89, 93–94, 105, 107–8, 109, 110, 115, 129, 185; Methuselah, 48, 52, 90, 93–94, 98, 109, 112, 115–16, 119–21, 130,

122, 146, 185, 189; Nahor, 40, 52, 91–92, 132, 146, 154, 159, 162, 165, 168–71, 175, 176, 199–200; Peleg, 49, 52, 91–92, 142, 146, 156–63, 165, 169, 176, 197; procreation ages of, 52, 132–33; redemptive significance of, 11–12, 24–25, 38–41, 42, 46; relationships between, significance of, 48; Reu, 52, 91–92, 146, 159–65, 169, 176, 198; separation work by, 142, 156–59, 165, 173–78, 182, 192–207; Serug, 52, 91–92, 146, 159, 161–63, 166–69, 172, 176, 198–99; Seth, 38–40, 42–53, 55, 59–60, 66, 78–85, 88–179, 194–208, 211; Shelah, 52, 90–92, 145–46, 152–56, 162, 176, 195–96; Shem, 38, 40, 43, 46–49, 52, 90, 92, 122, 127, 130, 132–33, 136–38, 143–51, 156–57, 162, 167, 175, 176, 177, 209, 211; structure of writings on, 42–43, 46; Terah, 44, 49, 52, 91–92, 132, 146, 159, 162, 169, 173–77, 200–203, 206; timeline of generations of, 42, 52–55, 89–92. See also specific patriarchs

Paul, 33–4, 36, 64, 72, 81; human weakness and, 104; ministry, 153; Messiah's coming and, 124; separation from sin and, 169, 170,196, 199–200; unity with God and, 82

Peleg: genealogy of, 47, 52, 91, 146, 156–63,